OLYMPIC AND HOSANNA. LIGIA. SEPTEMBER 2004

C000220321

Other titles by the same authors:

Watersteps Through France: To the Camargue by Canal
ISBN 0 7136 4391 9

When Bill and Laurel Cooper decided to spend the winter in the South of France, they took their seaworthy but half-finished Dutch barge *Hosanna* by an 'overland' route through the canals and rivers of France. Climbing the watersteps of the Massif Central, they passed through some out-of-the-way places, made a wonderful variety of friends, and had a great many adventures before they arrived in time for Christmas in the peace and warmth of the Camargue.

Here are the French, their folklore, customs and food seen through the eyes of two seasoned travellers who are always ready to take a fresh view of the unexpected.

Watersteps Round Europe: Greece to England by Barge
ISBN 0 7136 4399 4

After their journey through the French canals, told in *Watersteps Through France*, the Coopers cruised their converted Dutch barge, *Hosanna* around the Greek islands. Needing a replacement engine they hurried back to the UK to refit, meeting all kinds of difficulties, delights and disasters on the way.

This is the story of the eventful 2300 mile voyage home via the Ionian Isles, Sicily, Sardinia, Corsica, and then through France and back to Great Yarmouth. On the way we are treated to the Coopers' lively insight into the manners, customs and frustrations of those whose paths they cross on their troublesome journey home.

Sell Up and Sail 2nd edition
ISBN 0 7136 3948 2

This bestselling book is packed with first hand advice for anyone seeking to escape from the rat race and take to a life at sea. Considered the bible for longterm cruisers, it tells you everything you need to know – from the practicalities and pitfalls of early retirement, choosing a boat to live in, looking after her on the move, and organising your finances, to preventing ill health afloat, choosing suitable cruising grounds, provisioning in far flung places and deep sea voyaging.

Sail into the Sunset
ISBN 0 7136 3951 2

Sailors in their later years generally have very different requirements from their younger counterparts, as Bill and Laurel Cooper have discovered during their travels around Europe aboard their Dutch sailing barge. Covering every kind of boating from messing about in a dinghy on a reservoir to boating on canals, chartering, racing and retiring to live aboard, Bill and Laurel Cooper have drawn on their own experience to provide a wealth of practical information and advice for people sailing in their retirement.

Iaian & Margaret – Happy Sailing

BACK DOOR TO BYZANTIUM

To the Black Sea by the Great Rivers of Europe

BILL AND LAUREL COOPER

Bill & Laurel Cooper
"HOSANNA"

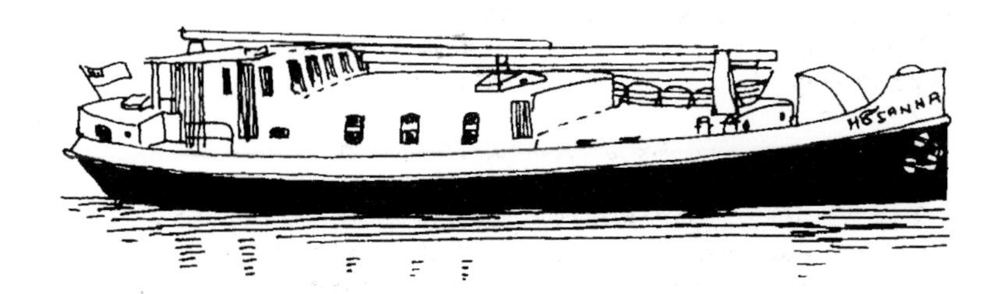

Adlard Coles Nautical
LONDON

Published by Adlard Coles Nautical 1997
an imprint of A & C Black (Publishers) Ltd
35 Bedford Row, London WC1R 4JH

Copyright © Bill and Laurel Cooper 1997
Illustration copyright © Laurel Cooper 1997

The authors assert their moral rights.

ISBN 0-7136-4637-3

All rights reserved. No part of this publication may be reproduced in any form or by any means – graphic, electronic or mechanical, including photocopying, recording, taping or information storage or retrieval systems – without the prior permission in writing of the publishers.

A CIP catalogue record for this book is available from the British Library.

Typeset in Garamond/Sabon 10/11 pt
Printed and bound in Great Britain by
The Cromwell Press, Melksham, Wiltshire

CONTENTS

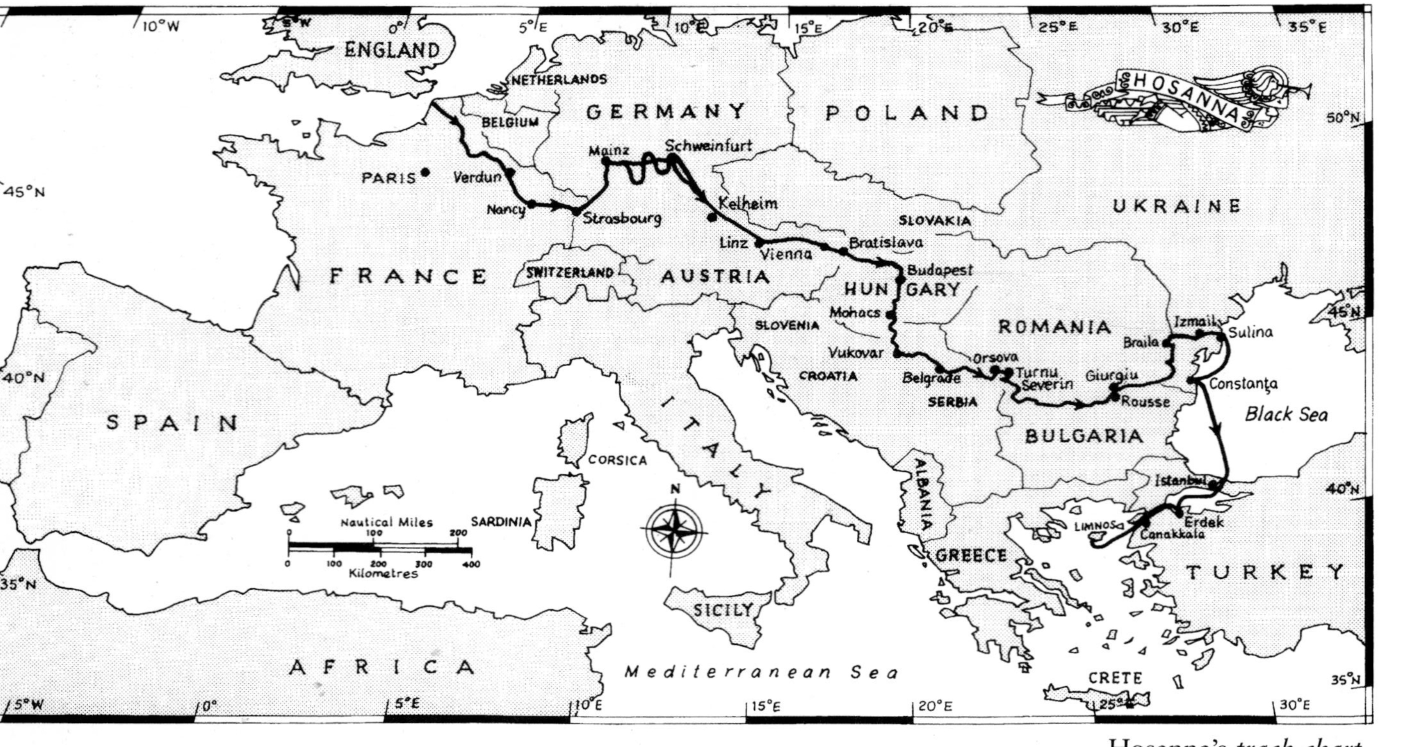

Hosanna's *track chart*

• 1 •
FLOODS IN FLANDERS
Arques

In *Hosanna*, our Dutch sailing barge, a bad winter had followed a bad summer, culminating in a cold wet January in the Pas de Calais.

Laurel wiped black mould off the sills of streaming wheelhouse windows for the umpteenth time, and dreamed of hot sun and blue water in the Greek Islands.

Bill did his umpteenth crossword, sneezed into a sodden handkerchief, and dreamed of cold beer on a warm day.

We live aboard *Hosanna*, and have spent the last eight years cruising the seas and waterways of Europe. The previous year we had lost our foremast in a September storm in the North Sea, and our three new engines had had teething troubles after expensive surgery. We sat gloomily in our backwater in Arques, near Calais, and listened to the rain drumming down. *Hosanna* is normally dry and comfortable, but for the first time we had mildew below decks. It whiskered the clothes at the back of our wardrobes, rotted vegetables in their airy locker and turned them, Cinderella-like, into damp mice. Even out in the supposedly fresh air the rope in our rigging grew green and slimy, and our cats, tiger-striped Tansy and fat, grey Bograt, sulked and hibernated below. Laurel's hip creaked and grumbled, and her bones longed for the sun.

We prayed for deliverance, as did most of Northern France and the Low Countries. Instead, the floods came. Nightly, television showed pictures of damsels, no longer young, rescued from floodbound attics by gallant *sapeurs pompiers* (the Fire Brigade). Bridges were immersed under torrents, and barges drifted helplessly in fast-flowing current. We thanked providence for our backwater in Arques, close enough to Calais for the floods to drain off to sea. Here, even in the worst of floods the water level rose by only 30 cm. Our mooring rings were underwater but reachable, and going ashore was possible with gumboots on. And we had an old Mini for marketing.

A few incidents lightened the gloom. One gale-blown Saturday at the height of the floods the *sapeurs pompiers* arrived at the slipway by *Hosanna*'s mooring. They were using inflatable dinghies to herd a couple of wild boar which the floods had carried into the water. The boars were swimming strongly but couldn't get out, until escorted to the slipway, up which they slithered in undignified haste and disappeared into the woods before even a Frenchman could get his hunting piece out and shoot them.

Arques itself is a small town full of glass factories. Those cheap and well designed glasses that you take on picnics or the boat, where breakages don't matter, are made here. Arques is also famous for the Boat Lift at Fontinettes, big enough to take a loaded 300 tonne barge and lift it 13 metres. It was built in the 1880s by an Englishman (who had built a prototype at Anderton near Manchester, in 1875) to replace a string of five locks, and was working in earnest till the 1960s; now it is a museum piece, and we had visited it last autumn, marvelling at the water-powered counterbalances. It is replaced by a deep lock with the same name, Fontinettes.

Our new mast arrived from England. Ten metres and 400 kilos of galvanised steel tube, it came over the Channel on a trailer, and we had to embark it. Bill contemplated the problem, wearing his new oil-skin. He hadn't had an oilskin until a month ago. This meant that Laurel, possessor of a well-used Henri-Lloyd, was always the one who had been sent out in the wet. Her protests had led to a dedicated search at the London Boat Show, trying on dozens of garments deemed suitable for a large and opinionated sailor of a traditionalist turn of mind. Nothing trendy; bright two-tone affairs in contrasting colours are not for him. He calls it having an independent mind. Several makers of waterproof garments now know his views.

At last he found an oilskin coat, sans logo, long enough to cover his behind. It buttoned down the front, was a traditional mustard colour, and a quarter of the price of those being sold for yachtsmen. It was intended for those admirable allweathermen: Breton fishermen. Bill had now lost all excuse for not going outside in foul weather. Laurel had greatly looked forward to this.

The waterlogged clay quay was too soft to support a mobile crane and had become a boggy skating rink. Bill slithered and swore as he rigged old spars across to the ship as guides and levered the mast inch by inch up them until it was safely on board. He hosed down his bargeman's rubber clogs (these and gumboots are the only footwear suitable in such conditions), and at last, with levers, tackles and wedges, manoeuvred the beast into a satisfactory position, and retired below to dry clothes and hot coffee.

The rain went on. Our plan had been to return to the warm Mediterranean coast of France by way of her picturesque canals as soon as the mast was aboard.

Bill was reading about Great Rivers one night as the wood stove crackled, the rain drummed on the steel roof overhead and rivulets trickled down the scuppers and out through the freeing ports. He sat with the book on his lap for a moment, and said, 'Why don't we go down to the Med the other way?'

'What way?'

'Down the Danube, to Istanbul. By the back door.'

'What does that involve?'

Laurel knew that a new canal linking the Rhine with the Danube had opened, but she didn't know the detailed course of the latter. It

Flemish houses

started in Germany (didn't it? or was it Switzerland?), went (certainly) through Vienna, and reached the Black Sea somewhere. The atlas revealed more: she was right about Vienna; few of us think of the Danube as anything but blue.

Bill did some homework, and found that information was scarce. He wrote to travel agents about cruising holidays. He phoned and wrote to the Foreign Office and embassies in the countries through which the river passes. He consulted lists of books in print, and got booklists from second-hand dealers. The last would turn out to be the most fertile, the penultimate produced a thin but interesting harvest, while Her Majesty's Principal Secretary of State for Foreign Affairs proved worse than useless. It would turn out that every bit of data that we obtained from the Foreign Office was wrong in fact, principle, and emphasis.

The most important thing we learned was that the river flowed through Jugoslavia, then torn apart by bloody civil war. Often a river forms a boundary between countries, but most boundaries in the Balkans have been clumsily rearranged by 'statesmen' without regard to the nationality, language, or religion of those who live there, leaving enclaves of difference which have proved explosive. In Jugoslavia, the land of the South Slavs, created by the allies at the expense of her neighbours after the First World War, and enlarged after the Second, the river flows through Jugoslav territory for 358 kilometres, and for another 230 forms the border between Jugoslavia and Romania.

We had often visited Jugoslavia in the early days of tourism. We had felt uneasy, but not threatened. Now that Germany's unilateral and ill-judged recognition of the break-away republic of Croatia had precipitated a civil war, the area of Jugoslavia adjoining the west bank of the Danube, once thought of as part of Croatia, had been brutally fought over and absorbed into Serb territory, some cities on the Danube being ravaged in the process. Apart from these episodes, most of the fighting had taken place away from the river. It was the situation in Serb-held, disputed, riverside Jugoslavia that we were concerned with, but neither the BBC nor the press bothered much about River Danube.

We consulted our children, both well-informed. Our son showed no surprise at our plan. Our daughter, an ex-TV journalist, reacted with a sharp cry of horror and dismay. 'Jugoslavia? You must be mad.' We would be subject to rape, pillage, kidnapping, extortion, or at best stormed at by shot and shell. She was nearly right.

Nevertheless there was a snowball-like momentum about the way we found ourselves buying maps, and inquiring about visas.

We may not go all the way, we told ourselves.

It might be pleasant to go a little further down the Danube than the Hofman family did in 1992; they got as far as Austria.

We could stop at the border with Jugoslavia.

We could always come back.

We informed a few tried and tested friends that we thought of going to the Black Sea, hoping that some would be able to come with us, but to our surprise they all seemed to be doing something different about the time we might be in central Europe.

'Are we being foolish?' we asked ourselves.

'No, we are only going to have a look. And no one says the river traffic is not getting through.'

We read in *Motor Boat and Yachting* of Nick Sanders, who planned to go down the Danube and back in a British Inland Waters narrow boat, from Black Country to Black Sea. He had obtained several sponsors, and had attracted media attention. This we did not want. Bill has a horror of attempts to navigate under artificially contrived circumstances. Sponsors and the media goad the imprudent among us to fill TV screens and news pages with super-hyped idiocies, and the pressures of timing they impose are inimical to well-ordered and careful ventures. They also change the natural course of events. Things are made to happen in front of the cameras, and gems the cameras miss go unrecorded. We prefer, having survived a good many adventures unrecorded in the press, to write about it afterwards. We did not consider Nick Sanders' enterprise as lunatic; a narrow boat should be able to make an inland water voyage, however long. We tried to make contact with him to see if we could exchange information, but failed to connect.

The idea of going south through France receded, and east down the Danube took shape. We took a quick trip to England with the Mini to talk to the children, raid second-hand bookshops for anything relevant, visit the Cash and Carry for stores, and get our teeth filled. Our last call before we returned on the ferry some days later was to B & Q. While there, the Mini, fully loaded and ready to go, was broken into and the top box of goodies stolen.

Pillaged. In England. This was irritating rather than disastrous; most of the things were replaceable, and the thief had mercifully ignored our precious second-hand books. He got the things you always take to Darkest France like Bramley apples, Marmite, and parsnips. We wondered what he would do with a map of Romania, an Eastern European phrasebook, and Laurel's HRT pills.

Back in France, a new shaft bearing was late arriving. Old boats were built in inches, and we could get only metric sizes in England. Germany seems to be the last place in Europe still making things in inches, but they deliver late, like everyone else.

The weather remained dreadful. The new bearing arrived, and on a rare fine weekday we took *Hosanna* to the nearby boatyard where the engine was lined up and the bed and stool for the new bearing welded in.

The boatyard was concerned mainly with the breaking of old barges, the principal products being rusty bits and noise. This did not seem to worry the neighbourhood geese and ducks, one of which had made a nest close to the bollard to which we attached our headrope. Our cats, enjoying the change of scene, watched the nest, but kept their distance. Laurel tried to ascertain which of the birds was to become mother goose, but found that all five geese or ganders sat on the nest as duty goose, and occasionally one or more of the big, handsome white ducks would also squat on the clutch and sit there with a soft and satisfied quack. We never identified the mother.

Among the nautical detritus lying about were many old anchors, and the yard generously gave us one, and loaded it on board as a reserve. They also craned on board our Mini. There was just room on deck for it; we hoped to land it occasionally for sightseeing.

By now it was April. With the blackthorn blossoming and the geese nesting, it was time to take on water and fuel and see to the final spare parts and ship's stores, get the cats vaccinated, and the hundred and one things that have to be done before a long voyage, including, always, some painting, when the day was dry enough.

We were as ready as we ever would be. We visited our hosts at the Base Nautique in Arques, taking a chocolate Easter bunny for their little offspring. We checked that we had on board both of our cats, and none of theirs, and bade farewell.

• 2 •

THE VOYAGE BEGINS
Arques to Noyon

We had sailed from Calais to Arques at the end of last season. Now on 5 April 1995, we left Arques for the unknown East.

'Nato preparing to withdraw from Bosnia', said the headlines, but we were too busy to notice.

It had been dewy and wet that morning, but a timid sun appeared, a bit hazy, warming the greening land. Never was there so much blackthorn blossom. The willows were faintly green, the weepers trailing yellow fronds, the woods misting over with the first veils of spring. It was a pretty rural day to begin an adventure. We locked through Flandres, waved goodbye to the workers having lunch at the glass factory, and with a last admiring look at the Boat Lift we passed our second lock of the year at Fontinettes.

We motored through an industrial landscape lightened by interesting graffiti: passing a bridge near Aire-sur-la-Lys, we noted painted in white on the red brick abutment in huge letters: 'La Pute est deuxième a droite.' (The Hooker is second on the right.) Was this a business notice, friendly advice, or had some poor woman offended the graffitist and was now being knocked up day and night, excuse the expression, by randy *mariniers* (bargemen)?

We passed backstairs Béthune, factories to the right, hamlets and fields to the left, barges moored on both sides, and a man out for a brisk walk on the towpath, CARRYING his dog.

Many barges waiting for cargoes at Béthune had no-hope names. Trade is declining, and huge subsidies go to rail and road freight. We saw names like *Sans Avenir* (No Future), *Futuna* which means, to put it politely, Messed About, and *Rien sans Mal*: Nothing without Pain. Among the Saints' names and *An-Jos* and *Perseverance*s they indicated a depressing outlook.

As often happens on the canals, when we felt like stopping in mid-afternoon there was either no quay or no bollards, and it was some hours later that we found a mooring between two commercial barges near La Bassée. Fifty kilometres was not a bad day's run, and because it was our wedding anniversary we had a good dinner of roast duck and apple crumble.

We had decided on our route. The floods in northern France were subsiding, but River Meuse was not yet navigable. The floods had done much damage, and the water flow remained strong, so that repairs had taken longer than expected. We would go an alternative route via Nancy, where we would have the choice of going down River Moselle, or through the Canal de la Marne-au-Rhin to Strasbourg. The journey to Nancy also had several alternatives, and Bill opted to go via the Canal du Nord, and Rivers Oise, Aisne and Upper Meuse because they are wider and deeper than the shorter route, making for easier navigation, higher speed, and fewer tunnels. Our experience of tunnels, some of them many kilometres long and taking hours to pass, was, to date, not good. It would, however, mean negotiating a great many locks, tedious to record, so apart from general explanations, we will mention only the eventful ones.

We started at dawn, the wind was strong and the traffic heavy, especially when we reached the Canal du Nord, the trunk waterway that serves the industrial and agricultural north. On either side of the canal huge lion-coloured fields swept to the horizon, almost unbroken by any tree or building. We were in potato country, and *Hosanna* was rising in this rolling land, and must have gone up 20 or 30 metres in just a few locks, with a lock every 1½ kilometres. From this new vantage we sometimes saw a vignette to break the rolling fields: a hamlet bordered with the intense green of a wet spring, embroidered with blackthorn copses, and lit with the yellow lamps of forsythia.

The cross wind which we were experiencing made waiting at locks difficult unless we made fast. It is courteous and advisable not to crowd too close to the gates if a barge is emerging, and this is especially true if, as she emerges from a tight-fitting lock, the wind catches her and blows her bows off line. If she is deeply laden this is less likely, but when empty she floats high and presents a big target to the wind, and must struggle for control. In this case the barge *Ve-Ge* was waiting ahead of us, and we kept well clear. Many of the bigger locks had 'guillotine' gates, rising from the water. You learn to stay in the wheelhouse until you have passed under the dripping gate, otherwise you get a dollop of canal water down your neck.

Having done it so often, locking was usually uneventful. Bill, being the more experienced driver, held the boat against wind and current while we awaited the green light. Once in the lock Bill positioned the boat close to a convenient bollard, which it was Laurel's job to lasso and make fast to our foremost bitts, as we were going *amont* (upstream). The water would enter the lock in front of us, sometimes with considerable force. In the big modern locks they have floating bollards which rise (or fall) with the water level. This makes life much easier; here we had to transfer from one bollard to the one above as we rose, or risk losing the rope under the water, still attached to the bollard, which Laurel had done yesterday in a fit of start-of-season forgetfulness. Fortunately Bill, quicker moving and with longer arms, had managed to extract us from that predicament. (This danger, and that of getting 'hung up' in a down-going lock, explains why a sharp axe is an obligatory item on the deck of a barge). Today as we reached the top, having successfully changed bollards as we rose, we had again the pleasant experience of a panorama of treetops coming into view, then hills, then fields, and then the lock-keeper's garden strewn with daisies, and a notice declaring that *endives* and *pommes de terre* were for sale, by the side of a barrowful of them. Yesterday it had been farm rabbits.

A misty sun was shouldering through the clouds as the gates opened. *Ve-Ge* started to move forward, with a great swirl of water behind his screw. This semicircular froth of disturbed water behind a moving barge is called the *gerbe*. Poetically named, the *gerbe* is powerful, and would have knocked us backwards had we not been prepared. We normally stay made fast until the water ahead of us is clear. Then Laurel flips the rope loop off with a practised flick of the wrist, which looks very professional. If it works. Mild panic ensues if it doesn't.

By mid-afternoon we were too tired to face seven more locks and a tunnel. We passed the industrial area round Douai and stopped on the edge of the agricultural village of Marquion, where there is a good quay. We stayed in; there was not much to go out for on a cool evening when walking is painful. As there were no main roads or other hazards the cats were given shore leave to play, and accepted with pleasure.

Our chief memories are a dreadful noise from a nearby factory and a wild catfight during the night, which turned Laurel out in her nightie with the shrimping net to rescue Bograt from the canal, where she was noisily, wetly, desperately clinging to a baulk of timber under the quay. She had stoutly defended her honour, and had dunked a large tomcat of indeterminable colour who was dripping off into the woods at speed. Laurel wrapped the drenched and shivering Bograt in a towel, and sat the cat on her lap with its nose in her armpit, feeling her gradually calm down, warm up, and switch on her purr. Once her little motor was going strongly Laurel put the towel in the warm airing cupboard, with the cat still wrapped in it, and went back to bed.

Next day was fine but cold. Barge traffic, if it does not go on all night, begins at dawn, and we woke to the threshing of screws as the commercial barges began their day at six. We followed two civilised hours later, after breakfast: which was always a good opportunity to check the cats. If they were not present and hungry for breakfast a search party would be sent out. They were both on board, and when breakfasted, would be ready to sleep in their respective cupboards, usually till mid-afternoon. Until they awoke, we could pass through locks untroubled by cats wanting an untimely run ashore. We waited and gave *commerce* precedence, as is customary; it is, after all, their livelihood, and we are mere *plaisance*.

We reached the tunnel of Ruyalcourt at noon. About a hundred yards from the tunnel the sides of the canal became steep, we passed under a high bridge, and came upon the barges that had passed us earlier that morning. 'No more astern are there?' asked Bill. No, we were '*la lampe rouge*', the last one. We were all waiting for a sand barge coming out rather slowly. Bill said, 'They've let *Ve-Ge* go first.'

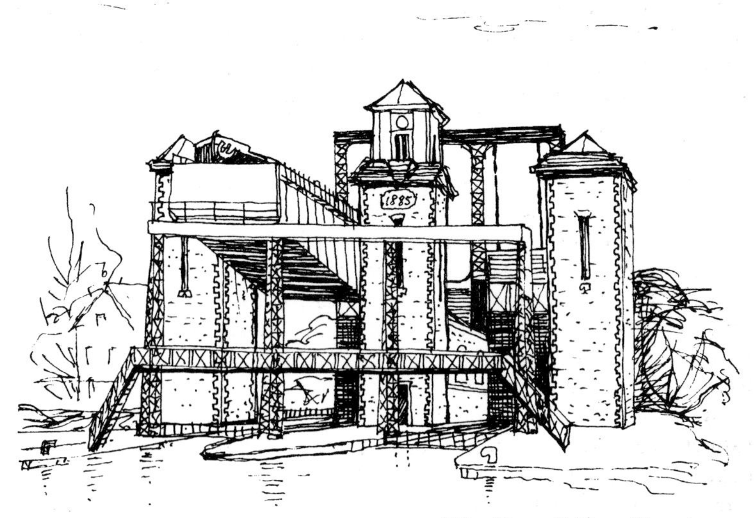

The Boat Lift at Fontinettes

It seemed sensible to let the faster, because empty, boat go first. Jilling about in confined waters with other boats can be difficult and requires concentration. The sand barge, *St Helier*, pushing a dumb barge in tandem, was probably bound for the glassworks at Arques, laden till the water was over her side decks. She was churning the mud up as she ploughed along the bottom in the centre of the canal. Passing her was tricky as the water she was displacing sucked us towards her; the technique is to remain almost still and allow the loaded barge to pass, giving a strong kick away when you first feel the suction.

With *St Helier* safely behind us we entered the tunnel. It is 4345 metres long and has a passing place in the middle in case of surprises coming the opposite way. To avoid mishaps we had taken in anything that projected beyond the hull. The tunnels are arched, and as you are going slowly and without much steerage way, the boat can easily touch the sides. Having once lost a starboard light that way we are wary now, and surround them with tyres in tunnels.

We were called to order over the VHF; '*Hosanna*, you are badly illuminated.' We had our navigation lights on and our stern light was working fine, but we had forgotten that the masthead light had gone with the lost mast. Laurel steered while Bill fixed up a temporary lamp before we reached the central widening part of the tunnel; just as well because there was a huge tanker coming in the other direction, with the unlikely name of *Venus*. Traversing the tunnel took 65 minutes. We were held up behind a particularly slow Belgian barge, but was he going to allow a *Plaisancier* to pass him? Not on your life.

It was an uncomfortable hour, for another reason. The tunnel took us underneath a large British war cemetery containing some of our hapless compatriots whose lives were thrown away by incompetent military leadership in the First World War. Once we had sorted our lights and passed the *Venus*, Bill, mouth in a straight line, was starkly aware of it, quoting Wellington's dictum that there are no bad troops, only bad officers, and adding bitterly that since Wellington we have had more than our fair share of the latter. He held forth, gesticulating, and as we emerged from the tunnel, he nearly hit a barge coming in the opposite direction.

Then we had time to notice little fairy steps at the canal's edge, made of aluminium. Elsewhere we have seen provision made for people who have fallen in to climb out of a canal, not an easy thing when the edge is high and made of smooth concrete affording no purchase. The steps turned out to be platforms to help ducks climb out of the canal where there is vertical concrete or sheer metal piling. The French are thoughtful in these matters, being very fond of ducks. Preferably braised, with *bigarrade* sauce.

We stopped for the night at Péronne, where the quay was full of puddles of unidentifiable chemical soup. Despite this it was far enough from the road to give the cats shore leave. Bograt, subdued since last night's fight and ducking, was sitting down very carefully. Gentle inspection of her situpon revealed swelling and severe bruising. Laurel murmured with some concern, 'I think my cat has been raped.'

Rape. In France. Which other of our daughter's predictions would come true, and us hardly started yet? Nearly all of them, as it happened, but in unexpected ways and places.

Bograt's attitude was philosophical, though her hurts took weeks to heal. She made no complaint, and dashed ashore in the rain.

On Saturday morning, Bill did some insistent engine room chores before we left under a watery sun. After yesterday's early start and long day's run (10 hours with 11 locks and a tunnel) we treated ourselves to a lie-in, and didn't start the day's journey till 0930. We recalled the Dutch barge *Helene* we had passed at Douai with a notice on it: 'Just Married – Sleeping late.'

We passed the tunnel of Panetterie, still in the Canal du Nord, with River Somme running on our left among the birchwoods. A pretty stretch, very different from the factory towns of Béthune and Douai; the woods were faintly spring green, and the trees tall and graceful. Among the birches were willows and aspens, and lower down grey furry kittenbuds clung to pussy willows, and hazel catkins bobbed and swung from the bushes at the canal's edge.

It was late afternoon before we arrived at Noyon quay. The canal is level with the rooftops of this ancient and historic town and we looked across the valley to the Cathedral, uncompromisingly dominant, founded by St Médard, whose Saint's day is to France what St Swithin's is to Britain: if it rains on St Médard it will rain for 40 days. We were a long way from 8 June, however. Tomorrow would be Palm Sunday.

It was a cold night followed by a calm, cool morning. Tansy did not appear for breakfast, and was found happily ratting in the nearby grain silos. We got a lift into Noyon, and enjoyed a second breakfast of croissants and coffee in the Café des Deux Bornes. Laurel bought bread, then sat in the café while Bill, the one with two good legs, went scouting.

His first duty was to find and reconnoitre the Michelin-starred restaurant and discover from its displayed menu whether we could afford to eat there. He decided to reserve a table; Sunday lunch is popular in France and he booked the last one.

Bill stopped to look at the De Gaulle memorial, which records the famous speech including: '...we have lost a battle, but we have not lost the war', which was largely ignored by his compatriots because they didn't hear it; the *grand homme* was at that time virtually unknown. Bill was accosted by a veteran: ('It empassions you, our history?' Evidently, since Bill once served with the French Navy off Indo-China.) The veteran took him behind the Cathedral and showed him where, in the ruins of the Bishopric, the Germans shot the Monsignor in the Second World War, and the pock-marked wall of the Cathedral where reprisal shootings took place, and the entrance to a tunnel connecting the Cathedral to a ruined monastery, by which one priest had escaped with his life.

Fifty years later, we were on the steps of Noyon Cathedral among the Palm Sunday crowd who carried, not the plaited cross or delicate fronds that we have in England, but great chunks of evergreenery. Some had tied theirs together as elegant bouquets, but others were carrying torn off branches of some size, even half a bush. The Bishop of Beauvais and Noyon had come to bless our *rameaux*; our palms. Cross our palms with silver, and we'll sell you some, seemed the motto of the gypsy lads in the square selling tatty bundles of greenery to those who had no gardens. *Hosanna* succumbed to this profiteering to the tune of ten francs' worth. Our green bundle smelt abominably of cat.

Laurel's name being what it is, we were struck by the Bishop's name being Hardy. He will never know how close he came to being a comic duo that Palm Sunday on the steps of the Cathedral. He was robed magnificently in scarlet, with a golden mitre and crook, and as we sang 'Hosanna in the highest' (with fervour, as that is the name of our boat), he began the blessing and we all raised our branches on high (blessing being a line-of-sight thing, like radio waves). We trooped into the church behind him, like Burnham Wood coming to Dunsinane.

The inside of the church was a surprise. Though the outside was square and blocky, the inside was an astonishing and soaring beauty, of columns and pointed arches, a gothic purity, austere and serene. There was no stained glass, no painted statues, no forest of hanging lamps, no banners, no colour at all except the Monsignor's scarlet and gold, the purple that shrouded the crucifix, and the green of our *rameaux*.

There were no embroidered kneelers either, and a stone floor, but it seemed we were not expected to kneel for prayer: the child beside us stood with his hands raised palms outwards in the *orante* position.

Calvin, the great reformer, who was born here and is given due recognition in the local museum, would have approved the austerity of this Cathedral.

After the service, with our brains and consciences washed pure, our fistful of blessed palm, and frozen feet, we took Sunday lunch at the Dame Journe. It was a very good lunch. We ate smoked eel, roast lamb and a *crepinette de lapin* with a red Sancerre.

Afterwards we walked slowly 1½ kilometres back to our boat. *Tansy* was waiting indignantly: Where the hell have you been when a cat needs feeding? Evidently she had not found a rat to her liking. Both cats showed a disquieting interest in our greenery, which Laurel had shoved raw into the shopping bag with the bread. The Bishop's blessing would undoubtedly have killed any germs, but didn't, seemingly, wash away the smell of cat.

We slept most of the afternoon.

• 3 •

POETS AND PUDDINGS
Compiègne to Rethel

We left the Canal du Nord, and joined River Oise, passing the industrial outskirts of Compiègne. We'd hoped to moor for lunch near the Armistice Clearing, where stands the historic railway carriage in which Marshall Foch took the surrender of the Germans in 1918. (In vengeful mode, Hitler made the French sign the instrument of capitulation in 1940 in the same railway carriage, which was then taken to Berlin in triumph, where the RAF destroyed it by bombing. The present one at Compiègne is a replica. These later details are not mentioned in French guides, such as the Green *Michelin.*) The River Guide showed a mooring, and we wanted to walk through the woods to the clearing during our lunch break: a welcome one, as often we snatch lunch separately while one of us steers.

There was no mooring, nor had there been one for donkey's years. The bank was shallow and unapproachable.

Farewell, Armistice Clearing.

That afternoon we ran aground twice. The fast river, full of floodwater, had deposited silt in unexpected places, in one case just in front of some lock gates. Powering out of such situations means that the filters for engine cooling water get clogged and have to be cleaned: Bill's job. He reported a sticky concrete-like mixture of clay, re-inforced with pondweed. Yuk.

Arrived at Soissons, we secured to a fine quay alongside a park near the Passarelle des Anglais. The day being dry and cold, we muffled up and went ashore. The market was closed, but we bought greengroceries at a magnificently domed and turreted *fin de siècle* building which had once been an hotel and smart café. In spite of the cold wind we found a sunny, sheltered corner and insisted on a drink outside. Hardy, we English, and desperate for a sign of summer. The sensible French were inside behind the steamy windows, drinking last summer's sunshine. When the first signs of frostbite appeared in our fingers we returned on board and lit our wood-burning stove, and on it grilled steak *au poivre*, with fresh peas and mushroom patties, a Bordeaux *cru bourgeois*, and strawberries and cream.

The following morning there was thick fog, so departure was delayed for more shopping and filter cleaning. We left at 1230 when the fog had dispersed. The current continued strong, though with all engines we made fair progress along the Canal Latéral à l'Aisne. We wanted to stop at Maizy, where old friends kept one of our favourite village *estaminets*, or small bar-restaurants.

We were going up through small locks, just big enough for a 38 metre barge, where the *éclusier* stops for lunch just as you get there. Nevertheless they are so much more friendly than the huge locks on the big canals. The lock cottages and their gardens are in attractive wooded country, and often there is a tall pear or cherry tree blossoming beside the lock. Usually there is a *basse-cour* (a poultry yard), sometimes a goat or two, and you can buy garden produce, eggs, rabbits and goat cheese.

It became, after the morning fog, a wonderful day. The woods on each side were full of blossom. When we passed seven years before, it had been autumn and it hadn't struck us that the haws then burning red in the thickets would have been may blossom in spring. Wild cherry blossom was everywhere, filling our heads with Houseman's poem, the cherry trees wearing white for Eastertide, and below on the left, River Aisne snaked beside us.

Further left, a ridge of hills was patched with colours, and so bright a green was the young grass and so fierce a yellow the rape seed that we were glad of the passing cloud shadows which muted them. On this ridge marches the Chemin des Dames, the Ladies' Road, used by the daughters of Louis Quinze when visiting their friend the Duchess of Narbonne.

Sloping up to the ridge were fields, hamlets, woods and orchards in blossom, the feathery green of poplar and birch, passing slowly and with no harm to body or soul. The blossom was so thick and widespread, welcoming the spring sun after a damp and flooding winter, that it seemed the ladies of France had thrown their lace curtains out into the garden to dry on the bushes.

Maizy is an awkward mooring against a sloping bank with insufficient bollards. When we finally moored after much tweaking, it was nearly 2000. We headed for the *estaminet*; Irène does not cook in the evenings out of season, so we drank their health and promised to return the following day.

Wednesday 12 April was misty and cool. Laurel wrote, and Bill changed the oil in all three engines. Ire invariably ensues. It does not matter how careful he is, he ends with filthy oil on his face, shoes, hands, arms, armpits, and if unlucky, his backside as well. It's simple enough for a motor car; you raise it on a lift, undo a nut, and let the oil drain into a well placed tank. Our engines are in the bottom of the boat, and the old oil has to be pumped into the can via two short lengths of plastic tubing. The treacly fluid pulses along these tubes, and if attention is relaxed for a millisecond, an end chooses that moment to flip out of the can and spray you from head to toe.

He managed without too much trauma, and went on to greasing and gearboxes.

Our friends Jean-Claude and Irène keep *Le Rivage*, which is also the Tabac, Newsagent, Bar-restaurant, and seller of torches, sweets,

Greengrocer's, Soissons

string, and the only two views of Maizy on postcards that exist. We were pleased that as usual the bar was full of friends, dogs and children, and that there were grey kittens in the cupboard under the counter. When old enough the kittens are temptingly displayed in a basket on the bar, and all find homes in a few days.

We were not allowed to take leave before lunch, and as the restaurant was busy so was Irène. It was 1400 before we sat down to radishes with coarse salt, French bread and new sweet butter. Irène's cooking always uses fresh and natural things, without making a fuss about it. Then there was chicken pie and salad. And as we were thinking: Oh good! a light lunch, just what we wanted: Lo! here came the Choucroute Alsacienne, a mountain of sauerkraut garnished with three kinds of sausage, chunks of boiled ham and slices of smoked pork. The wine, too, was from Eastern France, the Jura. 'It is a day of *bon souvenirs*,' said Irène. 'We conceived Sylvain (their youngest) ten years ago in the Jura Mountains; better not', she said modestly, 'go into further detail!'

The whole gang then trooped down to look at the boat, it having been unconverted when we passed seven years before. Then back to the bar for dessert and coffee, and it was 1630 before we left for Berry-au-Bac. This canal junction is noted for its *épicerie*, which sells goods needed by bargees. Because of the junction Berry is a waiting place for barges without cargo, and a stopping place for those with. We were hoping to buy rope, but it was 1900 before we arrived, and we took an hour to moor because of shallows. Finally we did the simplest thing and moored alongside another barge. The bar/*épicerie*/chandler's was firmly closed, so firmly that it looked as if it would be closed for ever; the windows were boarded up.

It was on a cold, clear, dry morning that we set out on the climb to the Ardennes. 'Dubrovnik under mortar fire' said the headlines. Dubrovnik seemed far away from the Canal des Ardennes, described in the Guide as 'very wild, impossible to approach the banks'. The trees and bushes, and the may in bloom came down into the water, and root and branch encroached on the canal. It seemed as if time rolled back when we saw a charcoal burner working on several carefully arranged piles of smoking logs. Dotting the banks were primrose and cowslips and wild violets, and sharp green spears showed where yellow flags would soon bloom. In our years in the Mediterranean we had forgotten the power and wonder of a northern spring.

At Asfeld we came across the first manual 'wind-the-handle' lock, and Bill went ashore to help with the winding. We were climbing, the lock wall was high above us, and Laurel was glad of her grannypole, an invention of our own. A removable stout steel pole, rising about 5 feet vertically between the forward bitts, acts as a steadier to hold on to when reaching for high lockside bollards, and jumping ashore.

There were more woodstacks at the lock at Pargny, but not for charcoal. They were immense and impressive. Bill chatted to the lock-keeper as they wound the gates together. 'I have wood always for at least two winters,' said the *éclusier*. 'It burns better and one can choose.'

It conjured up a picture of log tasting as of fine vintage wines: 'We'll burn some of the 1988 hornbeam from the forest of Signy tonight, not the 1970 pearwood from Grandfather's old orchard; I've laid that down for our silver wedding. And a nice dry crisp log it will be by then, with a good colour flame and a lovely bouquet.'

At Rethel, we found the municipality had provided a good mooring with picnic tables, rings, mown grass, a toilet block, water and electricity (for the three latter apply to the Bureau de Tourism or, out of season, the Mairie). It was both out of season, and out of working hours. We had two loos and a bath on board, plenty of water, and would use our own generator, as usual.

The last *éclusier* had recommended the restaurant near the station, so Bill logically headed for the footbridge that flanks the railway bridge over both canal and River Aisne. Getting up onto the footbridge involved an undignified scramble up a steep slope in a dense thicket of trees. Could this be right? Surely not! At the other end of the bridge was a blocking fence and a 30 foot drop. Down below us in the river the *sapeurs pompiers* were practising launching their rescue boat.

'How do we get down?' we shouted. They smiled and shrugged. 'Have you no parachute?' they jested. We had in mind to challenge them to get us down as if from a burning building, but they were busy retrieving their rescue boat and we thought better of it. We retraced our steps and very wickedly crossed the river on the rail bridge, absolutely *défendu*, but some sensible character had painted over the forbidding notice, so we could claim, if challenged, to be idiot tourists, forget our French, and plead total ignorance. Before arriving at the station we found a gate opening into a car park, and slipped through without having to explain why we were arriving on foot without a railway ticket.

The restaurant was worth the excitement. We ate the renowned Rethel *Boudin Blanc* (white pudding) on a bed of fried apples, followed by saddle of lamb. We walked back to the boat the long way, to settle and digest, and not grow too fat. We don't always eat out as much as we were doing then but, conscious of the culinary desert that loomed ahead in Eastern Europe, particularly in Romania, we indulged while we could.

On Good Friday, Laurel defrosted the hot cross buns laid down for the occasion and heated them for breakfast. Then we went looking for fish.

We ran some to earth at a *traiteur*'s, finding also that Rethel is rent by the War of White Puddings. In the 17th century, one Jacques Auguste Charamonde fled Paris because of illegal duelling, and came to Rethel, where he swapped sword for boning knife, set up as a *charcutier*, and invented the *Boudin Blanc*. The secret recipe was transmitted from father to sons, until now six *charcutiers* claim to be direct descendants of Charamonde, and to make the *only* authentic Rethel white pudding.

'What's in it?' we asked, when we bought some from the *charcutier* who displayed seven different kinds of sausage in seven different colours: red, brown, pink, fawn, purple, maroon, and of course white, in a pile three times the size of the others.

'The best white pork, milk, and eggs,' we were told.

'Do I boil it?' Laurel asked, thinking of Frankfurters. He tutted. 'No, in the *poèle*, the frying pan, gently, with a little butter. No need to prick the skin.'

He had done our cooking for the day. We had his crab scallops for lunch, with a salad of purslane, and that night we had salmon with sorrel sauce.

Sausages and the 19th century Symbolic Poets have little in common except the town of Rethel. The story of Rimbaud and Verlaine is so colourful that it out-Korda's Hollywood. Rimbaud, wild, sullen, gifted and evil, was born close by in the Ardennes, wrote astonishing poems from the age of 10, and ran away to Paris, where he went in for Black Arts and Dubious Philosophies, debauching himself deliberately in search of (he thought) a transcendental world. He was 17 years old when he wrote to the established poet Verlaine, sending him some of his poems, from which Verlaine took him to be at least 30. They met. Verlaine, married a year before, left his wife for Rimbaud, and the pair roamed France, England and Belgium until Verlaine, after a second attempt to murder his companion, was imprisoned. Rimbaud nearly died of the wound. He stopped writing two years later at the age of 20 and disappeared.

In prison, Verlaine converted to Catholicism and began to write greater poetry, though whether due to past sodomy or present suffering would be hard to say. Believing him dead, he published Rimbaud's work, and the absent and unknowing Rimbaud was greatly praised as he wandered anonymously from Sumatra to Cyprus to Abyssinia, working as a labourer; he came back to Marseille with a tumour on the knee. The leg was amputated but he died, aged 37.

The tortured Verlaine taught here in Rethel at the College after his release from prison. He horrified the residents with his drinking habits. He died celebrated but in poverty, and there was no crock of gold at the end of the Rimbaud either.

At some recent time a barge had unloaded timber on the quay. Bill put on his Witch-in-the-Dark-Forest kit and went out with a sack to gather firewood. He was picking up pieces of kindling, which we still needed every night, when a prince appeared in the shape of a frog: an elderly French gentleman, who owned the nearby small furniture factory. 'If you need wood for your stove, come and help yourself to our off-cuts,' he offered.

Bill accepted gratefully. In the workshop this generous man even cut up the pieces of oak, beech and pearwood into stove-sized pieces on a band-saw. In France mass-production of mediocre furniture is not so dominant as in Britain, and there is a tradition of small furniture makers that still continues. Bill was impressed by the stocks of maturing hardwoods at the back, and got the impression of a craftsman with great pride in his work. We embarked several sacks of off-cuts, well seasoned wood, which burned with welcome warmth.

The Navigation sent two young men to ask our plans for the ascent of Montgon. This Everest-like feat lay ahead of us: a staircase of automatic locks to the summit of the Canal des Ardennes, a rise of 80 metres over 8 kilometres by means of a chain of 26 locks. You do not stop (nor pass GO, nor collect £200), but pass directly to the summit, supervised by an *éclusier* to see that nothing goes amiss. The Guide recommends a whole day for it.

They were organising the rota so the *éclusiers* could have their Easter holiday. It seemed we were the only candidates for the staircase; the lower Meuse was still closed, so there was less commercial traffic than usual, and no other *plaisanciers*. 'We shall arrange it for you,' they said. We had the satisfying feeling that tomorrow, Easter Saturday, the entire Navigation would be working solely for *Hosanna*.

• 4 •
STAIRCASE TO THE ARDENNES
The ascent of Montgon

It was bitterly cold again, and we needed a wheelhouse heater although it was mid-April. We were trying to find some new-laid eggs for Easter Day, but nobody was about. Lockside hens are free range, with cocks for company, old-fashioned enough to go out of lay in the early spring.

There was a thick mist, which made it hard to see the gates of the locks, which were semi-automatic. Before these locks a wire stretches across the canal, and from it depends a pole, and you must seize the pole and give it a sharp twist to activate the lock. There is always an agonising wait while you think it hasn't triggered, but usually all turns out well.

At Attigny lock, where the houses had gardens and orchards and carefully tended allotments coming down to the banks, we found what we were looking for, as a pleasant lady in a blue pinafore brought us some new-laid bantam eggs.

At noon we approached the first of the Montgon chain. The locks are fully automatic and computer controlled, and as you leave one lock the next prepares itself and eventually opens. Then it automatically closes its gates behind you when you have entered, fills or empties the chamber as appropriate, and with bells ringing gaily spits you out towards the next one in the chain, 200 metres or so further on. A supervising *éclusier* was ready to start us off in good order.

It is forbidden to stop in the chain, and, once started, it was like childbirth, an inexorable progression taking several hours with no time to drink a cup of tea, let alone stop to make one. No time to do more than appreciate, as snapshots, the sight of a dozen cream-coloured Charolais calves clustered like brides under veils of may blossom at the water's edge. The low hills we climbed were pasture-land for multicoloured dairy cows; they charged downhill, thundering over the lush grass to look at us.

We could see water tumbling at the far end of the open lock, and River Aisne flowing below us on the right. We greeted our attendant lock-keeper, who would supervise us right to the top, as far as Montgon. As we rose in the lock the noise of the water became quieter. Bill and the *éclusier* discussed stopping for lunch. To our delight he was amenable to stopping in the lock: a rare chance to be seized with both hands. It would have to be a quick lunch, as the ascent could take 3 hours, and there would be no other chance to eat.

We started 40 minutes later due to Tansy having woken earlier than usual and gone walkabout. We found her under an evergreen bush and reluctant to emerge. Thereafter Laurel fixed 3 metres of red ribbon to her collar, as a useful clue to her whereabouts. Bograt was more a homebird, seldom wandered, and tumbled back on board like a shot from a gun if anything moved. Her experience at Marquion seemed to have taught her caution.

It began to rain near the top of the chain; a pity, for it hid the view down the valley, where the steep watersteps fell away behind us. By this time we both had backache and were chilled, as the wheelhouse doors had to be kept open to get a good steering line on lock entrances. Bill began to tire and misjudged No 3, hitting the lock sides as we entered. The jolt panicked the cats, who headed straight for their cupboards. Laurel took over, and made a perfect entry into No 2, but a total mess of No 1, the last lock. In fact Bill had to seize the wheel and put things right. She was tired too.

We had risen at 0700, and passed 6 locks before entering the chain of 26 at 1230, and were at the summit after a passage of 5½ hours more, which our *éclusier* said was good going. We moored at 1800 at Le Chesne, and in the time it would take to drive a car from London to York, we had covered 8 kilometres. At that pace our souls certainly keep up with our bodies.

We moored, as so often happens, in the rain; an easy moor to a welcoming gravel quay with a dustbin and a green hedge for the cats to play in.

We had the bantam's eggs for our Easter breakfast. Le Chesne (The Oak) is an agricultural village, and the general store was close enough to stock up with heavy gas canisters which cannot be carried long distances. We had a drink at the *Charrue d'Or*, the Golden Plough, a beer and a kir for 11 francs, the cheapest we had found in France for years.

We went again for a supper of lamb chops and chips. A cheap and cheerful place with a number of locals at the bar, where we had our coffee and *digestifs* after eating, and saw a notice on the wall offering a good price for *'chêne mitraillé'* (machine-gunned oak trees). Bill was puzzled, realising that the presence of bullets in the tree would ruin a saw. What, he asked, was the purpose of buying machine-gunned trees? Who would want them? Nearly all the woods around there, where armies had slogged it out for centuries, were composed of trees that had dozens of bullets in them, they told us. Until recently, their use had not been economic, but an enterprising sawyer had bought a metal detector and was able to avoid the bullets embedded in the trees, from which he made split rail fencing. But what must it be like to live in a place where every old tree is full of bullets? What memories must it bring shuddering to the surface?

Not only the trees got machine-gunned. In the square by the canal stood a beautiful late Gothic cross, replacing one that had been there

The Chain of Montgon

since 1207. It was pitted and flaked by the gunfire of countless armies, the warm stone scarred like an old warrior.

And in Jugoslavia too, the bloody conflict went on.

We left next morning in pouring rain. We had left up a TV aerial from the night before, and in the panic of getting it down before the first bridge, Laurel slipped and bruised her knee. She bruises easily, but any Boatwife knows what a bruiser a steel barge is.

We passed a watershed, and neared the Meuse. Down-going locks are more difficult to see in a barge than upgoing ones; when you approach an upgoing one the lock is empty, the walls stand up high on either side, and the entrance is obvious. Downgoing, you come into a full lock with only an inch or two of stonework above the water. This means pointing at an almost invisible opening which disappears altogether under the flare of the bows when you're 15 metres from it. All you can do then is hope you've got it right.

Herds of cows wandered in the wet meadows and came down to inspect our passing. Neither they nor the sheep seemed to mind the rain. But then the Lord provided them with efficient, fashionably coloured oilskins, breathable ones, and all sheep have been anointed with lanolin.

We seized lunch on the wing, a warming plate of ravioli, followed by chocolate Easter eggs. Not very well balanced, but it was too cold for salads.

The short tunnel of St Aignan, after lunch, was so shrouded in rain you could hardly see it. 'Light your headlamps,' said a notice, 'One way only.' But which way? There were no traffic lights. The entrance was awkward, right on a bend, and we ploughed through mud all the way. There were two manual locks the other side and nobody about so we gave a hoot, which produced a young man on a bicycle who took us through both and told us of a good mooring. It was only 1430 but the weather was wintry, and Laurel's knee stiff: time to stop.

We berthed in heavy rain at Pont-à-Bar where the canal joins the upper Meuse. We lit the fire, enjoying the crackling warmth of logs in the stove, and even the spit and rattle of rain on the roof, now that we were inside and at rest.

Laurel's bruise and the rain, together with arctic temperatures, induced a day's pause, as there were domestic chores and maintenance to keep us occupied. Bill put on his new oilskin and went for another gas bottle and new rope as Laurel was tired of the rough, hair-shedding junk that we were economically using up. The rope was white and smooth, though kinky and wilful, being new, but that would cure itself by stretching.

We tried the local pub. We entered followed by a blast of wind and rain which slammed the door behind us, and found the bar wonderfully warmed by an old wood stove. It had one of those notices which we so enjoy: 'Ramassage de Monstres' (Collection of Monsters). What leftovers from Jurassic Park were they meaning? It was the Municipality's infrequent collection of large items of rubbish: old mattresses, armchairs, the fridge that doesn't work. (For wrecked cars, phone first). There were no provision shops nearby, so we returned on board and passed a quiet evening, each with a bored cat on our laps.

We joined, with some trepidation, the upstream Meuse. Navigation remained closed below Charleville-Meziers, 14 kilometres downstream, which had been inundated in the January floods, when the river had been in flood throughout the Low Countries. They were repairing the damage, and hoping to reopen before the end of May. We had chosen this route to avoid the stoppage and were now going upstream towards Sedan, which had also suffered serious flooding. The signs were there: on the high banks the fence wires were strung and woven with grass sieved from the torrent as it raged past 3 metres above normal, leaving débris and shredded plastic caught in the bushes, up to a line as straight as a rule. After all the rain the current was strong against us, as we had feared, about 6 km/hr. Even with all engines we made slow progress, and found more locks giving trouble.

At Donchery most of the river careered off down a weir as we reached the quieter waters of the lock approach and triggered the radar beam successfully. The gates opened for us and closed behind us, and nothing happened. After ten minutes we pulled the 'red' alarm. A man came out of the cottage. 'Ah, someone will be coming,' he said. 'Me, I'm not on duty,' but he stopped awhile to chat about the vagaries of lock gates. 'It's the electrical contacts that don't always work,' he said, 'especially in the rain.' It took us 30 minutes to get through instead of the usual 10.

We passed the approaches to Sedan, which told us (in English) that in 500 metres there existed a Municipal Fluvial Haltingplace. It was up a side stream where we could just see a noticeboard and an overturned cabin. Nothing else. Judging by the television pictures we saw in January of the river roaring up to the top of the arches of the bridge, the Municipality of Sedan have more urgent things to do than replace the pontoons for the Municipal Haltingplace. Even the riverside houses quite high above the water had suffered; you could see the débris caught on the bushes where the floods had rushed through their gardens and in at the ground floor.

In the Meuse our tactics changed from those we had used in the Canal, where ship-handling is tricky because the boat almost fills the cross section of the canal, and water has to force its way past the moving boat. Rivers are wider, but present their own problems. To cheat the current we kept to the edges where it was shallow and the current less strong. On bends the current was stronger on the outside so we cut corners, not too close or we grounded, as these inside corners are also shallower.

The current in the river made entering locks difficult. On rivers these are built on a side cutting at an angle to the flow. You can't reasonably go full speed into a lock only a few inches wider than the boat: the consequences of misjudgement would be disastrous. One has to approach crabwise until suddenly the bows get into slack water while the stern is still in the flow and the boat swings wildly. You have to take your hat off to the professional bargee. When your boat behaves like a sulky and wilful child at every lock, it can leave you drained and tired at the end of the day, but unlike the professionals we could stop early, and when we saw an attractive *Halte Fluviale* at Mouzon, we decided to celebrate, for at noon we had been travelling for two weeks, accomplishing 431 kilometres and 90 locks. We winkled our way backwards into a narrow side cut and made fast. As we secured the last mooring rope to an ice cream advertisement, it started to drizzle.

Here we met other *plaisanciers*: a local school class in three boats, watched over by some desperate but dedicated teachers, who had sent their charges out to play football in the rain. Well, what would you do with them? A party of children then chased our cats good-naturedly in order to stroke them.

To escape boisterous children we put on oilskins, abandoned the cats to an overdose of affection, and went for a walk. We saw the Abbey (locked), the Felt Museum (closed), and a pile of *Monstres* awaiting collection behind the church, including the obligatory mattress (complete with bed in this case) and busted fridge, but no dilapidated armchair.

Thursday 20 April was a day of comparative rest. Domestic chores caught up with us. As the weather remained cold, and we needed more wood to burn, Bill cut up some of the broken wooden mast that remained from last September's dismasting. We got the chain saw out under the intrigued gaze of the schoolchildren, and very soon their teachers, who came along to assist and ask questions.

They were taking on water. We carry water to last at least six weeks, longer if we're careful, but their little holiday *pénichettes* need frequent filling. We were too late to advise them to hose down the tap first. Washing the tap before taking on water is part of our routine; the French walk their dogs on these pleasant quaysides, and the dogs love a good upstanding water tap. Municipalities never understand the need to raise standpipes above the jetstream of the average Alsatian.

Laurel hoovered the wheelhouse which was suffering from sawdust, plus bits of fibre dropped off our hairy rope, a certain amount of grass, mud, and cat fluff.

We also did some writing. Where else but on *Hosanna* would you boot a laptop computer by opening the fridge door? It's perfectly logical. Our low power system, which runs the TV, a little food beater, and the computers when the generator isn't on, works off an inverter which switches itself on when there is a 'call'. The laptop takes so little power that the inverter doesn't hear the 'call', but the fridge light is enough to trigger it. To check that the inverter is working, we switch on the radio, and if there is terrible interference, it is. *C'est la vie du bateau*, that's life on a boat, as a bargee friend of ours says.

The Felt Museum was open next time we walked past, and we went in to watch a demonstration. All you need to make felt from the raw material (wool or hair) is heat, damp, movement, and a little pressure, as most new Mums find out when the matinée jacket knitted by Auntie ends up the size and texture of an asbestos egg cosy.

Bograt fell in again that night, but this time she wasn't raped; just wet from what would be her waist if she had one, she being barrel-shaped, which is why she got the name Bograt; her Sunday name is Shadow, but from the beginning she was mischievous and got into trouble and got called Ratbag, and Rotguts, and Bograt. The latter stuck.

Friday was fine, but cold; 10°C at noon. We left our backwater as the Abbey clock struck nine, and followed the canal section past neat back gardens patrolled by strict rows of tulips, and prepared to rejoin the river. The Canal Guide gave us no warning of an unguarded weir, and as we passed the Sommer felt factory, suddenly, to our horror, the entire River Meuse was dropping off a cliff nearby to the right over an unprotected weir two or three metres deep. We saw it coming and revved up the engines to stem the current and avoid being swept sideways, but we were taken aback that there were no warning signs.

The valley sides were steep, sometimes wooded, and occasionally opened out into a plain. At Alma the lock-keeper told us that it was deforesting the hills which caused flooding; even two hours' rain goes straight into the Meuse and the current increases dramatically. This news was perturbing as we had had two DAYS of rain. There was none at the moment, and the sun was trying to elbow the clouds aside, but it was cold.

During the morning the river took us from the *département* of the Ardennes to that of the Meuse. We were now in Lorraine, and stopped at lunchtime at Stenay, another tricky berth up a winding side stream.

How could we pass up a visit to the Beer Museum in the Old Malthouse? It claims to have brewed the first beer in the world. But the word used is *mondiale* which often means 'in all France' (France *is* the world that matters, is it not?) or even 'all around here'. Brewing methods were explained, with a nod towards the Anglo-Saxons over the water who do odd things involving hops. There were tools, implements, gleaming copper mash tubs, wreaths of hops and examples of old advertisements of the Mucha school. The visit ended in the cellar with a taste of the local brew. Both museum and cellar were unheated, and the hot soup we had had for lunch had long since leached out of our bones. We were frozen. We opted for coffee which was available as an alternative. It was served with a slightly disapproving air by a bar lady who clearly thought these British lack strength and stamina.

We walked back past a huge old barracks, now empty of soldiers. Once France had great armies deployed here, near their frontier with Germany, with a second row of bases further back. Confident, at least in the short term, of peace, these large, ugly buildings stand empty. Soon France is to move away from the conscripted army, a feature of French culture since the revolution, and follow the British example to a professional, highly technical, but smaller, force. The following days would remind us sharply of battles long ago.

• 5 •

WARS AND RUMOURS OF WARS

Stenay to Toul

Stenay is off the river, up a narrow, curved, sidestream with a strong current from the weir. We would have to back out: bad enough in a car, where at least the tarmac stays still. Bill thought we'd be OK if we took it slowly, going astern on the outer engines, and ahead on the centre. Laurel would let go forward first, then we would spring the boat off and wriggle out.

It went better than we dared hope. We didn't touch anything and we didn't run aground, and fortunately there was nothing coming as we backed round the blind corner into the river. A tremendous thump under the boat cut short our glee. After two days of rain the river was running strongly, bringing heavy débris down, and we had collided with a tree trunk which was now bobbing away behind us. It didn't seem to have harmed us: our propellers are in cages to prevent such an accident doing damage.

During the long day we got used to the braiding and interlacing of the Meuse and the Canal de l'Est. We even got used to the unmarked weirs on the river, where the water would suddenly fall away on our right, usually the only tell-tale sign being uprooted trees lodged at the top.

What we didn't get used to, here in Lorraine, was the constant reminder of death in battle. As *Hosanna* rose slowly in the lock at Charny, the crosses of the French Cemetery came into view, row upon row in the rain, eerie, compelling. On the hills to the east lie five dead villages, never rebuilt after the terrible campaign that devastated the area in 1916/17, the Battle of Verdun, one of the most costly in human lives.

We saw on the hill the obelisk-shaped tower of the Ossuary where Douaumont stood, one of the vanished villages, scene of some of the most brutal and stubborn fighting in World War I. On each side of the tower extend wings where lie the bones of 130,000 dead.

These are merely the unknown dead.

The known, more than 500,000 of them, lie under their white crosses in the cemeteries that patch the hills around Verdun. The bodies of more than 200,000 Germans lie hereabouts, too. To the French it is a holy place, and some of that awe should touch all of us, their allies, for here they endured and held the German advance. It was a battle whose importance is often carelessly marginalised in British histories.

We were tired after 12 locks, and a bit subdued as we arrived in the City of Verdun at 1800, at a fine new municipal pontoon. We were the only boat there. There were working electricity points on the pontoon, which gave us free power. There was drinking water too, an excellent welcome for the nautical visitor to this fine city, in contrast to what we would find later in Strasbourg.

At the top of the quay was the Hotel Coq Hardi, whose restaurant we looked forward to patronising again. It is a place of character known to us since the sixties. The rambling hotel with its quirky staircase had been modernised, and the restaurant extended. A significant proportion of the clientèle comes from an American base in Germany, and there was a party of young soldiers nearby celebrating a birthday with a certain amount of cheerful, well-mannered noise.

The menu at 198 francs provided an unusual combination of poached egg decorated with leaves of smoked salmon. It was a delight to the eye as well as to the palate. There was a choice of roast lamb garnished with kidneys and sweetbread, or roast sucking pig. We had one of each, and we drank Toul pinot noir, the latter a disappointment, though our overall satisfaction was high.

Monday dawned with thick fog. The stream was running faster than when we arrived, and Bill decided the auguries were bad for navigation. This suited Laurel, who wanted to look round the shops.

The *éclusier* came to ask if we were moving on. With so few boats coming through they liked to plan their day, and there was friendly pressure to do it their way. A Frenchman wants his lunch, and it is pleasant and polite to tell him your plans and keep to them. We arranged to get under way at 1100 next day.

When we left Verdun, fighting the current, it was a spectacular exit: a weir, the lock, and a tunnel under the ramparts. We passed elegant high stone quays, with old buildings perched on the green and wooded slopes above them: a church above an ivied stone wall, a stained glass conservatory. Then with accustomed shock we heard a menacing roar increase, and saw ahead of us the great waves foam and cream, and clouds of rainbow-spangled spume above the weir, over which it seemed we were doomed to crash, since the alternative passage for navigation was not apparent till almost upon it. Through the binoculars we could now see the lock; we were expected, the gates were open. But the water level was high and the current boisterous as we bucked and struggled past the weir crashing over the sill to our right, and the approach was far from easy. We sighed with relief as we slid into the lock and the roar of the weir cut off behind us as the gates closed.

It was the first of a series of narrow locks, still unmechanised. Bill was winding one gate open while the lock-keeper wound the other; it's quicker if you help. As we emerged, high thick walls of ancient stone towered over us, and we passed through a tunnel under the fortifications, which were built in 1620 and reinforced by the military architect Vauban, 50 years later. It had been found impossible to widen the old river for navigation, for it would have entailed too much destruction of the fortress, and instead a diversion had been built, burrowing through the walls where they were least impenetrable. The noise of our engine echoed and thundered like the ghost of worldwar gunfire as we went through.

Bill photographed the swirl of water coming into one of the locks. 'For us it's not serious,' we said, 'but it's different for a little yacht, they get thrown about.' 'Ah yes,' said the lock-keeper. 'One tells them to moor at the back where it's calm, but always they want to go right up to the front. So we let the water in a little bit fast, to make them think. But they learn nothing, they pass all the locks like that! We have no problems with the Dutch or the English, even the Swiss and the Belgians: but the Germans! They know everything and there's always trouble.'

As promised on the map at the approach to St Mihiel we met the seven 'Dames de Meuse', seven huge stone buttes rising from the cliffs on the riverside, cork shaped, each one as big as a castle keep, set into a steeply green and wooded slope. Time has sculpted them into the seven Ladies of the Meuse, grey and craggy and Junoesque, and below them striped allotments ran down to the banks, as if the Ladies knelt with their aprons on the ground.

We arrived at St Mihiel, a town well known to American military historians, just before a cataclysmic thunderstorm broke over us. Half an hour later and we'd have been mooring in a downpour. We waited for the storm to grumble away eastwards and then walked in steady, but no longer torrential, rain to the Trianon restaurant. Not much to look at outside, but inside was an elegant Louis Quinze décor in blue-grey and cream with elaborate plasterwork and chandeliers, and very heartening food after the thunderstorm, good bourgeois cooking; salad of veal tongue, roast guineafowl, and a wine that was twice as good and half the price of the one at the Coq Hardi. Bill got his *fromage frais* at long last, and we both had an excellent *crême brulée*. It was raining harder as we walked back to the boat.

When we were very young and courting we used to go for walks in the rain, since there was nowhere else to go that didn't cost money. Sending passionate messages via our clasped hands, bony, wet and cold, we dreamed of our own future fireside, and the bliss of being able to talk in the warm if we could keep our hands off each other. Nowadays we had not walked in the rain much till the last ten days, but our fireside on *Hosanna* was just as comforting as we had anticipated, except that forty years on we tend to fall contentedly asleep.

It was still raining on the morning of Wednesday 26 April, but we walked into town at 0830. St Mihiel is the birthplace of the 16th century sculptor Ligier Richier, and two of his works are here. Before the supermarket opened at 0900 we could visit the church containing the *Descent from the Cross*, and the *Swooning Virgin*.

Lock and cherry tree on the Meuse

The church was open. It was gloomy, heavy stained glass filtering what daylight there was and no lamps lit. The sculpture of Mary fainting in the arms of St John is carved from a massive piece of walnut; it was in a dark corner, surrounded by a stout rail marked '*alarmé*'. Laurel suggested that Bill kept well back, remembering a débacle in Arles at a Van Gogh exhibition when by leaning forward he'd set the alarm off and we were suddenly surrounded by intense men in dark suits.

He did it again! We think he triggered it by idly swinging the shopping bag. The church shrilled with alarm bells for a few moments and we resisted the temptation to run. No one came, and we had time to appreciate the mastery of the piece, the tension of St John bearing the weight of the Virgin whose arms hang perfectly limp and relaxed. It was too dark to see the other sculpture.

In the supermarket two dames discussed the storm. 'My old one was watching Le Roogby. I told him: unplug, cheri, or you risk to explode the Tele, but he would not!' The local paper contained accounts of flooded streets, interruptions to traffic, and the number of television sets that *had* blown up. Back to the boat with dripping shopping, we cast off.

The rain wore long skirts today, and her smokey hems trailed halfway down the hills. Passing the locks was a damp and drippy business. Coming to the lock at Vadonville was a notice saying: 'Floods in the Meuse – the navigation presents dangers; inform yourself at the next lock.' We did so. 'Oh mon Dieu, is that still there?' said one of the *éclusiers*, 'We ought to put a dustbin bag over that.' 'It's been there since January then, has it?' said Bill. 'It's been there since January *last year*!' they said, laughing heartily.

At Commercy the Guide marks a good quay. 'Oh yes, there's a good quay, but...' an *éclusier* confirmed doubtfully. On arrival we were not surprised that he was doubtful. The quay had depth, there were bollards, and normally that is all we ask. But it had been let to a builder's merchant. Heaps of gravel almost hid the bollards, cottage sized stacks of breeze blocks lay about. Apart from a strip of grass at the quay's edge the ground was a yellow soup of mud. We moored nonetheless. We had intended a walk into town, but another thunderstorm dissuaded us.

Laurel had been looking forward to the Madeleines of Commercy, those little sponge cakes brought to France by King Stanislas' chef. She fancied one with her tea, but we postponed that treat till the next day, when we walked into Commercy to look at King Stanislas' summer palace and hunting lodge. The palace now houses the Post Office, the Mairie, the Tax Office and the Police, and is well maintained, which cannot be said of the horseshoe of contemporary buildings at its gates, which are elegant but dilapidated. If only the cafés and *petits commerces* which inhabit them could bully some cash from somewhere, the Place of the Horseshoe would be worth a visit.

The Tourist Office should have opened at 1030. We waited with our paper bag of Madeleines until 1100, having words to say about moorings and things. We gave up. Commercy got zero for *acceuil.*

It was foggy. No hills visible at all. Leaving Commercy there are warnings that the weir is a 'danger to navigation in times of strong water', and 'Traction à la Bricole' is 'interdit'. This phrase was beyond our French. It turned out to mean that pulling a barge along by manpower with a rope across your chest, as they used to do in the last century, was forbidden. 'That notice must have been there many a long year,' said the lock-keeper who explained it to us. Lock-keepers never see what's on the canal, because they travel between locks by road.

We moored at Pagny, a nice little village with a *Halte Fluviale.* Shortly after, the Tour Boat *St Mihiel* also moored, with a party of German youth on board. At 2200 a laden barge went by, slowly. All the same, she pulled out the bolts from our after mooring, they came clean through the soft aluminium of the pontoon. Bill took our stern line round a solid brick flowerbed after that. He doesn't think much of aluminium.

Shopping next morning, we complimented Madame on the pretty village and the provision of moorings, compared with Commercy. 'Ah, Commercy is *triste*, it's sad,' she said. 'Their Mayor doesn't care. Here we have a woman in charge. She sees things from a different point of view.' We agreed. Laurel needed a different point of view going back to the boat. The German lads had got tired of waiting their turn in the toilets provided, and were playing 'highest up the wall' at the back of the Mairie.

We were on our way to Toul now. We had thought of trying the Toul wine at our dinner in St Mihiel, for it figured prominently on the list. In conversation with Madame however, we raised the thought that we had not much enjoyed the Toul we had drunk at Verdun.

'That does not surprise me,' she said, 'it has its adherents, but I, myself, think it is over-rated.'

Just after we crossed into the *département* of Meurthe-et-Moselle, we passed through the tunnel of Lay St Rémy, the summit between the Meuse and the Moselle, and started descending towards the valley of the Moselle and the city of Toul. There were woods and singing birds on either side, and doubtless somewhere in the mist were the orchards of mirabelles, the little yellow cherry plums that are to Lorraine what cherries are to Kent, or apples to Worcester. They are made into conserves too grand to be called jam, and Eau de Vie de Mirabelles, which sounds so much more musical than plum brandy.

Arrived at Toul (never mind its wine), we found a pleasant *bassin* to moor in: the city had turned an old commercial basin into a smart yacht harbour. We had some difficulty berthing as it had silted up, but were glad of its electricity points and rubbish bins. There was company in the shape of a French motor boat *Garuda*, bound, like us, for the Danube, with whom we exchanged news, rumours, and information; and a Norwegian yachtsman on his way back to Norway via River Moselle. Toul is a waterway junction; from here you can go north to Holland, east towards Germany as we were doing, south down to the Rhône, or west towards Paris or Calais.

The Michelin Guide promised us a Red R restaurant within 100 metres of the mooring, and as Laurel was not in walking mood, Bill went in search of information. There was a party going on inside, but when he entered to make a reservation he was met with apologies. They had closed the day before for their annual holiday. Bill had now to look elsewhere. Alas, there was no elsewhere within walking distance except Le Fast Food. We do not come to France for that.

• 6 •
LA BELLE ÉPOQUE
Toul, Nancy, Lagarde

We left Toul heading for Nancy, a day's run of 31 kilometres and 8 locks. The Guide indicated a mooring in the town centre, and we planned to spend some days there over the May Day holiday weekend.

Because we could not get into small locks together, *Garuda* went first, 30 minutes ahead of us. As we approached the first lock, No 26, the gates refused to open. We tried to get the *éclusier* on the telephone, but could not raise him.

Laurel had painted the port rubbing strake the previous night. It looked as if she would now have time to paint the starboard one.

Bill's ears were steaming. There was a rainguage at the lock, a funnel-shaped affair about two feet off the ground. If they didn't hurry up, he said, he would falsify their weather records by a bit of creative micturation, which were not quite the words he used, but you get the drift. And Laurel could have done the painting before the *éclusier* turned up, looking flustered, and locked us through.

We passed the mossy ancient ramparts of Toul, waited for a lift bridge, nothing happening and nowhere to park; they were agonisingly slow to acknowledge our existence. When the bell rang and the green light came on, we went through a narrow gap listening to the *éclusiers* at locks No 27 and 28 excitedly discussing on VHF the absence of Monsieur 26, and a certain amount of ribald speculation as to the reasons therefore, involving a certain widow well known to all. Monsieur 27 had the gates open and the lock ready for us, as if to apologise for his colleague. A '*responsable*' who had witnessed our long wait said that it was not at all *normale*, Monsieur 26 had deserted his post. We will be kind and surmise that having seen *Garuda* and the Norwegian yacht through he thought that was that for the day.

After the third lock, where the line drawn on the cabin wall showed the height of the Moselle floods, quite as bad as those of the Meuse but less well televised, we entered the canalised Moselle. It was wide, and on each side were plains and woods of brilliant colour; a yellow field of rape-seed and the sharp spring green of the trees. This is a busy waterway, and ahead was a commercial barge. We had been spoilt for the last ten days with the long section from Pont-à-Bar to this point. Except for this morning, almost every lock had been ready and waiting for us; we had been through as quickly as was possible, so we had made exceptionally good time. It would be slower now, though nice to have company. Better still, the sun was trying to get through the cloud and it was warmer; Bill was threatening to take his jersey off and risk frightening the cats with naked skin.

It was not easy to have a hot lunch, and eat together as one of us had always to steer. 'Liverdun welcomes us' said Laurel, chewing, as we approached. 'Mediaeval city' declaimed the poster. '*Toutes commerces. Pharmacie*. Camping. Swimming pool, Yachting. Promenades in the forest'. Beautiful as the valley is, with the pretty little town perched on its own hill above the river, we were not stopping here; we were going on to Nancy. So we admired, as we passed, the ramparts and towers, the grey stone and red roofs and flowering cherries, the towered Chateau and the spire of the church crowning the town at the very top.

The bridge at Liverdun was a narrow mediaeval bridge with arches. The arch for boats to use on the waterways is marked with a yellow diamond, and those you don't use are marked with a striped red and white square, the nautical 'No Entry' sign. Picturesque as it was, bridges are built for road traffic, not for we barge people, and this bridge was at an awkward angle: the arch in use was difficult to negotiate, and they'd had to erect a wooden fender in one corner of it, to fend off barges hitting it on the turn. Being smaller than commercial barges, we managed to avoid clouting it as we passed.

The high wooded slopes on each side were clad with tall fir trees and birch, green with spring, among which houses were sprinkled, the sort of house where you come in off the road at the second floor and descend to the livingroom, and then another floor down to the garden, full of blossom and tulips, and lilacs in bloom.

After the second bridge at Pompey we turned right, as the barge ahead went off to the left down the Moselle towards the Rhine. This area is a maze of waterways, rivers, canals and cuts, and we had to follow the chart with some care. We were at the junction, coming off the main river: 'To Nancy' it said. 'Speed limit of 6 kph'.

Waiting at the top of the lock was a Tourboat decked with yards of net and pink posies for a wedding. Inside we could see five or six chefs in tall white *toques* working in the galley, and behind them an elegant dining salon full of guests, with net and posies everywhere. They waved their champagne glasses cheerfully and blew us kisses. We waved back, and made signals that we hoped would be interpreted as Good luck, God bless. We even managed to avoid hitting them, though the two barges were less than a foot apart as we crept past.

Under the motorway bridge three graffiti artists worked on immense and colourful murals on the stone abutments, intent and oblivious to our passing. The traffic crossing the bridge was equally oblivious to the artists below, and was intense, every other vehicle a caravan. It was a holiday weekend in France, characterised as a *jour orange*, a day when dense traffic can be expected. *Jours rouges*, red days, are even worse, and black days occur in one or two renowned bottlenecks like Lyon and Grenoble where traffic comes to a complete standstill. Because of the school timetable, it can happen that half France is trying to get away from Paris while the other half is trying to get back. And here we were passing the graffiti artists, all of us untroubled by traffic and orange days on the roads.

The industrial zones of Nancy spread on either side, Michelin tyres, scrap processing, metalworks, railway sidings, and an old building labelled 'Compagnie Générale de Tramways'. All shut and locked, the car parks empty, everyone gone fishing.

Nancy, like Toul, had turned a disused commercial basin into a pleasant yacht harbour. The Port de Plaisance was constructed by putting pontoons at right angles to the old stone quay, and finger pontoons off these. The only way for a big boat like us to moor was to weave past these herringbones and insert ourselves against the stone quay at the inner end, like a spoon in a presentation box. We really needed to be jointed in the middle to do it.

The longest bit of quay was not free, as a 12 metre hire-boat had parked in the dead centre of a 50 metre quay, thus leaving only two short spaces at either end. We were left with the second longest, which was perhaps a foot longer than the boat. Bill surveyed the scene with some dismay. As it was Saturday, people began to gather on the quay to offer advice, the loudest being a German from a small barge some distance back who had had to run hard along the quay to be in on the action. This self-appointed Port Captain shouted: (1) that we'd never do it and should go somewhere else, and (2) seeing our determination, tried to take charge with barking instructions.

Slotting ourselves into the quay beyond the projecting pontoons involved a right-angled turn between boats moored to the pontoons. It looked impossible and Laurel was as amazed as the crowd when Bill shaped up towards it.

'You'll never do it!' she whispered. Faithless soul.

'Yes, we will. Rig a spring (rope) from the starboard for'ard fairlead onto the last possible bollard on the quay, and with that, control the movement forward until we are almost touching that pontoon.'

She did. The crowd, which had grown to some 40 persons by now, watched spellbound. Some of them were helpful in the matter of distance off from the pontoon ends, but the German was barking completely useless orders, and we ignored him. Slowly the stern swung round. Eventually it gently nudged the blue boat which was the limiting obstacle. After checking that Laurel had no more rope to ease out to give him another inch, Bill gave a full ahead blast on all engines and the wash from our propellors thrust the blue boat and its pontoon back a foot, we slipped through the resulting gap and moored comfortably, and rather smugly. It had been a superb bit of ship-handling, and we had not touched any of the yachts. The self-appointed Port Captain behaved as if he'd just personally delivered a baby, but quietened down considerably on discovering that Bill was older than he was. 'You have done this before,' he said, accusingly. To have skill and experience, it seemed, was cheating. Laurel said quietly, 'Well done.'

'Getting out again should be fun,' was Bill's only comment.

'Feerst time in Nancy?' said the persistent German, recovered enough to take charge again, 'Feerst thing to see is Place Stanislas.' 'First thing,' Laurel said firmly, 'is TEA'.

But then *Garuda*, moored close by, told us that all shops would be closed till Tuesday, and the market closed at six, so we hustled thither in a thunderstorm, planning a military operation; dividing the shopping list in two, we completed it in twenty minutes flat, with shutters banging down all around us. We then walked slowly back with our booty, stopping at a bar for R and R on the way.

On Sunday 30 April we were unable to receive Radio 4. It had been fading for some days now, and we must have been at its limiting range except at sunset. From now on we would have to rely on the BBC overseas service for our news in English. *This is London*, said our radio, playing *Lillibulero*, almost a National Anthem for ex-patriots. *All-out war looms again in War-Torn-ex-Jugoslavia, due to the failure to renew the ceasefire. There has been a new outbreak of fighting in Croatia where government forces have been attacking*... on it went. We listened with attention. *The fighting comes as the Bosnian Serbs in disputed territory*... The clichés rolled on, and behind every cliché was a cruel and bloody fact. The Danube would carry us, if we continued, through *War-Torn-Jugoslavia*, with Serbia on one bank and the *disputed territory* of Croatia on the other. We would have to keep an ear on this.

Meanwhile we enjoyed the May Day holiday: the Feast of Labour, celebrated by a total absence of labour; even the locks were closed.

During the holiday weekend we walked long distances to see Nancy, which is part mediaeval, and part 18th century: the elegant and monumental buildings around Place Stanislas are 18th century. It is also a stronghold of Art Nouveau. The School of Nancy, as it is called, strongly influenced by similar streams (William Morris for instance, and Aubrey Beardsley in England, Ensor in Belgium, and the Jugendstil in Germany) threw up an astonishing collection of glass mosaicists, glass workers, wrought iron joiners, and architects of immense talent, whose work is to be seen in the façades and decoration of cafés, banks, shops and private houses throughout the town. We dined in decadent elegance in one of these places; the Excelsior Flo. It had booths of mahogany with brass railings like some of the *fin-de-siècle* restaurants in London. The ceiling was a masterpiece of vaulting that seemed like growing ferns, huge gardens of stained glass had been made into windows, green tendrils of wrought iron held chandeliers, and the bar was polished brass and glass and a magnificence of mahogany. Our meal, in company with *Garuda*, was cheap and excellent, and we revised our opinion of the wines of Toul, the Rosé called *Gris de Toul* was not bad at all.

We were able to dispense with our bedroom heater for the first time that night, the 1st of May!

Too late for the holiday, the sun came out on Tuesday. The Art Nouveau Museum was closed, but we had another look at the Place Stanislas, and the Restaurant Stanislas, the Hotel Stanislas, the Flunch Stanislas, and the Bar Stan, finishing up at the Tropical Aquarium, the only thing that was not named for King Stanislas.

In the entrance hall was a large tank, containing a fine specimen of Gymnotus, about four feet long. He is a kind of electric catfish from the Blue Nile, and was earning his keep as the Museum Clock. Wired to his tank was a cathode ray oscilloscope with lovely evengreen rhythms running on it although he was not doing much but think fishy thoughts. He acted as the quartz in the clock, which whole conception led us down such interesting conversational alleys as: 'What time is it by your fish?' 'Oh, my fish is slow, I shouldn't have gone swimming with it – these old fashioned fish aren't waterproof.'

After an early lunch we restarted our journey, enjoying the sun. Leaving was easier than our arrival as we'd moved into the longer berth the moment it was free, when no one was about.

We stopped the night at Dombasle, on a decrepit wooden pontoon off the mainstream in an industrial basin close to satanic mills which rumbled and belched, and poured awful things into several barges berthed at their quays (and also into the canal).

At the last lock before Dombasle we had been given a Télécommande and a sheet of instructions to open the next few locks. It was a device like that used to open garage doors by remote control; one points the gadget at a box mounted on a post about 400 metres short of the lock. The idea was to enable the hire-boats to stop where they liked, without upsetting the Navigation. We were suddenly into a holiday area in holiday mood with holiday weather, and the sun had brought out the hired boats like butterflies.

They love to moor in the middle of a quay, leaving no room at either end for bigger boats, and one hire-boat had moored right up to the gates of a lock so that we had difficulty getting out. Why, Laurel asked Bill, didn't you give him the rough side of your tongue? 'It would have ruined their video, wouldn't it?' said Bill mildly.

A hire-boat full of Swiss, which had also moored close to a lock which we had triggered, shot off the bank as we approached, and nipped in ahead of us as the gates opened. The gates then closed, shutting us out, and nothing else happened. Laurel manoeuvred *Hosanna* into the bank and held her there with the bow-thruster while Bill, irate this time, went to investigate. The people in the hire-boat had no Telecommand, and no idea of procedure. They could not go back, nor could they go on. The Swiss couldn't speak French so Bill had to call the duty *éclusier* for assistance on their behalf. It amazes us that substantial boats with a considerable capital value are hired out to persons with no experience.

We calmed down to enjoy the strange feeling of crossing River

The Excelsior Flo, Nancy

Meurthe on an aqueduct. Suspended high in the air on our water-bridge, we could see a weir way below, little pools and islands, and the tops of the willow trees. It was like flying. It became very peaceful, sheep baa-ed, birds sang, the countryside was lovely. The peace lasted until we found a tiny boat exactly in the middle of the quay at Lagarde, and had to moor for the night to a rough patch of ground near the lock. The Restaurant Bon Acceuil was closed *mercredi*: it was *mercredi*, so there was no *acceuil* at all. Never mind, the weather was so warm we had a barbecue. Until the mosquitos came out to play.

• 7 •

FIFTY YEARS ON

Arviller and Saverne

We left Lagarde before the sun had warmed up the countryside. Heavy dew hung over land and ship. Over the canal, twists of mist wreathed langorously, occasionally exposing the water surface, and in the lush fields of young corn the dew on the blades had damascened them like Toledo swords. Not much was moving as we parted the silent mist. The news at breakfast reported renewed fighting in Croatia.

We had climbed by now into the foothills of the Vosges mountains, and reached the summit of the Canal de la Marne-au-Rhin. Along the summit pound there were old bridge abutments barely wider than the boat, which necessitated strong concentration. It was a pleasant summit, passing by lakes and forests until we arrived at the basin at Niderviller. Faced with a choice of a difficult mooring, or an easy one which would have meant disturbing a choleric-looking Frenchman with a truckload of angling equipment, Bill opted for goodwill towards anglers, and churned up tons of mud in the shallows at the other end. This muddy cloud spread over the basin and disturbed the angler just as much as if we had berthed close to him. He got up, sighing deeply, and moved on. So much for good intentions.

We dined at the Tannenheim restaurant, and felt in a different country. So we were, in a sense: tomorrow, we would be in Alsace. It would be an interesting day; there were two summit tunnels, the Niderviller, which is about 500 metres long, and the Arzviller, which is 2.3 kilometres. We would descend into the valley of the Zorn by means of the Inclined Plane Lift at Arzviller. We would have to be up early, before the hire-boats.

At 0830 on a beautiful sunny morning of 5 May, with wonderful scenery loud with singing birds, it seemed a pity to plunge into two dark tunnels, so close together.

The light was red for the second tunnel, so we moored to wait. The hire-boat behind us wanted to pass, but we were not allowing that; one maintains station, so he was waved in behind us. The skipper then came along the bank and asked if he could pass because we were going slowly. Bill declined, pointing out that there was a speed limit on this dangerously narrow section. Fortunately he was German, and therefore law-abiding. The boat coming through against us took ages, but at 3 km/hr (the limit) a 2.3 kilometre tunnel does take 45 minutes. We were anxious to get past the nearby Arzviller boatlift quickly because it is a bottleneck. If we had let them pass they would have had precedence at the lift, and that would have held us up for at least two hours because the lift cycle takes an hour, and there were several boats in his party. We had always honoured the tradition on canals that one accepts one's place and sticks to it, and we didn't see why others shouldn't do the same.

It was a pleasure barge that came through at last, one like ourselves, and the light went green. The tunnel was rough hewn; some are lined with brick or trimmed stone, but this was carved out of the hillside, like a prehistoric cave; there were even patches of red and ochre which reminded us of the paintings on the caves at Altamira. A train tunnel ran alongside making the most alarming noise. When we emerged 35 minutes later we were into sunshine again... and began the descent to Strasbourg on the plain of Alsace. We were looking down a valley and could see, far below, the train that had come through the tunnel beside us.

The sloping stone banks were thickly wooded with silver birch and pine trees, and were provided with rope ladders at intervals, perhaps to assist anyone who fell in. We had the odd experience, in a boat at least, of looking down through treetops on to the rooftops of a hamlet. Imagine: being in a boat and looking down from a hilltop, like the Ark on Ararat.

We arrived suddenly at the Inclined Plane Lift as we rounded a corner. Everything happened fast: we scarcely had time to notice the crowd of tourists watching from the belvedere. A small hire-boat was already in the chamber, and when the officials asked our length they waved us in too, to the delight of the crowd. Video cameras popped up everywhere as we fitted in with a foot to spare. It was like coming on stage accompanied by a burst of limelight and the buzz of the audience, who had awaited us, the actors, for the performance to begin. The guillotine gates came down behind as we made fast, giving us the impression that we were late on cue.

We were still adjusting moorings when we realised that we were already moving. Downwards. In a bathtub. In times past there was at this steep slope a series of 17 locks within 3.8 kilometres. This was tedious to work and the delays to traffic were interminable. In places the distance between locks was little more than the length of a barge, making passing difficult. A proposal to build another lock staircase alongside was discarded in favour of a boatlift because of cost.

The effective part of the lift is a giant bathtub with gates at each end. The barge enters through a double gate, one of which shuts off the canal and another to close the bathtub. The barge is now floating in the bathtub, or chamber, which is then eased up or down the slope, a vertical distance of 44.55 metres, taking 20 minutes to accomplish instead of 8 hours to navigate the staircase of 17 locks, which the lift replaced in 1964.

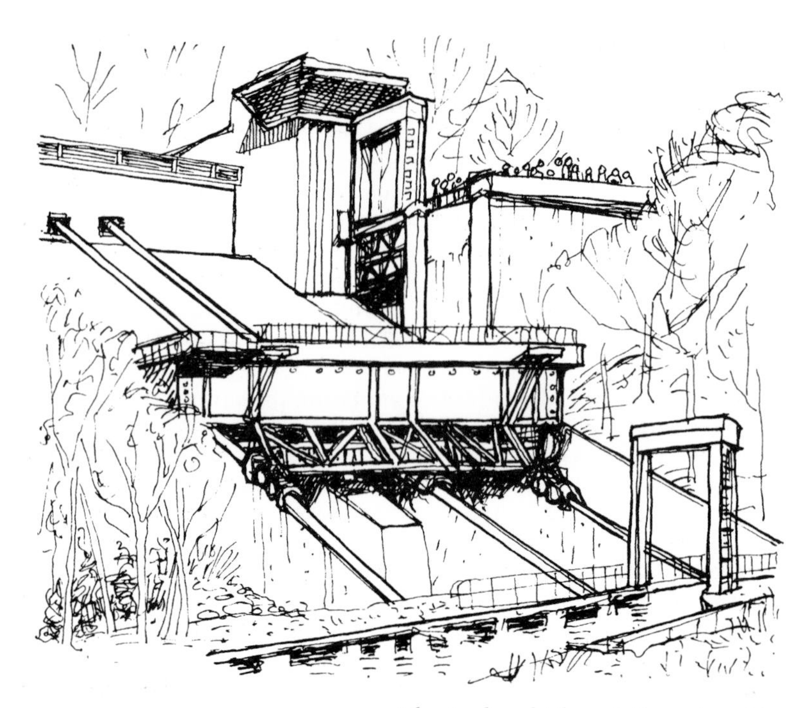

The Inclined Plane Lift at Arzviller

The chamber is very heavy, though the weight of the barge in it makes no difference because it floats and thus displaces its own weight of water. Whether the chamber has only water and no boats, or whether, as now, it was loaded with 80 tons of boat, it weighs the same. It is exactly counterbalanced, and the energy required to move it is comparatively small, only the friction having to be overcome. It is a fine piece of engineering, water wastage is reduced, and there is a museum at the top.

The descent had begun before we'd taken very much in; we now heard the Tour Guide and his excited audience receding as the whirr of the grass cutter below came nearer. The water in the chamber that contained us hardly shivered as we glided silently and majestically down, not a hitch, not a snag; like flowing treacle. Beside us the huge counterweight went up as we descended.

Below us a breathtaking vista of trees and glades bordered the silver ribbon which marked where our journey would continue. All this work in attractive countryside had not been without opposition, and undoubtedly there must have been scars for a time, but great efforts had been made to remove the more objectionable evidence, the landscaping was successful, and the lift not only benefits commerce, but also provides the population with an interesting day out.

It was hard not to feel like the *deus ex machina* gliding down from the wings of an ancient Greek theatre, harder still not to give an imperious and haughty wave to the adoring audience above with their video cameras. Below us there was only the man cutting grass, and he'd seen it all before. Anyway, he was busy.

A sense of friction told us that we neared the bottom. The gates opened, and we were in the canal again.

After that, anything could have been an anticlimax, but the village of Lutzelbourg came next, and suddenly it was as if we'd changed countries: not just place names (*burgs* instead of *villes*), but also steep wooded canalsides, chalet-like houses with names like *Edelweiss* and *Waldheim*, and a ruined castle beetling from cliffs, all showed we were in Alsace. Why else would the guidebook note the cement works at Hemming as a stop for lovers of Sauerkraut? (On close inspection there is the address of an Inn in small print.)

Lutzelbourg was pretty, full of flowering shrubs and gardens, and little chalets, and surrounded by forest. A cycle path ran along the canal, studded with Star of Bethlehem and buttercups, a path forbidden to all motors. Cyclists in neon nylon suits and crash helmets twinkled past as bright as the tropical fish at Nancy. The cherry blossom was over, and the woods were a hundred shades of green, including the more sombre robes of pine and fir. At the locks the apple trees were in bloom, in the gardens were lilac and wisteria, and at the canal's edge dandelion clocks and herb robert grew.

It was 1530, a civilised time to stop, when we reached Saverne. We locked through the picturesque middle of the town. We were the cabaret for the languid beer-drinkers at the cafés as we descended the deep lock, then along a short narrow cut which broadens and incorporates the ornamental lake of the Palace of Rohan, the Versailles of Alsace, opposite which we moored in some splendour. We had promised ourselves a pause to receive mail, to do maintenance and repairs, and perhaps a few day's rest too; we had been assured it was a beautiful town.

The pontoons were occupied by hire craft and there was no room for us, so we berthed at the main quay. We were able to get shore power for our work, and fresh water, and had an unobstructed view of the palace facing us over the lake, a huge chateau in the classic style. Started in 1740 as the summer residence for Cardinal Rohan who obviously cared little for the concept of ecclesiastic poverty, it was never completed because the Cardinal was involved in the affair of the Queen's necklace, and was obliged to flit at some speed. Cardinals were a colourful lot in those days.

Garuda was already here and Christian and Janine had found THE place to eat, the Maison Katz, an unbelievably decorated ancient timber-framed house, with panels between the frames further adorned with coloured plasterwork and woodcarving. Inside was as joyful as the outside; the largest plain surface was probably the bottom of our ashtray. Everything else was carved and printed and woven and betasselled and embroidered and illuminated and engraved and chased and etched, and in any spare receptacle: let's shove a bunch of dried flowers. It says much for the food, and the charming girl who served it, that we were able to forget our surroundings sufficiently to lift a knife and fork without worrying if we knocked over a corn dolly. Here we ate snails, Alsace style, very herby but no garlic; and fillets of Sandre, a delicious fish rather like pike, found in European rivers.

Saturday saw the start of another holiday weekend, so we had to do some shopping. There was a bank open, fortunately. Unfortunately the teller had never before seen a Coutts Eurocheque, and had to get the Manager and the Book of Rules.

Laurel sat by and waited, uncomfortably watching the queue grow uncomplaining, behind Bill. She had a long chat with an old lady in green wool, to whom French was obviously a foreign language too, successfully exchanging views on the sudden heatwave, and got a blow by blow meteo till Tuesday. The old lady then went over to speak to the receptionist, they both fell into Alsatian dialect, and had an excited conversation containing a great many cries of 'Jo!'

The day was very hot and sunny. Weeks of travelling caught up with us, and we slept all afternoon.

On Sunday, the Port Captain told us our berth would be needed for the Hotel Barge *Lafayette*. The only alternative was to double-park outside the péniche *Jumagu*, a boat's length ahead. This turned out very well, giving us privacy from passers-by and protection from the noise of a nearby fairground across the quay.

Our view of the palace was as good as ever. We found pleasure in its stone, the colour of old roses. We could see chandeliers twinkling behind tall ground-floor windows; candles also bloomed on the chestnut trees that rimmed the park outside. The lamps were lit because the Savernois were voting in the palace for their President, the President of France.

Cardinal Rohan had a family pride that was noticeable even in prerevolutionary French aristocracy. The gloriously arrogant motto of the Dukes of Rohan was:

> Prince ne daigne, Roi ne puis, Rohan suis
> (Prince I do not deign to be, King I cannot be, I am Rohan)

which displays a regal amount of self-confidence.

The palace was finished by Napoleon III as accommodation for war widows. Later it was used as a grain store, and then a hospital. Thus the interior is considerably less grand than the exterior. It now belongs to the municipality who have gutted one end and built entirely within the old façades an excellent theatre and conference hall; a completely modern edifice totally contained very successfully within a classic 18th century exterior. The other end of the palace contains a museum and is used for municipal functions.

Monday 8 May was the 50th anniversary of VE day. It was fine, but windy, and 1000 saw us outside the Hotel de Ville, next door to the Maison Katz. It was slightly less decorated, making up for it with the flags of France and Alsace and a balconyful of geraniums.

We were late; the detachment of soldiers from the *Centre Mobilisateur* was already in place, as were the *sapeurs pompiers*, stealing the show as always with their polished helmets and ceremonial axes. The *Musique Municipale* was already playing.

Here was the Deputy Mayor, greeting the officers, the dignitaries, his dear colleagues, and all of us on this important occasion, etc, etc. The ceremonies of the 50th anniversary of the capitulation of Nazi Germany were taking place this very day at Saverne, he told us, and made a long speech about it.

The Municipal Music played the 'March of the Second Division Blindé', and the first soldier fainted. The pupils of the Music School performed the *Ode to Joy*, with a few lovely squeaks on a strange assortment of instruments, then the combined choirs of the town and the Musique Municipale all joined in. One of the small singers was overcome, and had to sit down in a shop doorway.

And as the bugles played, medals were pinned on deserving chests far too young to remember 50 years ago, and wreaths were laid below the plaque which commemorates the liberation of Saverne by General Leclerc.

After a rousing 'Marseillaise', the Deputy Mayor invited those present to share a glass of friendship in the palace, and we were swept along in the rush up to the museum on the second floor, where there was an exhibition of Saverne under the German Reich.

A buzz of happy drinking chat led us to the room with the chandeliers, where we were given glasses of wine and giant pretzels, and introduced to two veterans. They were great friends, but had fought, having no choice, on opposite sides in the war. One, a flag bearer at the ceremony, resplendent in Navy blue and silver and blinding white spats, had fought in the desert, on the side of the Germans. His mate had escaped to the Free French and joined the Chasseurs Alpins. He showed us his campaign medals, and his big black beret, and through the tall windows we showed him our big black boat across the water. 'Come and have a drink *chez moi*,' he said, and later took us up the hill in his car to a small house that was almost a military museum. He had a collection of uniforms and regalia, of prints and books, that commands respect. French regiments guard their peculiar badges and idiosyncratic dress variations just as do the British, though because of conscription they have managed to keep more traditional regiments in being. French youth has up to now done compulsory military service; it is regarded as a citizen's duty to bear arms on behalf of his country, and they feel that conscription for a year or so reinforces this obligation. France, it should be remembered, has no Channel as a line of defence, and has been mauled by the Germans on three occasions in the last 125 years.

The exhibits that the municipality had gathered in the Palace of Rohan were more impressively comprehensive than we expected for a small town, and gave us to think more deeply about the occupation of France from 1940 to 1945. In spite of comic TV programmes, or

Canalside chapel near Niderviller

perhaps because of them, the sufferings that some (but not all) French people experienced are not much appreciated by the British.

Most know about the two main areas of occupation; the northern part of France, which was run by the German Army, and the southern part which was governed by the French Vichy collaborators. But the part of France we were now in had a rather different experience. Three *départements* adjoining the eastern frontier, Moselle, Bas Rhin and Haut Rhin, had been German from 1870 to 1919 when the Treaty of Versailles, which dished out parcels of land to the winners like a *département* store Father Christmas, awarded them to France, who had always claimed them as French.

In 1945 the Alsatian diarist, Philippe Husser wrote: 'The Germans have gone. The Americans and French have come. A new era starts for Alsace. Change of nationality! For the umpteenth (*combientième*) time? And for how long?'

When the Germans conquered France the Armistice made no mention of these *départements*, but the Germans seized them back nonetheless, and the French were in no position to argue. Thus parts of Alsace and Lorraine became once more part of metropolitan Germany. French identity cards were replaced with German ones, French street names were pulled down and the streets renamed in German, official documents were published in German, and even the letters on the taps were changed. More importantly, the people became German citizens; government employees had to take an oath of allegiance to the Führer (one lock-keeper we met had to swear allegiance to the man who had effectively ordered the killing of his son), and 130,000 men of Alsace-Lorraine were called up for the German Army. (They called themselves *Les Malgré-nous*). Any dissension or objection to the Germans was not 'resistance' but high treason. The office of Préfet was replaced by a German Gauleiter, an enthusiastic Nazi, who seems to have gone further than his official brief in the Germanisation of the country.

German as the official language was no hardship. Even to this day the dominant language of this area is German of a sort, though it is tactfully called a dialect of French. French it certainly is not. For example the word most heard for the affirmative is *Ja* (familiarly expressed as *Yo*), and many surnames would be quite at home in a German town. French citizens have difficulty communicating with the older people, and when Bill, who speaks good French, asked a local workman what a marquee was for, he came back saying that he had not been able to decypher a single word. It seems that some of the population cannot decide whether they prefer to be French or German, and communal loyalty tends to be pragmatic, depending on which country happens to be in the ascendancy.

Those wishing to be German were not much in evidence on 8 May. There had been an effective resistance movement during the war; allied airmen shot down were fed into the pipeline that got them back to Britain, bridges were occasionally blown up, and so on. These resistance fighters must have been extraordinarily courageous; they were far more at risk than those in the rest of France because of those local inhabitants who enjoyed the feeling of being German and superior. The rate of denunciation was high. We saw emotional photographs of one resistance hero (or traitor, according to your point of view), an *épicier*, and his family, his house, and some souvenirs of his belongings. His servant had found an incriminating paper in his dustbin, and had given it to her lover who was German oriented. The grocer was denounced, tortured, and then publicly beheaded. The Nazis evidently thought of him as sufficiently important for a special report on his capture and execution to be sent back to the Führer in Berlin. He looked a quiet, unassuming family-man, a shopkeeper in a small town, but what heroism!

Also on display in the museum were ration books, showing how strictly bread and coal were rationed, the latter a serious business in a land with such cold winters. There were photographs of Nazi parades in the town, of German soldiers in the streets celebrating, sometimes with civilians. War is an extreme form of sport: most of the bystanders find it hell and misery, while some of the players enjoy it as a lethal game. O U T spells out, and the bullet smashes into bone, or, as here, the guillotine blade falls on the traitor, who is held face upwards with his eyes fixed open, the better to see the blade fall.

In some photographs the spectators' faces were blanked out. The persecution of pro-Germans had been fierce, and the exhibition director, a history student at Strasbourg University, had wisely avoided reopening wounds that time was healing. There were uniforms too, some of German soldiers, others of the units of conscripted Frenchmen, badges, flags, and insignia, and these brought home the effect that a daily contact must have had. And in one cabinet, a yellow star, six-poignant, that had been worn by one of the *déportés* named on the town memorial.

Unlike most towns where the Second World War is commemorated with an extra plaque on the First World War Memorial (because France capitulated so early, there were few casualties in 1939–45), Saverne has a new War Memorial. The Gauleiter had ordered the destruction of the memorial to those French who fell in the First World War, a petty act, which we came across again in Hungary, where a memorial to the Russian dead at Mohács had been torn down after the collapse of Communism. No matter which side they fought for through accident of birth or homeland, the lot of the common soldier is unenviable enough to deserve the preservation of his memory when dead.

• 8 •
RHINESTORM
Strasbourg, the Rhine, and Mainz

We waited for mail and spares while resting. It was not a question of doing nothing; we rested by change of occupation. Bill made a new iroko deck grating for the verandah. The last had blown away in the storm that dismasted us last September.

The weather was warm and we could usually lunch out of doors though seldom was it possible to dine al fresco. We re-encountered Karl (Charlie), genial master of the hotel ship *Liberté*, which berthed astern of us when *Lafayette* left. We had first met him on River Saône the year before. He had a Rheinpatent, a document entitling him to act as a pilot on River Rhine. A Rheinpatent requires eight full journeys in the previous five years, and a personal log-book record for each trip. For the skipper who is not engaged full-time on the Rhine this can present a problem; the patent must be kept updated in the same fashion that an airline pilot has to log so many hours per annum for his licence to remain valid.

Better still, Charlie had been as far as Vienna, and could mark our charts for us. This is an important piece of homework when travelling: if you meet someone who's been there, you pick their brains. Charlie's information dropped into our notebooks like liquid gold. He would pilot us for nothing; the Rhine from just beyond Strasbourg to Mainz could be done in one long day's run, and would update his Rheinpatent. Thereafter we would be in River Main, and no longer needing a pilot. That settled, we enjoyed Saverne.

The *braderie* was a big event; it happens twice a year in Spring and Autumn. It was a grand sale-cum-market-cum-day out for everyone. The shops put out bargain stalls, the cafés and restaurants moved outside, offering sizzling sausages, waffles, pastries and doner kebabs. More than one of the latter said 'only the best veal used in our doner kebabs' – a tactful way of indicating that Muslims might safely partake. Market stalls filled the square and lined the streets. Everywhere was the lilt of the dialect; the Alsatian sings when he speaks his soft and gentle French, not native to him by any means.

The seller of new peas declaimed that they were fresh from the Midi: the first of the year, and the fat white shoots of asparagus were not expensive. We bought new geraniums, since no barge should be seen without them in summer, and our much-travelled veterans of two years ago had undergone 2000 miles of salt air and changing climate and had grown leggy and despondent, if still determined to bloom. Would the stallholder keep them for us till we were on our way back to our boat? Ach, Jo! Pas de problème.

That was the last fine day for a while; the weather changed.

The BBC told of intense fighting in the supply corridor to Sarajevo. In Saverne, the fairground was packing up, after one last day in pouring rain. So many people were there despite the weather that it seemed a good many family promises had come home to roost: 'Papa will take you next Saturday, Promis, Ach Jo,' and now it was raining and promises had to be kept, and tiny children with wide smiles were riding the Carousel, driving their very own (for a few moments) ambulance or train or dragon, round and round with flashing lights and roaring music; all Chiefs, not an Indian in sight. Half the stalls were selling gaudy sweets and cakes in primary colours and crude shapes: green frogs, pink octopus, chocolate turtles, and dusty looking biscuits like dun-coloured caddis. Leaning on one stall, a huge man in studded leathers, crash helmet over his arm, was dreamily winding his tongue round a web of candyfloss.

Looking at AdventureLand and SpaceWalk we exchanged views with a German-American, agreeing that fairs were all too high-tech now, and regretting the passing of the simpler rides, and the absence of skirts to be blown up as they stood over a grille, like the Marilyn Monroe poster; jeans were no fun. Being German he was astonished at the lack of regulations on the adult rides. Was nothing *verboten* here? He must have been tempted by unaccustomed anarchy; we saw him later, stolid and alone, a middle aged man with a wicked leer, venally driving an unregulated Dodgem car.

Were we enjoying Saverne? the Port Captain asked. Ach, Jo!

Except for a big shopping trip before we left, which was Ach Nein. Charlie had advised us that everything was dearer in Germany, and Laurel wanted our larder full before the border. The trolley came out of winter storage and we set off with big baskets, walking in the rain again, to Intermarché. Bill hates shopping, and comes only to help. He does this philosophically, mostly, but on this occasion his evident exasperation undermined Laurel's equilibrium, already upset by the awkward trolley, which after the winter in the forepeak was stiff and cranky and needed oiling: just as she did. We came almost to blows over the choice of toilet paper. 'Do you have to read every packet from end to end?' complained Bill, grabbing the nearest. 'We have now been here for twenty-five minutes and there are only three items in the trolley. I calculate we may reach the check-out at midnight.' 'YOU don't read the packets at all,' Laurel snapped, 'and YOU come home with raisin bread instead of wholemeal, and Harissa instead of tomato paste. Do you really want scented yellow toilet paper?' He dropped it hastily and we got the blue, unscented. There is too much choice nowadays: we sometimes long for the dark little shop in a Greek island where there is only one sack of rice, one vat of olive oil, and two kinds of cheese.

'Where to now?' said Bill.

'You've wiped my RAM,' Laurel said, 'I can't remember a thing I came for.'

'Where's your shopping list?' rapped Bill.

'I left it on the boat,' she said, sullenly.

We agreed that he should go and buy a tarpaulin at the DIY, and take a long time over it so that Laurel could wander round the store aimlessly reading all the labels.

Well, that was how he put it. Thus she was able to reboot her data bank and remember most of the things on her list, including some that she put back on the shelves as being too heavy, not wanting to overburden her donkey. Bill carried two big baskets, and she took the trolley with the tarpaulin folded across the top of its load. The trolley had only two wheels, a poor sense of direction, and a mind of its own at pavement edges, but it did bring home the bacon.

On the morning of Thursday 18 May the spares came. Rain fell heavily, but we left after a lunch enlivened by excitement on the opposite bank, where a car had slipped its handbrake and rolled into the canal, ending up totally submerged with its whereabouts marked by streams of bubbles. The police and *sapeurs pompiers* were there trying to get a winch on the drowned vehicle, the ambulance came and went again as the car was found empty and no life was in danger. When they let us pass, a crowd had gathered, under their umbrellas, but we couldn't stay to watch.

It was a short run to Dettwiller. Because of the pouring rain we stopped early when we found a quay set in wild woods, and had a supper of oxtail and dumplings, just the thing for a wet, cool night.

We had to get up early as Bograt, trying hard to burgle the crockie-jar (it has to be glass because she once, in frantic greed, gnawed through a plastic box) knocked over the kitchen pinger, and someone had to go and turn off the bleep. After that the cats decided it was breakfast time, and made pests of themselves until we admitted defeat and got dressed. As a consequence we were under way early for a morning's run to Vendenheim.

We had for months been trying to arrange a rendezvous with our German editors, and it seemed that they could meet us on Sunday at Vendenheim, near Strasbourg, which left us free to pick up our Rhine Pilot on the Monday.

We found a berth in a lay-by occupied by a cluster of Dutch barges, now homes to an assorted bunch of people, mostly ex-*mariniers*. They were friendly and helpful, and we were able to return their help in the matter of lifting a heavy engine on board a *tjalk*. The crane that was ordered had reneged as it was Saturday. Bill is very good at this sort of thing. He calls it seamanship. With planks, rollers and levers, and a minimum of push and shove, three of them slid the whole 800 kilos of engine aboard the *tjalk*.

We spring-cleaned the interior of our ship, as usual when expecting visitors, and painted the starboard rubbing strake.

Maison Katz, Saverne

We heard that Bosnian troops had fired Serb homes in Bihac. That was a good way from the Danube, on our map.

We telephoned Berlin on our new digital mobile phone, marvelling at the convenience of technology, hardly daring to believe that it would work. Our visitors would arrive next day.

We rang Charlie to fix Monday's rendezvous. Alas, he was unexpectedly needed on board *Liberté*, and couldn't come. There was minor panic, but from the *tjalk* help was forthcoming; brother-in-law had a Rheinpatent and would do the job half price, as his barge had been repossessed and he needed the cash. Here things got tricky timewise, as the pilot wished to start at Gambsheim, 13 kilometres beyond Strasbourg, at 0500 to do the trip and return by train in one day. The Rhine lock at Strasbourg would close at 1930 on Sunday and we must pass it by then. Our Germans were booked for tea at Vendenheim; if they were late, we could miss our pilot.

Sunday 21 May was lovely. The Germans were blessedly early and easy to get on with. 'Leave now, with us,' they suggested. 'Put us ashore at the last lock in Strasbourg, and we'll get a taxi back.' Problems evaporated. The knots of anxiety that had tightened for 24 hours untwisted and disappeared. We had a lovely run to Strasbourg, doing business on tea and scones as we went.

An hour and a half's journey brought us to lock 51, where Anneliese and Thomas, who seemed to have enjoyed this unusual way to have a business discussion, left us to find a taxi back to their car, and we went on towards the Rhine.

Charlie had warned us of a strong sideways current opposite the European Parliament Buildings, but we had no trouble, and were able to gaze in awe on the acres of glass and manicured lawns and landscaped setting that cossets our European masters. Even if we had had time to stop, there were no moorings for us in Strasbourg. The town council have not thought of visitors arriving by boat. The city is surrounded by unused docks and quays easily adaptable as a *Base Nautique*, but Madame the Mayor is too occupied with European politicians to consider peasants who might wish to visit their representatives. The Strasbourgeois should work a little harder for the privilege of housing the European Parliament.

The Rhine begets horror stories. The current is fast, the traffic intense and fast-moving, there are rocks and shoals and eddies, the Nibelungs and the Lorelei lie in wait, and the waterpolice would probably decapitate you if they found you, a boat of more than 15 tons, without a pilot (even though Bill once navigated an aircraft carrier). The wash from passing barges can capsize you, and when moored, the same wash slams you into the quay and breaks your crockery. We had time to think of all this in the lock, as it was huge. To our surprise we were the biggest boat there this Sunday evening, the others being two little motor boats and an even smaller speedboat. *They* didn't look terrifying. The enormous gates closed sideways, travelling across suspended from a gantry. We went up about two metres because the Rhine was running high, and nosed out cautiously from our hole, like a mouse knowing the cat is waiting. The motor boats turned right into Strasbourg. We turned left, through the empty docks, and out into the Terrible Rhine, giving way to two Dutch barges going upstream. We crossed to the right of the river, and proceeded downstream.

It was a bit of a letdown, really. We were the only boat in the wide river. No dragons, no fireworks, no hurricanes. We reached the rendezvous with our pilot, the lock at Gambsheim (13 kilometres in 55 minutes) and were about to telephone him when he climbed quietly on board. The lock-keeper was his cousin, he said, and had alerted him to our arrival. So, this was our cut-price pilot. Small, wispy-haired, glasses and hearing aid, and OLD! Instead of handsome Charlie of *Liberté*, we got André, more like Mr Pastry. He had no English, but spoke Alsatian, German, and strongly accented French. He asked a few sensible questions about the engines and steering, which modified our impressions. He saw us through the lock where the water level was only just below the PHEN (Plus Hautes Eaux Navigables) mark on the lock entrance. André said that if it rose overnight they would not let us go, but it was not expected to rise. The trend was downwards and navigation had just resumed after an interruption, which meant that traffic next day would be dense.

André helped us moor to the Ducs d'Albes, which are big piles called dolphins in England. They were 40 metres apart, to suit standard 38 metre barges, and *Hosanna* hung between them like a lonely shirt on a washing line. He then bade us goodnight till 0500, riding home on his bike which he'd left at the lock.

It was 21 May, 46 days after starting, and our voyage through France had covered 824 kilometres. We had been under way 154 hours on 26 days, giving an average speed of 5.35 km/hr, or 2.9 knots. If that seems a bit slow, remember we had passed 199 locks. It was faster going than we prefer for savouring the delights of France, but we had our sights set on Byzantium, still nearly 4000 kilometres of unknown waters to go, with question marks over the whole enterprise still in place, and with no prospect of a winter's break en route.

After a long day, tomorrow would be another, so we went to bed immediately after our meal, shutting the cats in, as we didn't like the thought of them attempting to funambule along our mooring ropes to the dolphins.

We were up at 0430, which astonished the cats. Sailors, with the scatological poetry of their everyday speech, call the small hours sparrowfart. The pilot arrived at 0455 (it was barely light) and he and Bill had cast off before the washing-up was finished. We headed out into the full force of the current which André estimated at 16 km/hr, and Bill passed the controls over to him. André was impressively confident, and impressively competent, though he could have done with a box to stand on in order to see ahead. We found him one. It was cold, thick jersey weather. André hung on to his cap and cardigan, but removed his jacket.

Below Strasbourg the Rhine has France to the left and Germany on the right, and Gambsheim was the last French lock. For the first hour traffic on the river was light, then it increased, and our pilot got more and more impressive. We were going fast downstream, well over 20 km/hr. The upstream traffic, having the harder work to do, choose which side to pass you. If they want to pass on the wrong side, ie starboard to starboard, they put up a big blue square panel, and you must then put up yours to show that you have seen and understood. Our pilot not only saw or anticipated blue panels long before we did, but knew how to take advantage of currents and eddies on bends to increase our speed. He wanted to be in Mainz by 1600 if possible, and that was 191 kilometres away.

We cleared Iffezheim, the only lock of the day and our 200th since Calais, by 0700. Now we had Germany both sides.

The river became narrower, shallower and faster flowing, and we needed two to drive. The amount of traffic increased markedly, and Bill was occupied with powerful binoculars spotting blue flags on approaching vessels, and at the same time monitoring our speed with a stop watch against the kilometre posts on the banks, as André wanted to know our progress over the ground, which was very different from our speed through the water. With a cruising speed through the water of 12 km/hr, we were able accurately to calculate the current. The maximum speed over the ground, he told us, was 20 km/hr, but he said that the police would not worry about 25 km/hr in these floods.

The blue flag system was causing us much more trouble than attention to speed limits, however, and a source of much more danger. Normally ships keep to the right when passing each other. This rule, unlike its equivalent on the roads where it is considered paramount, has temporary exceptions.

When river currents are strong, the shape of the river causes differences in current speeds, most marked on sharp bends where the water flows much faster on the outside than the inside. It can be so much faster that ships make little headway against it, and even if they can, they waste time and fuel. The custom has arisen, therefore, whereby a boat struggling upstream is allowed to cut the corners on the wrong side. The same concession is made where sandbanks or other obstructions cause the current to vary.

This is now enshrined in the regulations, and it is probably the biggest problem in navigating these fast-flowing rivers. It is not difficult to see that there will be occasions when ships have to change sides at the same time and place that ships coming in the opposite direction are also crossing over. It says much for barge skippers that this extraordinary manoeuvre seldom leads to collisions.

Upstream barges, called *montant* in French, become *bergfahrt* in German. All communication on the Rhine is in German, and there is much of it, which adds to the desirability of a pilot. A *bergfahrer* who wishes to pass green-to-green (ie keep to the left instead of right) will also broadcast on his VHF radio that he is going to *linksfahren* (keep to the left) as well as showing the large blue panel, or flag.

This is simple when there are only two ships. It is extremely dangerous in a crowded river with ships going in both directions, some overtaking, and some with tows spread across the fairway.

River Rhine is winding, and typically one can see 3 kilometres ahead. Bill counted 16 big barges coming towards us in such a stretch, up to four abreast, some blue-flagging, others not. (The ships in that short stretch kept 1000 trucks off the roads!)

In this apparent chaos André remained calm, and handled our ship expertly. It is not done to slacken speed, and Naval Officers who once carried out 'equal speed manoeuvres' know that constant speed can enhance safety.

Laurel undertook the task of displaying our blue flag when she was not preparing food for the navigators. When she disappeared to make coffee or get lunch, they missed her help. Like the professional barges we had mechanised our blue flag; we have a square blue board (*tafel* in German), one metre square with a white edge. This is hinged, and can be quickly displayed or folded out of sight, but is becoming inadequate for today's dense fast traffic: nowadays barges also display a white flashing light. Further on, in the Danube, we were to find that the blue board has been discarded by the most modern barges and a bright flashing strobe light was used alone, but the process continues to be known in English as 'blue-flagging', and is fundamental to big-river navigation.

Bill dislikes having a pilot on board. Her Majesty's Ships seldom take a pilot, and Navigating Officers were awarded a share of the money which the Queen thereby saved; unwillingness to take pilots is deeply ingrained in his system via his pocket.

André, however, earned his fee. Bill feels that he could have managed on his own if the river had not been in flood, and if it had not been the first weekday of navigation after a suspension, so that there were more ships than normal on the river. Even so it would have required hard concentration for the 12 hour, 191 kilometre passage, and above average skills. Small boats cope without much difficulty because they avoid the big boys by hugging the sides of the rivers. Bigger ships know pleasure craft are obliged to keep clear and can ignore them. Small craft that can be ignored are defined as under 20 metres long. *Hosanna* is 26.7 metres, so could not be ignored, and we had to maintain professional standards. Also, there are unwritten rules and conventions, and we had no idea what was being addressed to us in technical German over the radio. We were glad of our pilot.

We had a second breakfast, with eggs. Pilot drank tea, no milk, no sugar. He was a man of few words, and we learnt nothing about him. He seemed relaxed as he stood at the wheel, but his eyes were everywhere. We were far too busy to listen to the BBC news of Serbian attacks on UN safe areas.

Pilot asked Bill to take over while he had a quick lunch and a beer. Laurel whispered: 'You must tell him where the loo is.' Bill said, 'I did, but he went outside.'

The Rhine was 3 metres higher than normal, according to the *pegels*, stakes which read the water level, which pilots watch carefully.

The flow was fast, but our breakables had been stowed unnecessarily. Some waves broke over the bows, but nothing to cause concern.

We made better time than expected, and arrived off the confluence with River Main at about 1500. Because the two rivers flow strongly for most of the year, the confluence has been swept downstream behind a spit of land. This makes the turn into the Main from upstream very sharp, about 150°, and also blind. A barge in still water takes 500 metres to stop, and a downstream barge (*talfahrer*) can barely stop at all, so the turn requires prudence. Our pilot proved invaluable. He broadcast our intentions in German on Channel 10, and was answered by an obliging oppo round the corner that the river was clear. We then had to turn without being swept past it in the sluicing Rhine current. This led to a nightmare manoeuvre, commencing some two kilometres upstream, from which point we were swept downstream by the current while turning, and were therefore mostly broadside on. We had completed most of the turn when we arrived at the bridge 400 metres above the confluence and so passed under the right hand span stern first. Then we had to go full speed ahead trying to stem the current while crabbing over to the left to get our nose into the slower-flowing Main to avoid being swept downstream out of reach of it, unable to return until the floods passed. It was a sample of magnificent judgement, and Bill congratulated André, getting a gallic shrug in return, though there was a gleam of satisfaction in his eyes. 'It is that one is accustomed,' André said.

At 1610 we moored before Kostheim lock, four kilometres into River Main. Our pilot took his money with grave dignity and disappeared at once towards the railway station.

The village was Gustavsburg. The quay was a convenient height above water level, but we remembered that the river was three metres above normal, and it came home to us what range of levels the engineers have to allow for. Behind the quay was a high grassy levee, and behind that, below flood level was a neat housing estate.

So this was Germany. We are products of our generation. Bill's father had three ships sunk under him, and stories to tell of the German treatment of Greek islanders. Laurel's family had lost all their possessions in an air raid.

We brought with us no love for these people, but we were conscious that penance had been done over 50 years. Most of those we would meet were not born in 1945. We were in a country where we didn't know the language, bar about 20 useful words. What's more, we were 200 kilometres into it after the day's run, too far from the border for anyone to speak French. We would test the water, see how we got on, and reserve judgement.

• 9 •

THE MAIN ATTRACTION
Frankfurt, Aschaffenburg

The first thing we saw on German soil was a notice at the quayside saying 'Das betreten ist verboten.' We understood that. It means don't tread on the grass, and with pricking eyes Laurel thought of summer holidays with her grandparents in Cambridge, where, as Brooke says of 'Grantchester', you are NOT forbidden to tread on the grass. We were to learn that Germany is highly regulated and law-abiding, and almost everything is forbidden.

We took Rupert Brooke from the shelf and Laurel read 'Grantchester' aloud. It was more poignant than we remembered, especially as the lilacs were in bloom, and we suddenly felt a long way from home. There were tears in Bill's eyes too; Brooke is a favourite of his. We had visited his grave on the Greek island of Skyros two years before, anchoring *Hosanna* offshore and walking up the stream bed to the olive grove, just as his coffin bearers had done three years after he wrote 'Grantchester'. But that's another story.

While eating supper on our verandah, we met our first German on his home ground. A couple approached and sat on the quay with their little dog, asking questions. The dog was called Lady, and they were Corrie, and Günther. We invited them to a glass of wine and managed to communicate an enormous amount with our small German and their better English; Corrie was Dutch and Günther was German, and the enormous barge that had berthed ahead of us an hour after our arrival belonged to them, would we like to look?

She was called *Böhmerwald*, and was a hundred metres long, the size of a destroyer, and was run by Günther and Corrie Steffen, plus one crew who lived forward. It took us minutes to walk her length. She had a wheelhouse that went up and down on a hydraulic pillar, and Günther demonstrated how he raised it to see over the top of a cargo three containers high, or lowered it to go under a bridge while a closed circuit television camera in the bows relayed the view ahead. His driving chair was ergonomic, and the most comfortable we have ever sat in; long hours are spent in it. The switches and dials were like the cockpit of an aircraft, the skipper sat at a U-shaped console with everything he could require within reach: joysticks for steering and for the bow-thruster, throttles, controls for generators, compressors, auto-pilot, radar, radios both VHF and HF, and domestic radio and TV too, with three satellite dishes outside. It was air-conditioned for the summer, as it was effectively a greenhouse, complete with exotic plants in pots, Corrie's influence no doubt. What Hollander could be without plants in pots? Bill and Günther played with various controls for some time. Bill's judgement was that everything was well thought out, and would make the ship a pleasure to handle. The skipper owned the boat and had designed the wheelhouse himself. Many ship-handling problems are made worse because naval architects do not understand how ships are handled. The fittings in an owner-driven boat are always better laid out.

The enormous engine (2500 hp) was in a room the size of an aircraft hanger and as clean as a hospital operating theatre. One could walk about in a white coat and remain unsmutched, like Jonson's lily. Bill was greatly at home, admiring the workbench, neatly stowed machine tools, and welding gear. Then it was shoes off as we went into their livingroom for coffee, because Corrie is Dutch. It was, of course, immaculate. The only note of disorder was a brown cushion on the floor. We talked about many things, and understood each other perfectly. Boats, big or small, are common ground, and we were in full flow when the dog Lady suddenly attacked the cushion, and raped it in most unladylike fashion for several minutes, ending with a spasm and little cries of orgiastic ecstasy. Günther and Corrie took no notice, and we tried to follow suit. It would have been beyond our linguistics to ask if their dog was trans-sexual or just queer. In any case we were relieved and pretty happy with the amount of communication we had achieved in a language we don't know.

Germany was going to be OK.

We trod the forbidden grass to walk into Gustavsburg the next morning. (Günther told us the notice does not apply to bargees, who have the right to cross the grass to get to the road.) The town was scrubbed to clinical cleanliness. There were no stones where there should be earth, and no mud or paper on the swept and scoured pavements. Bushes, plants and trees looked fresh from a flower shop, and not a dead twig or a dry leaf was in sight. We were in difficulty with our rubbish, which we had brought with us as usual, hoping to find a bin. There were plenty of rubbish bins, all different colours, all locked. It became clear, anyway, that separation was necessary. There were three bottle banks side by side, one for green, one for white, one for brown glass. Fortunately our bottles were in a separate bag. But the rest of our gunk was all in together. Would we use blue ones: Old Paper? brown ones: Kompost? green ones: Biodegradable? Two other colours we were unable to decipher, but there were no scarlet bins with skull and crossbones for dreadful old gash-pirates like us who don't sort their rubbish. We dumped it in a bin under a lamppost which had a reassuring mixture of coke tins and greasy food wrappings in it, and Laurel murmured to herself:

> The dustbins stand in coloured rows.
> That's for these, and that's for those.
> Blue for paper, black for tin,
> And one for putting nothing in.

Gustavsburg was like a seaside model village, there was a lilypond outside the Post Office where we bought some stamps (one mark! That's nearly 50 pence for a stamp!) and some fruit and vegetables at a chic fruitique close to a fountain. Suddenly we'd spent eight quid. Heavens; we should be living on potatoes and pig's feet at this rate. We should have known it was a Tiffany's sort of fruit shop: it had a designed interior and its own emerald green paper bags, specially printed. Strawberries cost like rubies, the green pepper could have been an emerald, and the apples were red and green, tourmaline. We could think of no precious stone for the courgettes, and were thankful that we had resisted an avocado (3 for 10 francs in French markets), here it would have cost like jade. We walked back through the garden village and were quite relieved to see, unkempt upon the pavement there, a German unofficial turd. Just the one. A whisper of welcome anarchy.

Böhmerwald left before breakfast, waving, off to Duisberg for a load of coal. We left too, bound for Frankfurt.

We were now in River Main, much narrower and more winding than the Rhine, and the current much less strong, about 7 km/hr, but it was now against us as we climbed towards the watershed of Europe.

It was a 3 lock, 32 kilometre day. In the first lock we were summoned to KONTROL. Bill took all the papers with him up to the office, and came back grinning. He had explained what we were doing, and after a phone call for clarification, Authority had decided that we need not pay canal dues. '*Alles frei*' they said. *Wunderbar*, especially if food was going to cost so much. We then went through a blizzard for a few kilometres, which seriously cut down our vision and filled the wheel-house with fluff, which also settled on the water. There were woods on either side, so it must have been thistledown. Here? In Germany? Surely thistles would be *verboten*.

The river proved to be not so difficult, though we could make little sense of the German being used on VHF channel 10. Bill had hoped to manage with common sense and extra care, but the German authorities carry out maintenance work very thoroughly, and introduce one-way working whenever they are dredging, or building up the banks. One-way traffic is not controlled, and it is up to skippers to sort out precedence from opposite ends of a 500 metre channel out of sight of each other round a sharp bend. We narrowly avoided an accident, and got ourselves abused. At least we suppose it was abuse. Bill said that had the boot been on the other foot, he would have abused the other skipper, so he accepted the rebuke. We had transgressed a convention, not a law, because we had not been able to decypher what we had heard on VHF. Our German is far from adequate, but skippers do not speak pure, well-articulated German. There are many accents and colloquialisms, much technical jargon, and apart from Dutch and Belgians speaking German as non-natives, there were also occasional crews up from Austria, Slovakia, and Hungary. We did not notice the nationality of the skipper whose wrath we had incurred; he flashed past on a bend, very close, and we were concentrating hard on hitting neither the other ship nor the bank.

The Germans, joking, call Frankfurt-am-Main 'Mainhattan' because of its skyscrapers. We made fast to the MainKai just after 1500, leaving a respectable distance between us and the luxurious hotel boats that occupied much of it. This apparently good mooring, a fine stone quay in the city centre, turned out to be uncomfortable because big barges passed at full speed (in spite of limit signs), and we would surge forward until our sternrope twanged as tight as a guitar string, our bows would crash against the quay, then bounce out again for us to surge aft and repeat the process the other way. With the quayside bollards inconveniently spaced, the stretch in our nylon mooring ropes was sufficient to allow us several feet of movement. However, there was grass, there were trees and benches, and no cars allowed; so the cats were let out when they woke up. Across the road which flanked the quay was a row of coloured houses that reminded us of 18th century Annapolis, and behind them we could see the spire of the Dom. Bill got out the old hairy rope and used it aft to take the chafe, with the new one a little slacker in case the hairy one parted. Then we walked into the town.

It was warm. We found nice old buildings, and nice new ones, a square with a fountain, full of stalls selling food and flowers, beer and wine, with plastic covered trestle tables and benches to sit at. It was the MaiFest, a spring celebration of flowers and wine and beer. We got a glass of wine at one stall. 'You get one mark back when you return the glass,' said the waitress. Bill had to go to a different stall for beer, with a different set of tables. We asked, half-joking, mindful of the segregation of rubbish, if we were allowed to sit together, having bought our drinks at different stalls. 'There will be no problem,' she said gravely.

In this big business city, home of the prestigious Autumn Book Fair, we were astonished to find that credit cards were little use. Germans appear to have a deep distrust of plastic (unbiodegradable: orange bin) and like primitive communities they like cash in the till.

When we returned to the ship we found our mooring ropes slack: our stern rope had dislodged the huge block of granite that formed the corner of the quay. Something must have gone past deep-laden and fast to cause that. The hairy old rope had done its stuff, but its hitch had tightened on the horns of our bitts, and needed a hammer and spike to free it, leaving hairs embedded in the paint.

It was a neat quay, and Bomber Harris with the might of the RAF had failed to damage it. Never mind, the Royal Navy did it in the end, though it took fifty years for us to get round to it.

Bill made a recce and found the market while we were at the MaiFest. Laurel can never resist a market within her walking distance, and set off early. She would not be buying much, she thought, if prices were that high, but she needed some research. Given an adequate supply of marks she could have bought anything she wanted at Frankfurt market, probably even elephant meat (but only if ordered, and not till Friday). Not only was there fruit and vegetables from all Europe, but from every corner of the world: mangoes, lychees, guava, starfruit, kiwis; there was Italian pasta, oriental rice, Indian chutney and Japanese sushi. Chicken and game was upstairs with the fish, separate from the meat downstairs. Laurel bought broken asparagus tips, which were cheap; 200 grams, which got her a funny look, but she needed only enough to make asparagus tart. She explained to the Bakerlady that she needed bread to keep. 'This weighs two pounds,' said the Bakerlady, displaying a large oval loaf, as brown and shiny as a chestnut. 'Ein kilo,' agreed Laurel. She nodded, pleasantly surprised that this foreigner knew about kilos. 'Vill keep a veek,' she said. 'Four marks 80.' £2! Ouch. But it was lovely moist brown bread under the crust, smelt of malt when you cut into it, and it kept, as promised.

We mustered the cats and left soon after 1000, and had to wait longer than usual for the locks, as traffic was heavy. A double pusher waited ahead of us, but was too long to get in with the barges already there. We were small enough to fit in, so we went before him. At the next lock we also had to wait, and for the first time had to understand what the *schleussenmeister* was saying to us over the VHF. We could not get used to being called a *sportboot*. A huge Dutch Barge *Gudrun* from Rotterdam came past from behind us, and we caught the words *sportboot*, and *komm gleich*, and assumed, rightly, that we were to follow her.

In the lock with no floating bollards, rising and changing the rope to a higher bollard four or five times, we still had time to notice the playpen on *Gudrun*'s deck. It was as big as most people's front room, with high steel mesh walls, two swings and a bouncer, a slide, and numerous other ways of amusing two highly active children in it, leaping about like budgerigars.

We were heading for Aschaffenburg; where the chart showed that an old lock had been turned into an off-river mooring, where wash from passing barges would not hurt us. We had had a panicky phone call from Janine on *Garuda*, who were ahead of us at Würzburg, saying they were having a lot of problems: there was nowhere to moor on the Main, there was no room, everywhere was full of little boats.

We pulled off the river at 1800 into a treelined arm, under the rose-red Schloss Johannisburg, built by mad King Ludwig. There was a long quay and plenty of room, but with the usual fierce notices saying 'Only for Hotelboats' and 'Only for the WSV'. We made fast to a mooring belonging to the Kriegsmarine Old Comrades Association, whose clubhouse *Orion* looked closed. Bill felt that 6 years of open conflict which ended 50 years ago ought to lead to some accommodation if anyone turned up to protest. We stayed and lit our barbecue on the side away from the quay. No one complained.

Thursday was a holiday in Germany. It was Himmelfahrt. Now, we've got to stop falling about when we hear that word; yes, we remember 30 years ago driving across Germany on the motorway, and the kids in the back giggling every time they saw huge signs saying Ausfahrt and Einfahrt. The youngest was learning to read and his elder sister egged him on. There are worse ways of teaching children to read than a rude dictionary. No, we must be serious about this word, because it means travel, journey, movement, voyaging: all the things dear to us. Himmelfahrt, therefore, means a journey to Heaven, and thus: Ascension Day. Shops were closed, the sun shone, and the cycle path was busy with whole families out for a day's biking, little ones in seats behind Papas.

The BBC told us of Nato war planes poised for action after the attack on the safe area at Tuzla. A long way from the Danube, we thought, smugly.

The Hafenmeister introduced himself. If we wanted water, move 100 metres back, and he could provide, next to his restaurant barge. Now, please, as it was a holiday and the restaurant would get busy later. So we moved; and realised that giving us water caused him considerable work. This was Germany. It was a cycling path, and the tap was on the far side. Cyclists holding holiday posies must not stumble over hosies, landing on their sun-kissed nosies. The Hafenmeister unbolted the dozen or more bolts that fixed a metal cover to a conduit across the road, laid the hose in it, and rebolted the cover. You really had to admire the elaborate precautions taken to protect the populace. We wonder how many council meetings it took to sort that out.

We washed down the boat, which was grubby, and got rather wet ourselves as the water pressure was high; luckily the day was warm and sunny. The cats hated it. Bograt made for her airing cupboard, and we thought Tansy was in her chosen den, but when the hose water drummed on the dinghy-cover it flushed her out, and she leapt straight through the waterjet. She retired to the wheelhouse, furious; and spent the next hour washing.

We'd shoved the hose end into the inlet to fill our tanks when a young Englishman in shorts introduced himself as Peter. After the hard work of washing down we were ready for a beer, and invited him to share one. He worked as a bricklayer, the money was better than in England, and he was able to help us with some phrases and customs we had not understood. We mentioned the separation of rubbish. 'Oh, they are really into recycling,' Peter said, 'All tins have to be washed clean, have the tops and bottoms removed, and then be squashed flat. If you don't do this, after a few warnings they charge extra, and rubbish collection already costs an average householder an enormous amount.' We could well understand it, with each household provided with five different coloured bins, all new and shiny.

We moved back, nicely full of water, to our berth, and had a quiet afternoon apart from bikers and hikers admiring our sleeping cats.

A nearby boat owner invited us for a drink. Walther was practising his English, being in love with New Zealand, and wishing to go there when he retired to join relatives. We remarked on the air of festivity, and he said: 'Oh, It's not just Himmelfahrt: what you call it?

Ascension Day? It is also Father's Day. The club boat has taken the Fathers for a day trip, with much beer. Soon they will be back, very drunk and singing.'

Sure enough, half an hour later, the Club Boat *Johannisburg* lurched round the corner from the main river, reeling a little, and very musical. She was an old, nice-looking river boat, with 20 or so carousing Fathers on board.

As they moored up, Walther took us to talk to them, and they gave us litres of beer, even though Laurel hardly qualified as a Father. They sang us an old shanty from Hamburg: 'Einmal'.

> 'Once more we'll sail to Bombay, once more to Singapore,
> As long as, in the end, it's Hamburg Altona once more.'

Altona is the district in Hamburg where the sailors live. They embraced us tenderly as we all sang 'Auf wiedersehn', and we pictured them hiccupping home, full of beer and sausage, and jolly rogering their wives in order to be Fathers again by Ascension Day 1996.

After the holiday we shopped, just in time as the weather broke. The headlines yelled, shocked, that the Bosnian Serbs were using Nato hostages as human shields against air strikes.

We left on Saturday after a night of thunderstorms and pouring rain.

Aschaffenburg moorings are in an arm of the old river where it went through a lock that is too small for modern traffic. The lock gates have been removed, so there is current through the moorings which keeps the water wholesome. We decided to try to rejoin the Main via the disused lock. The current was not strong by our berth. We nosed past the little craft, their crews just up and breakfasting. It got narrower and shallower, and our determination faltered, but by now we were committed as the channel was too narrow to turn in, and to thread our way backwards, downstream, through all the small boats was unthinkable. Onward then. We put our nose into the old lock chamber between the stone walls. It was 8 metres wide, and in the narrow confines the current was rampaging. Bill gave *Hosanna* normal full power and she barely inched forward, pushed about by whirlpools sweeping through the chamber. Laurel took the wheel (there was little choice over which way to go) and Bill went to tweak the throttle cables, squeezing 200 additional revs out of each engine. It took over 10 minutes to cover the 60 metres of the old lock chamber, moving forward in little spasms, but once the stem got through the top entrance the skin friction eased and we started to accelerate. The danger was not yet past, however. The confluence with the Main was close, and there was a mass of whirlpools. Bill shot through them before easing speed.

'Don't ever let me do a tomfool thing like that again,' he commanded. Laurel sighed. 'Try and stop him,' she thought.

• 10 •

THE MAIN PROBLEM

on to Schweinfurt

From Aschaffenburg to Miltenberg is a four-lock day. It was not far, a day's outing for the Aschafenburgers, who promised that Miltenberg was beautiful, with an easy mooring just past the bridge, on the right.

We dodged canoeists and speedboats out for a Saturday spin, and came to the third lock, Wallstadt. A splash of foam to the right of the lock showed where the weir was. There were several barges waiting, and a dredger was working. We settled for a long delay.

We were lucky to get through at all. It was an hour before we settled into the lock with two other barges. A man with a heaving line stood by the gates, and once we were in, he heaved it across to the other side, who hauled in the line and an attached wire, led the latter to a hand capstan, and winched the gate closed. This tedious process had to be repeated for the second gate, which they left halfway shut. They opened the vannes of the upstream gates and a tidal wave came down the lock shooting *Hosanna* 5 metres backwards, and noisily slamming the gates shut behind us.

The skipper of the neighbouring barge confirmed a power failure caused by the previous night's thunderstorms. The lock was isolated in the countryside, and the team of men had been brought in when the number of waiting barges built up. The system was laborious and time consuming, but it worked. We watched the upstream gates open laboriously one at a time by the same wire rope and capstan system, taking ages because transferring men and gear from one side of the upstream gates to the other involved travelling the 200 metre length of the lock, across the closed downstream gates, and back 200 metres along the other side. The big barges eased out of the lock and we were free to follow.

The berth at Miltenberg was occupied by a floating crane about 60 metres long. We made fast, at their invitation, to the barge *Fiducia* already moored alongside the crane. Only later they told us that they would be leaving at 0600.

Going ashore meant crossing both barge and crane. It was not easy to cross the barge, several feet above us, and worse still the crane, which had nowhere you could put down one foot and a walking stick, most of it being taken up with huge steel piles and useful looking

Market Place, Miltenberg

winches and reels of wire, but it was worth it to see Miltenberg's half-timbered houses and charming setting, with St Jacobus' church and the castle of Mildenburg looking down, snootily conscious that its spelling with a D and a U sets it apart from Miltenberg with a T and an E.

We had our first meal out in Germany, at a *weinstub*. These offer a rough equivalent of English pubgrub, but cost more, due to strong currency and large appetites. We ate pork chops with salad; the mushroom sauce didn't taste of much, and the salad was sogged in runny dressing, so we poured it off into the ashtray. Massive portions: there are no small helpings in Germany. Even the children eat huge platefuls.

Bill had a litre of dark, strong-tasting, satisfying beer (a litre was the smallest measure served), and Laurel had *trocken wein*, in a glass the size of a small bucket. Franconians are proud of their wine. The cooking was mediocre, the atmosphere friendly.

We stood off at 0545 next morning, as *Fiducia* left at exactly 0600, and we re-moored to the floating crane for a pleasant, warm day. We went ashore for another of the excellent beers, but barbecued our own pork chops on board. We have a stainless steel barbecue suspended over the side on a bracket with a hole underneath to which Bill connects a 12 volt air-pump used for inflating air-beds. This blows the charcoal fire into almost white heat like a blacksmith's forge and produces beautifully grilled meat, far better than the *weinstub*.

Bill, like men everywhere, lords it over the barbecue, displaying fits of temperament, and downing cans of beer when not putting plasters on his burns. Laurel, of course, is doing the real work in the galley so that the lord and master can delude himself that he is cooking the supper. We would be barbecuing many pork chops over the coming months; we hadn't realised it yet, but east of the Rhine Europe eats pork, pork, and pork. Not little bits at a time, but great wads of the stuff. Soon we would face our first haxen, the knee of the beast, entire and whole and perfect, sitting on a plate, alone, as big as the head of St John the Baptist. One of these would fill the two of us to bursting, and then our doggy-bag would feed us for another two days, as well as providing off-cuts for the cats.

The crane team got us up at 0700, as they were moving on, but before casting off and leaving they had to position three huge piles 45 cm across and about 15 metres long, that hold them in place on the river bed when working. These had been lying on deck, and had to be raised and slotted into the vertical tubes, a delicate job because they weighed about 2 tons each, and fitted exactly into the tubes.

All this happened close by our breakfast table with a cacophony of metallic grinds and screeches which scraped down our cringing spines like a fingernail on a blackboard. 'Langsam, langsam,' the workmen said encouragingly every time we winced.

It was 0915 before they trundled away, with unexpected majesty for something that looked like an upturned gateleg table. We did a quick shop, and left at 1100 for Wertheim.

We had trouble at Faulbach lock, on a silted bend with dredgers everywhere. The restricted passage was marked by yellow buoys and notices, one saying 'beware of crosscurrents', and others warning that practically everything was *streng verboten*. A red light forbade onward progress. A huge container ship emerged from the lock; we had little leeway to give him the room his gestures indicated he needed. We decided we could move a little closer to the line of yellow buoys that marked the shallows – as Bill said, gloomily, he would push us there anyway. He did. With a propeller measuring about 2 metres across, he took every bit of room we could give him, and the echo sounder showed little water indeed as he edged past us about a metre away. We later realised that one of the forbidding signs was merely the logo of the dredging contractor.

We came to Wertheim on the Main in the rain. (The rain in Spain may fall where it likes; in Germany it falls on Franconia.) All the berths said they were *Nur fur Fahrgastschiff* on ostentatious notices with big letters. We lay off while we debated the prospects, not being terribly sure exactly what a *Fahrgastschiff* was, but guessing at hotel boat. Eventually we decided that in the European Union we were unlikely to be sent to a labour camp, so we fell back on our usual policy when faced with incomprehensible orders: act wet and apologise if Authority objects. We made fast to the extreme end of the long quay, and prayed to escape notice. Only one hotel boat turned up, there was room for five more, and we were left in peace. Opposite us was a car park beneath a road which was clearly a flood wall, and a pedestrian walkway with flood gates so that water could not inundate the town. When the rain cleared we went for a walk in a charming small town. We did some shopping, managed to find an unlocked rubbish bin in the car park, and then returned for a supper of pork (what else?) and beans, with a Bergerac wine.

It poured all next day. Visibility was poor, which was a pity, as the little villages we glimpsed through curtains of rain were picturesque places. Traffic was light and we had a couple of locks to ourselves, choosing to berth near the rear gates. This enabled the keeper to let the water in fast, which speeded everything up.

We struggled to translate a forbidding notice warning us of some danger ahead. The dictionary was unhelpful, *saltzen tonnen* (saltz with a T). Salz with a Z is pickled cucumbers; were we being warned to beware of tonnes of pickled cucumbers? Very sensibly they gave details of the kilometre post where this danger was, so we should see when we got there.

Near Homburg we chanted in chorus: 'where the hats come from' and found our pickled cucumber in the shape of flashing lights and red buoys, the sort of dredger with a mudpump, and a floating crane: everything but motorway cones and red ribbons. Drenched souls worked in oilskins. Homburg, almost invisible in the rain, was like many little Bavarian towns, perched on a steep forested hill.

We berthed at 1530 at Löhr, beside a welcoming barge *Spessartor*, named for Spessart forest nearby, where Siegfried was treacherously killed while hunting. The berths were for *Fahrgastschiffs* as usual, but the *marinier* lived locally, and in Germany, like everywhere else, it pays to know your way around. He confirmed that the *Fahrgastschiff* was a hotel or restaurant boat, hated by bargees because they had too many privileges.

We'd done 40 kilometres, and had almost reached kilometre post (Kp) 200 in five travelling days up the Main. When we considered that whistling down the Rhine we did 191 kilometres in one day, we realised the difference between down- and upstream. There were still almost 300 kilometres more climbing before the watershed, after which 50 more would bring us to Kelheim, where the navigable Danube starts its headlong rush to the Black Sea.

Löhr was another of those pretty little Bavarian villages with crooked streets and pink cobblestones, rather hard to walk on, and a strong impression that Snow White would be making gooseberry tart just round the corner of this half-timbered house, and on that high footbridge up there, silhouetted against the sunset, we should at any moment see seven little men with picks over their shoulders, hi-hoing home. But it was not Disneyworld. It was much more detailed, the carvings on the houses much finer, the colours more subtle, less new-looking, and the houses very individual, some narrow and five storeys tall, and some rambling into farmyards, and everywhere tubs and pink stone troughs of flowers, and little fountains.

We were smitten with the crucifix before the gatehouse at Löhr. It had a semicircular hood over it, as if the good Lord had been housed in a telephone booth, for Instant Communication with the Most High.

Rubbish was a problem again; the bins on the quay were locked. Too many people used them, it seemed. You should only use them if authorised. It appeared that we *would* have been authorised, but the garbage-gauleiter was off duty, and had taken his key home with him. We'd taken our bottles ashore expecting to find the usual green, white and brown bottle banks, but we walked a long way to the Post Office without finding any. In the end Bill left a small bag of rubbish and one bottle in each picturesque lamppost bin for coke tins and ice cream wrappings, and hoped no one would follow the trail back to our boat. We had *bratwurst* for supper. Mit mash, onions und salat.

The last day of May was still grey and mizzly and the weather forecast held out no hope of improvement. In Jugoslavia, the UN was reported in disarray.

As we approached Steinbach lock we saw on the bank at the bottom of the riverside steps an old woman bending to pick grass for her rabbits. So we thought. And then she hitched up her knickers and went back up the bank to the car, where her husband must have said: 'Here, you'll be all right, dear, no one will see you down by the river...' BUT here was *Hosanna*, slowing down for the red light at the lock. People with cars seldom think of traffic on the river.

We made Würzburg shortly after teatime, passing under the Alte Mainbrucke, the 15th century bridge adorned with 12 admonishing saints. Still raining. On leaving the lock, under the Festen Marienburg, there was a fine quay for pleasure craft, 50 metres long and a pontoon, inside which we could have moored had not the 8 metre motor boat *Calypso* been in the middle of the only space we could occupy, and reluctant to move. We were wet and tired, and there was nowhere else to go. We decided to be bloody, bold and resolute. Said Bill: 'Then he vill mein fender becom.' He shaped up to berth our 27 metres and 60 tons alongside the motor boat, using her as a cushion.

This need not be as life threatening as it appears if done with care. Bill is not bad at ship-handling, and can, when conditions are right, place *Hosanna* literally to the inch. He wouldn't try it with a cross wind or tide; he knows his limitations. Here he was aided by a strong but steady current, which enabled him to keep fine control while moving very slowly over the ground. Nevertheless, the view from the motor boat must have been daunting. When we were about a couple of feet off, they lost their nerve and offered to move. We backed off while they pulled their boat about 8 metres along the quay, which gave us all the room we needed, and we berthed. Magnanimous in victory, like that scoundrel Siegfried, who came here often, Bill thanked *Calypso* for their courtesy without displaying any noticeable sarcasm, and invited them for a drink. We passed a sociable couple of hours, and they marked our maps for us.

This incident, contrasting with our welcome reception alongside the two commercial vessels, points up the different approaches of the professional and the amateur. Professionals of all nationalities find it second nature to assist each other; the profession is exacting enough without adding to difficulties. Amateurs, used to competing for the last parking space in their motor cars, take a different line: 'I got here first – you manage as best you can.' Until persuaded otherwise.

Würzburg is a city which features in all tourist guides. When the rain fell to a light drizzle we visited the cathedral of St Kilian, who was the apostle of Franconia until martyred in the 7th century. It seems as if the main export of Ireland in those days was saints, assorted, proselytising. All over Europe one finds churches dedicated to devotedly industrious Irish saints. We looked Kilian up, which wasn't easy. O'Hanlon's *Lives of the Irish Saints*, a reference work not often carried in boats, gets to the K's only at volume seven. St Kilian's relics are respectably housed in Würzburg, though the RAF attempted to dislodge him during the war when the 11th century cathedral was badly damaged.

One contrasts the ascetic and cruelly terminated lives of these early saints with their apostolic successors, the prince-bishops of mediaeval times (such as Rohan in Saverne). In Würzburg, the prince-bishops built themselves a fine palace, the Marienberg, which makes the Palais at Saverne look like a village hall. This palace lowered at us from its hilltop across the river. In nice weather it would have been a lovely view. We debated getting wet, for we had no personal transport. Bill was finally deterred when he discovered (as he might have expected) that the decor inside would be baroque. He likes baroque music, but he was not going out in the rain to look at a wedding cake, he said firmly. He is a fair-weather tourist.

After not visiting the Marienberg, we left next morning in the pouring rain. We were not quite quick enough at the lock as two Dutch barges came through and took station ahead of us. John Major refuses to bow to Serb blackmail over British hostages, said the news, foreboding.

'Well,' said Bill, in the tone of voice that Latin students translate with *nonne*, 'Is the idea to see out our brief terrestrial span observing Franconia in the rain? Or do we wish to see a little ray of sunshine in

Greece this year?' He had hit upon a thin patch in Laurel's armour. It was she who vociferously longed for sunshine. We felt we were not making progress. Our advance eastwards was slow, since River Main lurches across Franconia via an immense W, so that for days we were progressing north or even northwest, and finally almost to the southwest, with no choice, as this was the only route. The converse was that, unlike road travel, one seldom took a wrong turning.

It was a bad day's travelling, and though soothed a little by the news that the hostages in Bosnia had been released, irritability was not far below the surface. There were many locks, and for some reason they all appeared to be badly managed. Barge skippers were surly, not to us for we kept out of everyone's way, but crews and lock-masters shouted at each other. At almost every lock we waited while arguments took place.

A slight but welcome smile was caused by passing Winterhausen on one side of the river, and Sommerhausen on the other.

In Kitzingen lock a little Dutch boy about four years old was helping Daddy, taking the great loop of rope and putting it over the bollard for him. He was wearing Klompen, which are no longer wooden shoes, but rubber in bright colours and his were red. Then he tried leapfrogging over the bollard but it was too high; he was only a little chap, learning already to be a bargeman.

It had been convenient following the two Dutch barges, since although it slowed us a little, every lock was open our way until what we hoped would be the last lock of the day, at about 1600. Now, at Fahr, the Angelus rang out across the water as we passed, time all little barges were in bed, but here we were, still steaming, with nowhere to lay our heads.

We emerged from another snowstorm of airborne thistledown, peering around for a mooring. At 1845 still not a sign, and we were still following our two Dutchmen. Well, we should all have to stop at 2200, when the locks close. After some thistledown went up Bill's nose he suggested a glass of wine. We rationed it to half a glass, as we were driving, but it cheered us up until we were reminded that stopping at a lock meant starting again at 0600.

Oh, what fun boating is!

We desperately scanned the maps for a mooring, but not one of them could be approached by a boat even half our size.

This is the surprising feature of boating in what could be a picturesque and popular waterway for water tourism. Business and pleasure shall not mix in Germany. There is undoubtedly an element of that in the absurdly draconian regulations governing pleasure boating there. These are a minefield of ineffective, useless, bureaucratic nonsense that the new overlords of Europe are trying to ram down the throats of the rest of the community. They, an almost land-locked nation, know what is best for seafarers!

We had to continue. We had started at 0900, and it had been a hard day manoeuvring while waiting in turbulent weir-races for our turn at busy locks. The rain, and the morale-sapping thought that we were travelling west, had not helped enthuse us. We had hoped that at Garstadt lock, which we reached after 12 hours travelling, we would be able to stop at the lock's quay. Some locks have useful quays for waiting barges, or for overnighting, though they become uncomfortable once traffic re-starts. Nevertheless!

We were disappointed. On the downstream side the quay was almost wrecked, and mooring was impossible. In any event the lock-master, who had clearly also had a bad day, ordered us sharply into the lock and we complied. There would surely be a quay the other side, but no, that was under repair, so on we went into the darkling. Schweinfurt lock would close at 2200. We knew there was a good quay the other side of that so we hastened, following our Dutchman's stern light in the dark, but we did not stand a chance. At 2215 we turned right into the industrial hafen at Schweinfurt, while he went on to the lock to await its opening at 0600. We made fast to a high quay for loading scrap-iron, heated up some Konigsburger Klops, swallowed them down with some reviving alcohol, and fell into bed.

The next morning we had difficulty extricating the ecstatic cats from the huge heaps of scrap metal which they regarded as a feline nirvana. After the ultimate in enticements (second breakfast) we had just shoved off when a big barge appeared round the corner wanting our berth. Good timing.

Joy of joys, a hazy sun; we had almost forgotten what it looked like. And here was one of the best quays to date, through the lock and into the weirstream at Schweinfurt. It had bollards, it was protected from the suck and tug of big barges passing, it had a landscaped park running along it, and trees to screen off the railway. Plus it was only 200 metres to the town centre. We made fast gratefully, using good ropes because there was a noticeable current, and decided to stay for Whit weekend.

We were about 600 metres above the weir where a hydro-electric station hummed like a contented bee-hive, on Kp 333. We spent a lazy weekend enjoying the town, almost entirely rebuilt since the war, but not without character.

Janine of *Garuda* phoned on Sunday: they were stuck near Kelheim as the Danube was in flood and navigation halted. If the rain which caused this continued, there was not much point in hurrying on because all the berths would be full of waiting craft. After a wet winter and a wet spring, followed by a wet summer (the wettest we could remember) we were not surprised the Danube was in flood, the rain had scarcely stopped for weeks. We'd lit the fire several times, and the sunny day that occurred once a fortnight caught us in Guernseys and oilskins.

On Whit Monday the weather improved, the sun appeared and so did the River Police (*Wasserschützpolizei*). We had travelled more than 500 kilometres on German waters without so far being checked, which amazed them. When accosted by men in uniform, especially carrying guns, there is a golden rule: BE POLITE. Even Bill, who resents bureaucrats on principle, acknowledges this rule. When two courteous policemen asked if they could come aboard, Bill said, 'Why not? I'm going to have a beer, what about you?' They replied cautiously that they might like one later, but perhaps they had better get the business done first. Bill had been looking forward to his beer.

'Who is the Captain?' (Very good English.)

'I am.'

'Ah so.' It is interesting that both Germans and Japanese use the same expression in the same circumstances.

'And from where do you come?'

We told them we had crossed France and come down the Rhine.

'And who was in command in the Rhine?'

'I was.' answered Bill. This is strictly true for whether or not a pilot is on board, the Captain remains in command; legally, a pilot is there in an advisory capacity.

'Do you have a Rheinpatent?'

'No.'

'Why do you not have a Rheinpatent?'

'The last time I took a larger ship than this up the Rhine I did not need a Rheinpatent.'

'When was that?'

'It was a warship in 1947. No one asked then for a Rheinpatent.'

There was a long silence. The two policemen exchanged a look, and then gazed at Bill. He stared back. After a minute or two he added: 'And I think I am better at navigating now than I was in 1947.'

The senior policeman looked out of the window, where it seemed, he found inspiration. 'Ah so,' he announced, and suddenly smiled. 'Then you are entitled to an honorary Rheinpatent. It is in the rules.'

We felt the tension disperse. Bill sensed that perhaps he had been a bit brusque.

'Sorry to appear abrupt,' said Bill, brusquely. 'It is a military habit.'

The policemen understood, but were curious. 'But the Rhine has been in flood. Did you not find it difficult?'

'Yes, I did. It was so difficult that I took a pilot. I am not a fool.'

At this they laughed outright, and it was time for the beer.

'And now,' they said, gratefully wiping the froth from their moustaches, 'About your ship.'

Our ship's papers were in order, but there was a little problem. The British government as licensing authority considered us to be a pleasure ship, or *sportboot* as it is known in German.

'We have *sportboote* under 15 tonnes, and *sportboote* over 15 tonnes.' said the senior policemen.

'Well, that's no problem. We are clearly over 15 tonnes.'

'But you are more than 20 metres long.'

'So?'

'So you cannot be a *sportboot*. A *sportboot* is defined as being under 20 metres long.'

'But not in the rest of Europe, and this is Europe.'

In the end they decided that this was far too important a matter to be decided by a sergeant and a constable, and they would need to consult Authority. It being a holiday, they were reluctant to disturb Chancellor Köhl, and we all decided in an amicable way to adjourn the meeting until Tuesday morning. We would not be moving on, we promised, and our visitors departed assuring us that Germany could surely solve this problem in a reasonable way (we still had a few doubts) and we had a pleasant day's rest.

On Tuesday morning Bill was invited along to the Headquarters of the *Wasserundschiffartsamt*. It was explained by a senior officer that a Gilbertian situation obtained:

WE WERE a *sportboot*, a pleasure craft, and therefore MUST give way to commercial shipping,

BUT we were over 20 metres long, so did NOT have to give way to commercial shipping, and had right of way over *sportboote*. As *sportboote* on inland waterways could not be over 20 metres, we could not be a *sportboot* in Germany. This left two possibilities. We could be a *beruffschiff*, but as we had no hold and no cargo, this was an unconvincing definition. We had however indicated to the officers that we wrote books on board; therefore we could be considered an *arbeitschiff*, or working boat. Bill saw no possible objection to that.

However if we were an *arbeitschiff*, we would require an inspection to ensure we conformed to the regulations governing them, entailing payment of a modest fee for the inspection, and then, as an *arbeitschiff*, we would be entitled not to yield priority at the locks to commercial vessels.

'The only thing which would present a problem would be the inspection. It is known that Britain has different requirements. Perhaps we should ask you a few questions.'

Our safety measures, since we were a seagoing craft, were more than satisfactory. We had correct lights, the blue board, lifejackets, and an excellent first aid kit. It transpired that the only things that would cause difficulties in Germany would be gas, and our Halon fire extinguishers, which are banned in super-Green Germany. Bill, who was once a salvagemaster, has fought some fires at sea, and maintains that Halon is so far and away the best fire-fighting substance for use in ships that to ban it is to condemn seamen to death. He would not dream of using anything else. As he points out to Green friends, he has no intention of using the stuff, but if he needed it in a rare emergency, rain forests would come a long way down his list of priorities. The senior police officer was sympathetic to this, so passing over the Halon question he came to our Butane gas cylinders. These are stored above deck level, with holes for ventilation and drainage over the side, in accordance with best UK practice, but in Germany, this is not enough. We began to understand why German boats in Germany depend on alcohol cookers, which in our view are far more dangerous. The rare explosions in gas-fitted boats are far fewer than fires in boats with alcohol cooking. The German pondered for a moment. 'Our rules are perhaps over-cautious.' He paused. 'But, please try not to explode before you get to Austria.' Bill paid 43 Deutschmarks for the *Schiffsattest*, and felt it was cheap at the price. In the office next door he was given his *Schiffsattest*, his Honorary *Rheinpatent*, valid also for the Danube, and a book called: *Donauschiffahrtspolizei-verordnung*, which was the rule book for navigating both Rhine and the German Danube, and which we should by law know and carry.

The whole episode passed with great good will, and good humour, and Bill felt that he could not fault the behaviour of the German *Wasserschütspolizei*. A bureaucracy with wise and flexible administrators, who can temper stupid regulations to fit the situation, or heave the book at malefactors, is probably the best form of government available.

It was an astonishing piece of luck that all was regularised in view of the events that were to occur the following afternoon, when the lack of the correct certificate might have caused an offence, and the whole terrible affair might have had a very different outcome.

Those old enough may recall that fifty-odd years ago almost every day the BBC announced air raids on the ball-bearing factories at Schweinfurt. Someone had an idea that Germany would surrender if these factories were obliterated. He forgot that neutral Sweden was happy to sell any ball bearings Germany needed.

The US Army Eighth Air Corps bombed the factories by day, and the RAF by night. They succeeded in flattening the town, but did little damage to the factories, though there were temporary interruptions in production.

Both of us, Bill in particular, were re-examining our attitudes as we travelled through Germany and met her people. Throughout Bill's early training, he was taught that they were ENEMIES. Freud says that our personalities are conditioned by our experiences in infancy, but an important input into the conditioning of adults is surely the culture in which they spend their 'apprenticeship years'. Bill was having a hard time adjusting in spite of our friendly reception.

We spent the afternoon in the Spittalsee Bunker, which had a 50th anniversary exhibition in it. It was grim. We went with Ingrid, whom we had met in the supermarket. She was just the person we needed to translate the captions; she'd been born in Silesia, which was then German, but is now Polish. The family had to flee from the Russian advance; her father, a physician, was taken prisoner, and her mother was killed in an air raid in the last weeks of the war, leaving Ingrid, 16, to care for younger brothers and sisters. She became an American citizen.

One long wall of the bunker was filled with obituary notices from the wartime newspapers, each with an iron cross printed in the corner. Starting off six to a page, they decreased in size as casualties mounted and newsprint got scarce, down to the size of a postage stamp. The bomb damage pictures included photos of Coventry and the London blitz, just to keep the record straight. What moved Ingrid most stood among some objects of the period – a pram, a tin bath, an old radio, and a free standing cooking range, enamelled blue. 'I cooked for the youngsters on a range like that,' she said, 'when I could get anything to cook. When I could get wood to burn.' In the forest where they lived they could gather fallen branches only. Cutting wood was forbidden.

Schweinfurt, meaning Pigford, has not the grace of Oxford, and is not in the guide books. There is little of its thousand year heritage left. It did not rebuild its mediaeval buildings stone by stone as Frankfurt did. This was a working, not a University town, and they rebuilt in a pleasant no-nonsense practical way, no avant-garde monstrosities, and no pastiche baroque. Fifty years on, the gardens are mature, the trees have grown and the buildings have settled in as if they'd been there for centuries. We liked it very much. We were walking back from the bunker, crossing the quayside park, when we realised that something was amiss.

Hosanna was in midstream with her mooring ropes trailing in the water, and drifting steadily towards the hydro-electric station.

• 11 •
HAVOC AND HEROICS
Schweinfurt

It was the sort of nightmare one dreads. In broad daylight, in late afternoon, we viewed the scene with disbelief. As we came through the little passage under the railway, it took valuable seconds to realise that *Hosanna*, our only home, was in grave danger. There was no barrier above the hydro-electric station, which was still humming its little song as if nothing whatever was wrong. If *Hosanna* were to arrive broadside on, as she then was, she would straddle two of the station's supporting piers, and might be capsized there by the force of water flowing under her. If she were to turn end on, then she would disappear inside the large opening where the water began to fall, and God only knew what would happen.

She had been left well made fast with four substantial ropes, heavyish hawsers over an inch in diameter, with breaking strains of 12 tons each, a huge reserve of strength. Two of them, called breast-ropes, held the ship at right-angles to her length, and two more longer ropes, known as springs, left the ship in a forward direction; they were meant to take longitudinal strain, in this case current of 4 km/hr.

No loops remained over the bollards on the quay, so it was unlikely the ropes had parted. As they were trailing in the water, the assumption was that vandals had deliberately and mischievously cast her adrift in the current.

There was no time to consider this, however. *Hosanna* was a good 30 metres out in the stream, and moving steadily. There were no rowing boats that we could borrow. Laurel offered to swim off, but Bill forbade her. In this current of cold water, and with no easy means of climbing on board, he did not want a drowning to add to his misery.

He set off at a smart sprint for the hydro-electric station, which was not something an asthmatic of his age should do. He raced across the bridge past the power station to the lock-keeper, asking him to call the water-police boat, and saw him leap to the telephone, but it was the power station he called, and not the police. Bill ran back across the weir and rang the power station bell. He hammered on the door. The turbines were running, sucking water in. There was no response. The station was unmanned.

In despair Bill looked over the parapet. *Hosanna* was long past the row of warning buoys, the limit of safe navigation. One of them had caught her and swung her round so that she was in line with the current instead of being across it, and she was drifting stern first down to the hydro-electric station intake, under Bill's feet, into unseen dangers. He presumed the ship itself could not actually reach the turbines, but her trailing ropes and wires could, and would do great damage. He knew that the power station intakes would be designed to accelerate the water flow. *Hosanna* could be capsized, certainly badly damaged.

As he stood there, badly out of breath, he saw that she would pass with her poop about 10 feet beneath him. He had a chance, and took it. As her stern came below him, he dropped down onto the poop, sprawling as he landed. *Hosanna* was travelling at about 1 metre a second, so had 26 seconds to pass under the parapet. On the fourth of those seconds she struck the base of a work cabin on wheels that hung on rails from the parapet, presumably to service the intake. She bounced off this with a noise like a bomb on a ball-bearing factory, paused a moment, and continued her way in. Bill stopped only to pull in the stern rope which was hanging dangerously near the propellers, and then dashed into the wheelhouse and started the centre engine.

As the engine roared, Bill put her into full speed ahead before starting the others. *Hosanna* started to move ahead, but she had been on the swing as she entered the tunnel, and with her stern still in the power station (actually under the parapet) there was no possibility of steering her. She took a sheer, and as she gathered speed with 3 engines she headed for shallow water close to the bank and there ran aground.

Bill paused for breath. The immediate threat was met. He pulled in the other ropes. Then he tried to get off the mud, but could not do it sideways. He had to back off the mud the way he had gone on, and manoeuvre her once more stern first into the very tunnel of the power station, but this time so as to point towards deeper water, then full ahead again to shoot clear.

Laurel watched all this, helpless, from the quayside 600 metres away. She sobbed twice, and then prayed, having nothing much else to do. At first she lost sight of Bill altogether, then suddenly saw him on the parapet. She heard the crash of the collision, and saw him leap on board from the power station, like Errol Flynn in a pirate movie, saw him pull in the ropes, saw him run aground and work the bow thruster to try to get off.

It was an impressive piece of boathandling, even without the heroics. As *Hosanna* re-approached her berth, Laurel hooked up the breast-rope from the water with her walking stick and dropped its eye over a bollard.

Bill was white with rage, and red with over-exertion, his mottling changing with every gasping breath. He was in no state to make the ship fast. He felt sick. He was too out of breath to speak, otherwise what he might have said to the bystanders could have caused a war. Laurel stepped on board, saw to the mooring, switched off the engines, and took command of her husband.

'I don't think,' she said, 'that men of your age should be doing a kilometre sprint. Have a brandy.'

'Good heavens,' said Bill. 'Are you going to get it for me?'

'I'll get you anything,' she said. 'Tonight you are MY HERO.'

Bill had a stiff brandy, believing that strong alcohol disperses adrenalin. Having cosseted her Captain, Laurel then looked for her cats. Who knew what vandals might have done to them? As usual, when there was noise and disturbance, they had sensibly taken refuge in their separate hideouts: one in the airing cupboard, and one in the cupboard on the verandah.

Then, of course, we shook like leaves for quite a while. We couldn't sit, we couldn't stand, we couldn't settle to anything; the adrenalin was running extremely high. We decided against taking tranquillisers, and we had another slug of brandy each, and then the cats made us laugh, and we began to feel more like human beings. There is no doubt that an incident like that screws you up to a pitch that few people reach, and you have to come down one way or another. We weren't hungry for a long while afterwards.

We speculated on the kind of mind that enjoys such mischief. We had been cast off before, in Savannah in Georgia, but we were aboard and noticed in time. It had happened in Cambrai in France; again we were on board and could take action. This was the nearest we had been to disaster.

We wonder whether the vandals stayed around to watch what happened afterwards. At least we had acquitted ourselves well. We could be proud of managing with no help from *Wasserpolizei*, bystanders, indeed without any assistance whatsoever. We had got ourselves out of trouble unaided as we usually do, and were pleased about that.

After a decent interval for recovery we checked for damage. By the grace of God there was none, though the impact had jerked some books off our shelves, a bottle of shampoo was upended and weeping quietly into the bathroom carpet, and the Salvation Army mug we kept the parsley in was broken. We found on the poop a large galvanised bolt, apparently sheared off the power station. All in all, a small price to pay. It is significant that our ship's log for that day contains no entry for what we did after 1800 that evening, and neither of us can remember what it was.

The police did not arrive until the following morning, closely pursued by the *Wasserschutzpolizei*, the Direktor of the power station, and the local press.

Bill was suffering from reaction, so Laurel coped with most of it.

An accident report was required, and done with the least possible fuss. Our documents were squeaky clean. After some discussion in German, which centred on the fact that the incident was due to the act of persons unknown, and was neither accident nor negligence on anyone's part, the power station manager agreed that there would be no claim for damages, which were not in any event serious. Everyone heaved a sigh of relief. Apparently, if there is a claim for damage, the investigation takes on a different dimension. We kept the sheared bolt.

Bill recovered his physical condition, apart from stiff muscles, as the morning wore on, but he was very depressed. He sat for a long time with his upturned hands on his knees and his head in his hands, the position his father used to rest in when he came home exhausted from the fishing. Bill moaned silently; the only way of describing it.

The newspapermen returned, wanting pictures. The police returned, and Bill had to surface for a bit. They had taken several statements, and were convinced the culprits were American servicemen from a nearby base. Apparently they had done this before. There were 14,000 men at the base, with little to do. There would be no hope of tracing them because the US authorities were unhelpful and unco-operative with the civil police.

Bill wondered if there were any competent officers at the base. It was a rhetorical question. 'Officers who cannot keep their men out of mischief should retire and run a nationalised industry,' he said, and Laurel contrived to redirect the interview before he got carried away. She told the police that we were too relieved at recovering our home safely to bother with charges against persons unknown. The senior policeman was very sympathetic, and pleased that we were not going to make an 'incident' of it.

Later, the Chief of the *Wasserschutzpolizei*, who was very interested in our voyage, came to say he had been in touch on our behalf with the German authorities at Passau, down River Danube. His news was gloomy. Ships *were* getting through Jugoslavia, which was one thing, but they had to pay a tax to the Serbs. There were reports of theft and demands for money, on no known scale, and without receipts, so that one surmised it was illegal. The ex-Jugoslav Army were ill-disciplined and more or less looking after themselves. There were rumours of big cargo barges, carrying armed men, running the gauntlet with their windows blocked up with steel plate, of bullet marks in them, rumours of piracy and pillage, and guerilla bands taking whatever they wanted at gunpoint.

Though most of this seemed to be hearsay and rumour, we knew we would have to think carefully about going ahead. Bill seemed to have lost his enthusiasm, and moved about as if in shock. Laurel, who has been a Samaritan, knows a little about depression, and detected ominous signs. Bill started to write letters to our children, friends and associates to say we were giving up, the project had beaten us, and we were coming back. She let him write.

On the TV news we saw wild floods at Passau where the Danube is joined by River Inn. More heavy rain was forecast. Nothing seemed to be in our favour. It was surprising therefore that at bed-

Old crane, Bamberg

time Bill responded positively to Laurel's suggestion that we go a bit further.

'At least let us feel Danube water under our keel before turning back,' she said.

'All right. It's a bit early to give up. We'll find some of those Barge Captains who have done the journey and talk to them ourselves. Let's go down to Vienna, at least.'

'Or Budapest. *Garuda* was bound for Budapest.'

'Budapest, perhaps.'

Bupapest. Perhaps.

• 12 •
BREAKFAST IN BAMBERG

On Wednesday our picture was in the *Volkszeitung*, describing us as *weltenbummler* with an account of some of our voyages, so everyone knew who we were; one of the policeman asked if his friend could take a photo of himself standing with us on the boat. Five bob to speak to us now we've had our picture in the paper. Many people stopped to talk, expressing sorrow and shame that such a thing should have happened in their town. We were touched and grateful for their comfort and encouragement, and took strength from it.

We left after a night of heavy rain, not intending to go far, just to get moving. Bill had noted a possible stop about 90 minutes on at Hassfurt-hafen, and the *Wasserschutzpolizei* said it would do us fine.

The small *hafen* was crowded with commercial barges. We made fast to a friendly Dutch boat, but he was soon summoned under the loading berth; loading would continue like this day and night with all the concomitant noise, so we shoved off. Shortly after, at Knetzgan lock, we were reprimanded for having fendered ourselves with motor tyres. We know it is *verboten*, and we also know that it is tolerated; not one lock-keeper had complained so far, and this was the 232nd lock on this voyage. We were the only ship in the lock. We hauled in the offending motor tyres, after which the keeper let the water into the lock so fast that the violent disturbance threatened to damage the ship, especially with no adequate fendering. We were a comparatively small craft in a big lock so we hastily cast off and Bill used all three engines and bow-thruster to hold *Hosanna* as stationary as possible in the middle of the maelstrom. It was deliberate spitefulness on the part of the lock-keeper.

As the racing water calmed down Laurel had to restrain Bill from venting his displeasure in rough sailor's language over the VHF radio. He contented himself with leaning out of the window and making an uncharacteristically moderate gesture.

We had to wait at the next lock for a barge to come downwards. As she left, we noticed that she came from Budapest. Somehow this cheered us up. We would soon meet Captains who could tell us something.

After another half hour we poked our nose into a creek at Eltmann, and made fast opposite a small marina. We had hoped to lie at the marina itself, but its fittings were far too fragile for a boat of our size, so we wriggled across to what was described on our chart as a *betonkai*. This ferro-concrete platform did not look strong either. It was about 11 metres long so that we overlapped by 8 metres at each end, backing into an alder tree at the rear. The mooring rings were inadequate, so Bill took a long rope ashore and ploughed painfully through a jungle of nettles with leaves as big as soup plates and made the bows fast to a sycamore, then Laurel threw him a long rope for the after end, which he made fast to the alder.

It started to rain again, and the large battery charger failed. Filters were not obtainable at the nearby garage. It was not a very successful day's cruising, but at least we were on the move again.

We had a disturbed night, to add to the grumbles. Traffic passing on the river made waves in our creek and caused us to scend in our berth and bang against the *betonkai*, and our cats met, noisily, a patrol of German cats led by a coal-black *Obergruppenführer* of ferocious demeanour and magnificent whiskers.

We disentangled ourselves from the alder before leaving. Its loving embraces left branches and twigs all over the deck. Laurel swept up the evidence, fearing the next lock-keeper might say 'Ach! I know where you moored last night! Not content with savaging the hydro-electric station at Schweinfurt you now damage one of our beautiful alder trees!'.

At mid-morning we entered the Rhein–Main–Donau Kanal (RMDK) at Kp (Kilometre post) 384. We had covered 1367 kilometres since Calais. Later, two small yachts passed and warmed our hearts by giving us a round of applause. We began to realise just how unusual a sight we were in these waters.

Coming into Bamberg, which we had long looked forward to, Heikell's guide tells of a mooring at the Kettenbrücke. We counted bridges to locate the right one. A *Pegel* or post for 'Vier brucken' marked the headroom under the four bridges, plenty for us. A new bridge spoilt our counting, but we established the right one, with two beautiful 200 metre quays, just where a tourist boat might want to lie to visit this gem of a town. They were quite empty and enticing, but we could see no bollard. Two possible bollards turned out to be ducks, and you can't very well moor to a duck. There was not even a bench, fence, or lamp-post to moor to, let alone a tree. A notice saying 'No mooring' would have done fine.

We had to come a kilometre back and moor to a concrete quay belonging to the WSA, the River Authority. We expected to get chased off, but as it was pouring with rain we decided to stay until chased. Laurel is the better wheedler, so she went up to the offices for permission to stay the weekend. She found a young man who spoke English, and was sure it would be OK, and consulted the Direktor. The Direktor was not a wise and flexible administrator. Laurel heard words like 'problem', and 'Wasserpolizei', and all kinds of negatives. The young man being on her side, she produced the Schweinfurt newspaper cutting, to prove that we were responsible people who didn't leave their rubbish in the wrong bin, and wrested the grudging admission from Herr Direktor that there was nowhere else we could go, and that a blind eye could be turned if we left promptly at 0700 on Monday, before work started. Delighted, she agreed.

We lit a fire in the saloon, spent a lazy afternoon indoors, dining on chicken and mushroom pie, followed by *clafouti*. It was a quiet secure berth.

Saturday morning was cloudy but dry and we planned to spend the whole day as tourists in Bamberg.

When Laurel was a child she learnt a German folk-song called 'Ach! du lieber Augustin'. When she was evacuated up to Yorkshire, she found that the same tune had very different words:

'Don't put yer muck in our dustbin, our dustbin, our dustbin,
Don't put yer muck in our dustbin –
Our dustbin's full.'

Here we were with our rubbish looking for a German dustbin again, walking into Bamberg through a riverside park, and every litterbin was full.

We had a lovely day in Bamberg. It was a long walk, but there were benches at intervals. Bamberg is one of the most beautiful towns we have ever visited. River Regnitz (a tributary of the Main) flows right through the centre, dividing itself round small islets, on each of which there are beautiful buildings connected by beautiful bridges. We had something of the pleasure of walking round a Venice in miniature on this bright morning. At the top of a hill was the Domplatz, a vast cobbled square where stands the Cathedral, the Alte Residenz, which is Renaissance, and the New Residenz, which is 17th century.

The Town Hall, a small building covered with paintings, sat astride a bridge in the most picturesque place possible, over the Regnitz river. On one side, if you looked very carefully, you could see where a painted Cupid suddenly developed a three dimensional leg, which stuck out into the gutter.

We sat in the pedestrian precinct for refreshment, with an accordion playing in the background. Walking through, as conspicuous as a peony in a bed of parsley, was a Scot, in full regalia – kilt, glengarry, sporran and bagpipes. We weren't quick enough to ask him what a nice Scot like him was doing in a place like Bamberg.

We knew what the locals were doing. At 1030 they were already joyously tucking in, indoors if wet, outdoors if weather permitted. Coffee, cakes, ice cream, followed by beer, doner kebabs, and sausages of every kind including currywürst, and almost anything that once flew, squawked, or squealed, cooked and sliced copiously into a sesame bun. More serious meals of Gargantuan proportions were consumed inside the restaurants.

Breakfast was being taken on the table next to us. For an inclusive price of 14 marks (£6.50) this is what they got: choice of tea, chocolate, espresso or cappuccino. A basket of assorted breads and rolls, with butter. Jam, honey or Nutella, and orange juice. Then it got serious,

The Dom organ at Bamberg

a huge plate of Parma ham, shoulder ham, salami, assorted sliced cheeses, followed by another huge plate of scrambled eggs. Then, just in case they were still faint with hunger, they could have extras in the shape of muesli, hard-boiled eggs, yoghurt, and croissants. And the eating day had only just begun...

Our attempted visit to the Dom collided with an organ concert which Bill said he was not prepared to undergo. The organ is not Bill's favourite instrument; he thinks it is environmentally unfriendly. As the Dom bell rang out we found a quiet terrace nearby, it being warm and sunny, and had zander and buttered potatoes.

We returned to the Dom; there are pearls of Gothic sculpture there, including a 13th century statue of the Bamberg Rider; an unknown young man on horseback, believed to be St Stephen, first King of Hungary. His aspect was regal and dignified, reminding us of the Delphi Charioteer.

The tomb of Henry the Second (the Saint) and Cunegonde his wife, buried here, was carved with intriguing scenes from their lives: Cunegonde falsely accused of adultery, Henry being miraculously cut for the stone, an operation which, in those days before anaesthetics, was best achieved by the surgeon with the sharpest knife and the fastest reactions, in this case St Benedict.

The statue of Adam which once adorned the porch has been removed to the museum in the old cloisters next door, ostensibly to reduce the effects of atmospheric pollution, it being a coincidence that a substantial charge can now be made for seeing it. The face was memorable, handsome and good, all the dignity of man before the fall.

Fifty yards upstream of the little Town Hall was a weir about a metre high, with the water in spate crashing over it, and endeavouring to paddle up the rapids were kayaks covered with arrogant graffiti, containing multicoloured dare-devils in crash helmets, intent on doing themselves an injury. We watched one windmilling his paddles in about 20 attempts to scale the cascade, but got tired before he succeeded, and turned our attention to the water fowl in the back-eddies, playing with an abandoned blue balloon blown by the wind.

We also went to look at a bit of industrial sculpture: the old crane on the passenger boat quay, and looked in vain for possible moorings nearer to the centre of town.

Laurel was by now painfully feeling the effects of a bridge too far, so we sat down for the smallest ice cream we could find, still enormous (we requested two spoons).

We returned, slowly, to the boat, having enjoyed walking almost 4 kilometres, a bit at a time. Laurel was in pain so Bill cooked sausage and mash, a menu within his culinary capabilities.

The question of what to do on Sunday was solved for us. In the first place it started to rain, and secondly, the batteries were almost flat, and it was urgently necessary to dismantle the big charger and find the fault. This took time. Two separate fuses had blown, which was hard to spot, and we had only one spare cartridge fuse, so Bill had to improvise from a card of Woolworth fuse wire. It worked, and our hungry battery had a square meal. The weather turned colder. On Saturday 10 June we had eaten out of doors; on rainy Sunday, we had to light our fire again in the afternoon in order to keep warm.

Flaming June.

• 13 •
RUNAWAY RIVER
Nürnberg to Kelheim

Mindful of our promise, we left Bamberg at 0700; the Direktor waved goodbye from his window and we had an uneventful journey to Nürnberg, where a dual carriageway clung to the canal. There was no room for us at the Motor Boat Club.

Some distance past Nürnberg was a good quay, 3 kilometres long. We chose a point where the noisy road wandered away from the canal and left only a cycle track lined with grass and woods. Two charming fishermen came to welcome us, saying that what looked like a hotel barge moored some way ahead was a disco. They said, disparagingly, that it went 'rumba bumba' all night. Perhaps because it was Monday night we had no rumba bumba at all. As the quay was some way out of Nürnberg we didn't see the beautiful mediaeval city, capital of Franconia, Nürnberg of the Meistersingers, and Albrecht Dürer, and the Nazi Party. Bill, interested in history, would have liked to see the Luitpold Stadium where Hitler made his speeches.

On Tuesday we reached the Main–Donau Kanal. It was broad and modern, so we were surprised to find no floating bollards in the locks, one of which was 18 metres tall – we had to change our rope over 13 times. The lack of traffic also surprised us; we went through nearly all the locks on a green light. We saw two boats come up from Hungary, but had no opportunity to talk.

Eibach lock, however, was closed against us with something coming through. So we stopped and made fast and Laurel took Tansy for a walk on her red ribbon. Eibach must have been the start of the most recent section of canal, because there were floating bollards, which made things much easier. The next few locks would be even higher: we were going up the last gigantic watersteps to the top of Europe, to the watershed. Each lock was about 25 metres high. A feature of these modern locks is that they save water by having huge tanks at the side: when the lock empties, water goes into these tanks instead of being poured off down the canal. Almost three quarters of it is saved; an ingenious device for summer when water is short.

At mid-morning we saw ahead the astonishing but unmistakable silhouettes of an English canal narrow-boat and its butty, and came up with Nick Sanders. His two brightly painted boats named *Unspoilt by Progress* were on the way back from his trip to the Black

Sea. We stopped and roped the boats together (fortunately no barges were coming in either direction) and had half an hour of useful chat.

He had descended the Danube in mid-winter in bad weather, and the butty had sunk at one point. Conditions had been very hard for his small under-powered craft, and to return against the current he had needed a tow back to Regensburg. We gave him our sincere congratulations; we would not like to do it his way.

Chats between fellow travellers on lonely roads are a vital part of voyage survival, sharing information and passing on advice, and we had been severely deprived since *Garuda* had pushed on ahead. Much of what Nick told us would come in handy, far more valuable than anything we obtained from official sources. And best of all, he had done the voyage! Spirits soared. We had needed a Captain's report, and his was about the best we could possibly have, at a time when we sorely needed reassurance that the journey was possible at all.

We were approaching the last lock before the watershed. It had the awkward name of Hilpoltstein, and was another 25 metre lock. This section of canal is new, having been opened in September 1992, and the landscape was still scarred, though great efforts had been made to restore a rural appearance. Success is in sight; trees are growing.

These summit locks are very tall; behind this one were green forested hills, and once we were through we should be in the summit pound. The gate came down behind us, a massive thing, with cages in front to keep débris out. It was like being in a concrete cathedral, from Atlantis perhaps, as the damp walls towered above us, smelling of river mud, and colourwashed with pond green slime. To add to this underwater impression the bollards moaned in their housing as they rose, singing eerily like whales under the sea. Looking up from the bottom the cathedral was roofed with a vault of blue, patched with wispy cloud. We came up the 25 metre rise faster than lifts on the London Underground. So did 3000 tons of Dutch barge ahead of us, an economical use of energy.

We emerged into the summit level, and at 1435 on 13 June 1995, *Hosanna* passed the European Watershed. We were at the top of Europe's waterways, the watershed between the North Sea and the Black Sea, 406 metres above sea level, 1332 feet, certainly the highest *Hosanna* has ever been, and possibly the highest achievable by a proper ship sailing all the way on her own bottom. The highest we had been before was 340 metres, at Langres, the watershed between the Channel and the Mediterranean, in central France.

Laurel was singing: 'Hosanna in the highest, Hosanna evermore'. She was as high as a kite with excitement and expectancy. From now on (if we went on) we would travel downhill all the way to the Black Sea, another 2485 kilometres. It was still 71 kilometres down the staircase to Kelheim, and the confluence with the Danube itself.

The feeling of altitude was such that we almost expected snow when we came out of the lock, it looked Alpine, a beautifully scenic stretch with the pine woods and the sloping grass banks on either

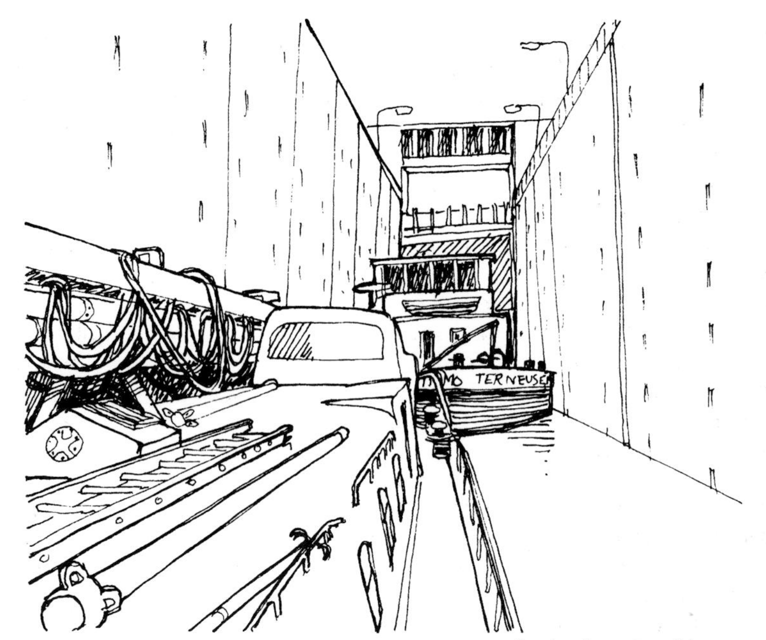

In the lock at Bachhausen

side, cropped by sheep. The wild flowers that grew on the banks were so profuse and beautiful that one had a feeling that Nature didn't quite do it alone. Nature, when left to herself, has a habit of sprinkling far too much yellow about. Suddenly the view opened as the land fell away, little white church towers appeared with their Victorian sugar-shaker tops, and we could see in the distance, beyond blue forested hills, the shadowy mountains of the Bavarian Forest.

We passed the *denkmal* (monument) on the south bank marking the watershed itself, having come a long way, 1515 km (819 nautical miles) since Calais. In the Guide is a picture of the opening ceremony of the RMDK on 25 September 1992, which took place at this spot. Our picture shows immense crowds on the banks, hotel boats, and the firehoses of the fireboats spraying like fountains, a festive scene with crowds of people and a brave show of flags. Today there was one other barge ahead, and nobody on the banks at all. This was built as the biggest waterway carrying the most tonnage in Europe, but the Jugoslavian war and the collapse of Eastern Europe had decimated the traffic.

We found a good, isolated quay on our left at Kp 114, with bollards perfectly spaced for us at 25 metres, so we stopped the night. Though fine by day, it was cool for mid-June with day temperatures of about 17°C.

Fields rolled away from the canal bank, to a village maybe 2 kilometres away. The cats rolled on the ground in ecstasy, the skylarks were singing, the clover was blooming in the grass, and everything was lovely.

Fifty metres away they were cutting the hay with that summer sound of puttering tractor and the summer scent of mowing. Only the farmer and his wife were working; like old times except that they had 'his and hers' tractors. When her man disappeared farmwards with a full load, the farmwife's curiosity drew her towards us on her redolent clogs, and Laurel had a nearly unintelligible conversation with obbligato of skylarks. '...Wie fahren?...Schön, eh? Jo! Genauge! Schuss! Auf Wiedersehn!' We agreed that the air was good, that the weather was right for haymaking, and she was astonished that we carried our house on our backs so to speak, like a caravan, and that we had a kitchen and a bath and a bed, and electricity. It does sound grand when you say it like that. She was also intrigued by the two cats, who were ecstatically hunting fieldmice among the clover; luckily the haymaking machine was a good way away.

Early on Wednesday 14 June the skylarks watched us waiting for the first lock downwards, and the BBC reported that the Bosnian Serbs were massing for a big offensive. As long as all the fighting stayed in the west, away from the Danube...

Bill swilled the decks with the nice new water from the top pound, unspoilt by progress through countless slimy locks. We had not understood what the lock-keepers were telling us over the VHF, and they had had the courtesy to come and explain that two big tows of barges were arriving, and that we might not get in at the same time. It could be a long wait, the barges were not even in sight yet, and then the second came a long time after the first. It was the longest wait yet on the whole journey, two hours and twenty minutes. Apparently a pleasure craft was waiting at the other end, and when she came up, we could go down. The weather remained uncertain, our haymakers were nowhere in sight in today's drizzle.

A Dutch barge came up from behind us, took his priority and went in, but there was room behind him for us. Going downhill, we used our after bitts in the locks, as the water now came in from astern and swept us forward.

After the lock we slowed down for a boat with a blue flashing light close to the shore, with frogmen working. Our usual principle is not to look too closely at what frogmen are looking for, or worse still, have found, but in this case they were using an underwater pneumatic drill, doing repairs.

We had come to the beautiful Altmühl Valley, where forest clad hills climbed up from the canal, and organpipes of grey rock stood like watchtowers in the forest. Through a grey mist of rain we saw guelder rose and wild flowers, and some stalwart fishermen under umbrellas.

We passed a most attractive little village with chalet-like houses at the foot of a green cliff crowned with rocks but there was no mooring. The *raison d'être* of the many huge and expensive hotel boats was beginning to be apparent; it is the only way to cruise these waters and enjoy the scenery, otherwise moorings are for commercial barges, and

Lock cottage on the old Ludwig Kanal

tiny *sportboote*, whose havens are too small for sea-going boats to get in. We would like to have stopped, we were tired, and sick of the rain, and apart from anything else we needed bread; Laurel had had to bake some because we'd been unable to buy any for ages.

During the afternoon we came across traces of the old Ludwig Kanal. There have been previous attempts to connect the northern rivers of Europe to the Danube. The Romans thought of it, but without locks, which had not been invented, it was not feasible. Charlemagne attempted it just before the year 800, but the engineering was unsatisfactory and it was never completed, though traces remain. The next attempt was by King Ludwig I, and was for those times a first-class endeavour: thousands of men and some early mechanical diggers were employed. The project, just over 170 kilometres from Bamberg to Kelheim, was begun in 1836, and opened in 1848.

It followed the Regnitz valley to Nürnberg, then cut along the Sultz valley to Dietfurt, and down the Altmühl to Kelheim. Its summit pound was 457 metres above sea level. It took barges of 32 metres length and 4.45 metres breadth carrying about 100 tons of cargo. Long enough for *Hosanna*, but not wide enough.

Negley Farson travelled along this canal in his small yawl *Flame* in 1925 and afterwards wrote the classic *Sailing Across Europe*. We had much enjoyed reading it, 70 years on, the more so as up-to-date information was hard to find. Already by 1925 the canal was falling into disrepair, and Farson had difficulty making progress. Possibly his was the last passage from coast to coast before the canal closed, for he met no other traffic and took many lock-keepers by surprise.

The route of the old canal comes close to the new one near Mühlhausen, and follows the same path as far as Ottmaring. From then on the two canals are in and out of bed with each other, the old one weed-choked and overgrown with trees, with remains of old locks and lock-keepers' cottages, colourwashed a pale salmon colour and with arched windows and doorways. They were preserved after building the new canal; and the landscaping has been most sensitively done, blending in with the forested hillsides down to the canal's edge with sweeps of grass, plantings of trees, and the inevitable cycle path. There were riders out with their crash helmets and brightly coloured suits even on this wet day.

At 1530 the rain became torrential, and we made fast to an isolated quay at Haidhof. It was securely fenced off from the countryside, though whether this was to keep us from robbing the population, or to protect us from Bavarian monsters, we cannot say. The cats soon found a hole through into a sandpit and were happy; we just pulled the blankets over our heads and lit our fire to keep warm. For the latter part of the day's journey we had been travelling above cloud base. The rain continued. When we look back on this journey we shall tell our friends: last June we spent winter in Germany.

There was a scheme to enlarge the Ludwig Kanal to carry 1500 tonne barges, and work started in 1922, but there was little progress until 1933, when Hitler came to power. When Austria joined Nazi Germany in 1938 work was speeded up, both in the canal and in enlarging the canalised Main. The war interrupted work and though it re-started afterwards, it never had priority, and it was not until the end of September 1992 that the last part was finished. Germany was reluctant to complete it, fearing that barges from the Warsaw Pact countries, all government-owned and massively subsidised, would give her own barge fleet unfair competition. This fear was entirely justified, and the problem today occupies the European Union Transport Commissioner.

At Schleuse Kelheim (Kelheim Lock), the last on the canal, we came across our first Danube *pegel*. We did not pay it much attention. For one thing, Heikell's Guide advised that: '...unless you are familiar with the (*pegel*) system (it) is best ignored.' For another, Bill had been summoned to the lock office with the ship's papers, and by the time he returned *Hosanna* was far below him, and Laurel had to manoeuvre the ship under a ladder so that he could descend. This took our minds off *pegels*.

Charlie, near Strasbourg, had counselled close attention to the *pegels*, and it proved better advice than Heikell's. We soon learned that it is dangerous to ignore them and negligent to fail to understand the information they supplied. This is something anyone following in our wake should master before they reach the Danube.

If we had read the *pegel* properly it would have told us that the water level in the Danube (4 kilometres ahead) was 5 metres above normal. We tried to find a mooring in Kelheim town where the quay looked inviting, with nicely laid out flower beds at our deck level, but there was no room for mooring anything other than tripper boats of which there were many, it being the feast of Corpus Christi, a public holiday in Bavaria. A quick dash to the shops was fruitless, or rather breadless, as they were all shut for the holiday. We had moored illegally under a bridge, and had to leave before we were spotted. They spot things like that in Germany.

We had not intended to join the Danube just yet, so our long-anticipated arrival occurred suddenly and precipitously, and we hardly had time to read an almost unnecessary notice saying 'Donau: kilometre 2414', and realise that far from being the Blue Danube this swirling river was mud-brown with silt, laden with large débris, and travelling at 20 kilometres an hour. It was a shock, after the comparative peace of the River Altmühl to find ourselves in a raging torrent with ambitions to become a waterfall.

We 'knew' that the Danube was in flood, but a theoretical appreciation of this fell a good deal short of reality. We were riding a runaway horse, and the torrent bucked and kicked and tossed its mane in a shower of spray. We had intended to cross to the shelter of the commercial port on the opposite bank of the river. It was immediately obvious that all our skills had to be concentrated urgently on avoiding being set down below the basin entrance, because if we were carried past it, we might never get back.

If we had known how often we would be faced with this situation in the days to come, we might have turned back then and there, though it might have taken all day to claw our way back to the junction with the Altmühl.

The Danube was about 150 metres wide here, and the current strength differed as one crossed. In the centre it was wild, and it was as well that Bill had not lost much ground in the easier part. We were swept downstream sideways so fast that we both feared that the task was impossible, and the pitching and rolling of the swinging ship, barely under control in the whirlpooling water, frightened us, but after passing mid-river the current eased, and we got our bows into the slack water of the *hafen* entrance.

Inside the basin all was calm. The water lapped close to the top of the quay. On the right on entering were two big Slovakian tugs and their tows. Other quays were occupied, but at the very end of the basin was a vacant spot, just our size. We made *Hosanna* fast with some relief. 'I'll never be able to drive her down in conditions like that,' Bill said, shaking his head. 'The current must have been more than 20 kilometres per hour. We would be totally out of control!'

He went for a walk through the deserted port, while the cats gambolled happily in the adjoining woods, which excited frogs were trying to convince us was rainforest. It had stopped raining, so Laurel cleaned up the rubbing strakes in the hope of a chance to paint them, watched approvingly by the Slovaks. Bill walked as far as a marina 2 kilometres down-river to see if there was a possibility of a berth for a few days. We needed a rest, and we also needed to work, both boat-maintenance and writing. We are always amazed that almost alone in Europe, the English do not regard writing as work.

('What do you do?' we are often asked.

'We write books.'

'No, I mean what *work* do you do?')

When writing, we need 230 volts for the computers, and we need it also for power tools for maintenance. Our own generators are noisy and expensive to run, and themselves need routine maintenance, and if shore electricity is available it makes a quiet change.

Herr Rammelmeyr, who owned the small marina, spoke excellent English and was hospitable. Of course he could find us a berth, and of course power was available, and of course he had craftsmen to help. Herr Rammelmeyr offered to hold a place for us till conditions improved. Given the floods, no one else was likely to take it.

We barbecued lamb chops on the quay that evening and the captains of the Slovakian tugs called by to exchange greetings. We offered them some cognac and had a limited chat in a pot-mess of German, English, French, and Slav. Bill showed them a postcard we had of a Mississippi tug pushing 72 barges; they were fascinated by this, and with cheerful goodnights invited us on board *Saris* the following evening.

In the morning the Hafenmeister appeared and told us that but for the *hochwasser* (floods) we, a *sportboot*, would not be permitted to use his *hafen*. We showed him our certificate as an *arbeitschiff*, which mollified him considerably. No one could leave anyway, he said, because navigation was suspended. The flood level at the next lock had risen to the cut-off point and the river current was now 20 km/hr, making all navigation dangerous. Had we not seen the *pegel* at Kelheim lock?

Horror-struck, we realised that ignoring the *pegel* could have cost us our ship, even our lives.

The Hafenmeister had become quite affable. We would please leave as soon as navigation resumed because the *hafen* was only for cargo boats, and would soon fill when barges could get upstream again. We might have to move anyway, as would the Slovakian barges, if the level rose another 20 cm; everybody would have to raft up on the highest flood-quay. We promised co-operation, and then asked if he could authorise the crane to lift out our little car. 'Better,' he offered, 'we do it by fork-lift truck and there will be no charge.'

So the Mini was landed and we drove into Kelheim Altstad. Bread at last! Kelheim (pronounced Keelheim) is a pleasant town with an attractive square where we had lunch out of doors in baroque surroundings, but showery weather. The small town has three gate-houses, on the west, north, and south, while the eastern side is guarded by the Danube itself. The water was still rising as we drove back to *Hosanna*, lapping within an inch of the top of the quay.

We visited the Slovakian tug *Saris* after supper, and were entertained by two captains, Mihel and Miroslav, who proudly showed us their tugs, state-owned, of course. There was a small mess room with a black and white television for the crew, a simple galley, a washing machine and dryer that they were very proud of. They are big tugs, about 64 metres long, and square-ended in order conveniently to push dumb barges instead of towing them. Their two 2000 hp diesels were Swiss built. The wheelhouses were well fitted, including air-conditioning, and

The Alte Stadt, Kelheim

like the one on *Böhmerwald* were on hydraulic lifts, so we had the obligatory juddery ride up and down.

Then it was choice of orange juice or strong brandy, elbows on the oilcloth in the Captain's cabin. His sleeping quarters were visible through a connecting door, a clean vest hanging there on a string. All the tables on board had standard issue oilcloth on them, but the Captain's had a lace runner as well.

And they were off: three Captains together, with maps and diagrams and Captain's chat, so when Tansy came, wailing, to fetch Laurel back, which she did very firmly, seeing her safely home to *Hosanna* before disappearing into the resoundingly croaky woods, Laurel left them to it.

Bill stayed on, going over charts, marking data books, and asking advice. There was no language in common, but seamen communicate easily. As soon as Bill opened the page at, say, Gabçikovo or Nagymaros, they knew what a sailor would ask, and they made drawings and used arrows and internationally known symbols. They let him pick their brains most generously, and they were reassuring about Jugoslavia. One of them had been through about a month before, there had been no trouble. The transit tax amounted to $2 per tonne of freight + ship tonnage, and had to be paid in full in cash dollars on entry to Jugoslavia. One would get a receipt. There was no problem with thieving or being boarded if one anchored in the designated anchorages, the only bother being with the so-called diesel pirates. These were comparatively gentlemanly pirates who wanted to buy diesel oil in order to evade sanctions, and would pay for it in dollars (presumably those taken off us for transit tax!). Our chief problem would be with the United Nations sanctions team at Mohács, who were supposed to prevent such sales.

Bill returned cheerfully, quite a few brandies later, with a great deal of useful, not to say priceless, information on how to get *Hosanna* through Serbia.

The next morning the water level had started to fall a little. We took the Mini and drove along the river banks to Regensburg, where Bill had a look at a few possible moorings and talked to a friendly lock-keeper.

Regensburg, ex-Ratisbon, is a difficult place to drive in because of a one-way system in which all roads cleverly lead outwards from the centre and everywhere else is a pedestrian precinct. Bill cheated by sticking to the riverside, driving along the quay, and ending up right in the town centre. We had our lunch at the Historic Sausage Kitchen, the oldest in the world, with Filipino waitresses. In dirndls.

It is on the quay by the old stone bridge, the Steinerne Brücke, built between 1135 and 1136, an impressive and handsome work with 16 arches and 310 metres long. It can still take motor vehicles such as buses: how many bridges built this century will still be usable in 850 years, we wonder? We ate watching the Danube sluicing through the narrow arches.

There was a difference in water level between the upstream and downstream sides of the arch of over half a metre, a slope of about one in twelve, which very nearly qualifies as a steep hill on a road, let alone a river. The thought of a 60 ton vehicle without brakes shooting that through a gap of only 7.7 metres made us shudder. Downstream of the arches the whirlpools extended for 100 metres or more; we wondered how the bargees of old used to cope with it. (They no longer have to because there is a marine by-pass.) Barges were smaller then, but even so they were bigger than *Hosanna*; perhaps they were patient, and would wait for calmer times.

Yesterday the floodwater had been over the quay and the Historic Kitchen tables had only just been put back in the open air in anticipation of a fine Saturday; they were doing a roaring trade. We were next to the Sausage Roast, within a few feet of the Danube, and there was a wonderful smoky smell of roasting sausages and the refreshing tang of beer.

We visited the Rathaus, a lovely mediaeval building, and halted at a window thinking it was a bicycle shop, but it turned out to be unicycles. If ever you wanted to buy things to construct your own circus we can now tell you that you can in Regensburg; this shop sold the juggling rings, the Indian clubs, the bright spangly balls, even imitation eggs for jugglers. There was everything a budding magician could want, and a library of books on juggling, magic, circuses, and kite flying. There was also a shop selling everything in miniature, beautiful models of anything you care to think of in the domestic or artisan line, exquisite hand-made dolls-house furniture and fittings to scale.

We crossed the old bridge and walked along the flooded banks to the museum of Danube river transport, the Schiffahrtsmuseum, housed in an old steam paddle tug. Originally built in Germany and called *Ruthof*, it was later sold to the Hungarians and renamed *Ersekcsanad*, and now bears both names. Down below there were models of types of craft that once plied the Danube, drawn by enormous teams of horses.

Trade had once consisted mainly of downstream traffic carried in the so-called Ülm crates. These were roughly built barges, quite big, which went downstream with the current and were broken up at their destination after discharging their cargoes. The upstream traffic was then limited to valuable cargoes (salt was an example) and the upstream boats were long and slim so as to tow easily.

It had all changed with the arrival of the paddle-driven steam tugs, originally brought to the Danube by the English. These had enabled traffic to be two-way. Nowadays most of the traffic in the upper Danube is by self-propelled barges of between 1000 and 2000 tonnes. Dutch crews dominate; we had the impression that Dutch barges outnumber German ones by about two to one. Perhaps the main beneficiaries of the RMDK are Austria, who receives the goods, and the Dutch who carry them. The Dutch are not only competent, but also daring, navigating in conditions when most others have stopped.

But even the Dutch were not going into Jugoslavia. Everything would be different down there, where only the Iron Curtain countries dared to sail.

Just as we were completing our interesting visit to the old tug the heavens opened with one of those downpours that gives one the impression of being submerged in a jacuzzi. Bill was tired of coping with motor traffic, Laurel's hip told her that the weather was damp, and could we go home now, so we drove back to Saal in the rain.

Later, when the rain had ceased and we were sitting on our verandah, several other members of the crew of *Saris* and her sister-ship dropped by to look at our Mississippi postcard. The Slovakians (and the Hungarians, Bulgarians, and Ukrainians, but not the Romanians) tow by pushing dumb barges lashed tautly together ahead of them. Our aerial view of a tug on the Mississippi pushing 72 dumb barges became legendary as time went by, and tug-masters all down the Danube would come over to us unexpectedly for a sight of this postcard, which represented quite an achievement. We did not want to spoil the fun by telling them that the event on the Mississippi was not a genuine commercial tow; it had been posed specially for the photograph, and the 72 barges were each smaller than the Danube barges. So do myths begin.

Laurel served haxen with onions and white sauce for supper. Since discovering them in a restaurant, we now found that they grew ready cooked at the butcher's, cheap, delicious and copious. Most Bavarians can eat one each. It was probably the most enjoyable German dish we came across.

The river level was falling noticeably and the tugmasters prepared for resumption of navigation on Monday morning. We too rose early. Work started at 0600 in the *hafen*, and sure enough the Hafenmeister appeared at 0740, asking us pleasantly to move as the berth would be required later. He allowed us a last minute shopping trip to Saal village for perishables, and then the car was re-loaded on board and at 1105 we left.

Getting into the marina with the river in flood was daunting. Bill had already studied the problem from landwards.

The entrance was angled downstream at about 45° so that the basin was protected from the current. The cut through the levee was 12 metres long, and 8 metres wide. *Hosanna* is 4.70 metres broad. The current at the edge of the river was over 10 km/hr. We could stem that, without any problems, and could have crept upstream near the bank and turned in, except for a new bridge being built close below the entrance.

The chief problem of entering the narrow cut was that our bows would be in the slack water of the entrance while our stern would be still exposed to the strong sideways current in the river. For some seconds therefore, the boat would be subject to a violent turning force, and common sense indicated that the entry should be made as fast as possible to minimise the time while thus out of control. One had to make all the manoeuvring decisions in advance and then hope they were the right ones, otherwise the damage could have been extensive.

Fortunately Bill got it right: he put our nose into the cut at full speed, and suddenly we were through and making desperate efforts to stop before ploughing into the moored boats opposite. We were left with an awkward sternboard berth, having to wriggle ourselves backwards into a very narrow space, but there was no current and little wind to worry about, and we wriggled back into the berth like someone squirming into a swimming costume a size too small.

It was tight ship-handling. What a pity no one was watching!

• 14 •
SEX, CHAOS AND ENERGY
Regensburg

We had much to do at Saal. There was engine maintenance and painting on top of all the normal cleaning, housekeeping, cooking, and shopping. Living in a boat isn't all lazy days: the maintenance is heavier than with a house, though one saves on gardening. Bill hates mowing lawns, so he has to put up with engines.

Mail arrived, and some was not too late to answer. We found an engineer who finally made sense of our refrigeration system, by reducing it to a kit of parts and putting it together again.

Herr Rammelmeyr builds expensive motor yachts destined for the Mediterranean. They go by the German canal system to Hamburg and the long way round by Gibraltar. They are beautifully fitted out, and a significant part of his work force is British or Italian. We were hailed at lunchtime by Jim, who said 'I knew it was *Hosanna* when I saw you, there isn't another boat like yours.' We last met him on the Greek island of Limnos on board *Faith*. He had to work hard here, but the pay was good.

Gradually we ticked things off our programme. Once, when we initiated the first-ever long-distance cruising symposium with *Yachting Monthly* we discussed with Geoff Pack, an experienced liveaboard sailor, the extremes of fitting out boats. He favoured the Keep-It-Simple rule. The question is: How simple? We had made our first long cruise in *Phoenix* in 1954 with our six-month old daughter on board. The yacht had no WC, no wash-basin or sink, no engine, no electrics whatsoever, and the sole means of cooking had been a primus stove. We had a wonderful cruise, but Geoff didn't mean that simple. Did he?

Hosanna is at the other end of the comfort scale, with a washing machine, spin-drier, computers, microwave, sanders, drills, and so on, and she has three generators to supply the juice for them. Whether the time we save by having machines is used up by maintaining them is a moot point. It is usually done by the skipper, as deep-sea call-out charges tend to infinity. Washing clothes by hand is hard work, but is it worse than changing engine oil, or doing one of those repairs that boat machinery always seems to need? And if Bill did the washing and Laurel the oil changes would the polarisation be different? The debate continues and will never end, but our 'norm' moves inexorably in the direction of comfort as we grow older.

On 21 June we heard of the death of Tristan Jones, who in 1985 went down the Danube from Regensburg in great discomfort. By Friday 23 June the floods had subsided; it was time to press on. Bill tested our anchoring arrangements to make sure we could let go quickly in an emergency, for going downstream fast gives one little time in emergencies, and we had not used the anchors for ages. In the upper Danube the bottom is rocky and offers poor holding.

Regensburg is not far downstream, and seemed a good trip for the first day, which was cool and cloudy, broody with thunderstorms. The river level had fallen by a metre, but was still running strongly and we faced a similar problem to that on entering the marina. It was easy to manoeuvre inside the basin in still water, but as soon as the bows left the channel the current seized them and pushed them downstream towards the new bridge pier, and we could not turn to avoid hitting it until our stern was clear of the exit. We were travelling at 3 metres per second and for 9 seconds we were out of control. We missed the bridge pier by a whisker, but side-swiped the temporary light buoy marking it. The hollow clang was audible for miles, but the buoy bobbed upright again and we were off.

Immediately after the bridge we met the *Wasserschutzamt* boat struggling upstream against the current, bearing a small crane, and a stack of navigational buoys on board. 'My God!' said Bill, 'they have been quick. We only hit it a moment ago.' They were on a routine post-flood check of river marks, to restore them to their proper position if they had been swept out of place. Or knocked aside by passing *Hosanna*s.

The Danube was still over its banks in places. We timed it at about 17 km/hr, about 9 knots, but this has become a comparatively tame stretch of river since the building of the Bad Abbach barrage and lock. Considering what we had seen at the height of the flood, we renewed our respect for the mariners who used to tackle this river in the old days, and wondered what the wilder parts after Regensburg would be like. For economy we used low power to motor with the current. When going against the stream one wants the adverse force at work for the minimum time so one goes full speed. Going downstream one wants the favourable current to do as much of the work as possible; all one needs is steerage way.

The hills on each side rolled away into the blue distance, rocky with outcrops of limestone, and clothed with dark green pine trees. The houses in the villages were occasionally low-lying enough to have had their lovely pastel colours marred by the recent floods. Kapfelburg had a little church painted a beautiful pistachio green, with a grey slate steeple and a little clock face on it. We passed signs warning us of weirs, and a big whirlpool, which we discovered to our enchantment was called a *strudel*, so an *apfelstrudel* pudding is an apple whirlpool. There was a bridge without much room under it, and we had left up aerials and flags, and even spread an awning over the poop hoping for a sunny day, but we just got under. When the sun came out, the Danube was green, reflecting the forest colours and the grass and the willow trees on its banks.

It was a swift, uneventful voyage of 31 kilometres, and we were soon off the fast-flowing river and on to the still water of the canal by-pass round the city. We locked through at 1600 and found a big quay with all berths occupied except one short space that suited us.

We berthed. 'Oh, look,' said Laurel, 'there seems to be a bit of a market.' That was the understatement of the decade. The crop of beer tents and barbecues that were popping up like mushrooms on the high grassy bank was just a tiny fraction of Regensburg's Bürgerfest, a huge biennial junket for the citizens, to which 100,000 visitors were expected.

At 1700 there was a wham of decibels well above pain level, and we thought there'd been an explosion nearby. Then behind the trees we discerned twin mouths of hell, black and silver amplifiers, big as blocks of flats, and realised with sinking hearts that we were moored in the middle of the Rock Festival. Two more woomphs beat through *Hosanna* like depth charges: the first 'HUH' testing the amplification equipment, followed by 'one-two-three's, giving the effect of a heavy artillery bombardment. 'We'll have to leave,' said Bill. Laurel agreed; it was not bearable. Mercifully, after five minutes, things settled to a more sensible level and, although loud, the music was tolerable. We felt the beat sweep over the high quay and into our verandah like a waterfall, but at least we had some protection. Just as well, as it was non-stop 12 hours a day, 36 different groups, for the whole weekend, Britain well represented by the inaptly named Pretty Things, among others.

We could have eaten at one of the stalls, where there were fish and sausages roasting, but we chose to eat at home, after a wary wander round. People in strange hats were selling incense and T-shirts, and souvenirs of Woodstock. A great many people came from the other parts of town. Apart from the bank by our bows being a popular place for the men to get rid of their beers into the water, and some people camping round the auditorium (there was a faint smell of pot from groups of 50-year-old hippies) everyone was extremely well behaved and there was nothing to worry us. The music ceased promptly at 2300. What a relief that was. In Greece the summer discos go on until 0600, and are much louder.

We woke at 0600 to the noise of turning screws from the big barges near us. Commerce continues inexorably, during weekends and festivals alike. The barges at either end of us left, leaving us in the middle of the quay; not a good place. Sure enough during the morning a number of barges wanted to berth so we had to move. After our third move that morning, Bill became a little depressed. He was finding the voyage hard enough physically, entailing as it did some difficult ship-handling problems, and the insecurity of berthing was getting him down. Everything here was geared to very big barges, and we were bottom priority. So when one of the barges which had berthed in our former place told us he would be staying overnight and invited us to berth alongside him we accepted with relief. Much better for you, he said, and we agreed, realising that as well as enabling us to go into the city together to see something of the *fest* (we had almost given the idea up) we would no longer be against the quay in a mixed rain of cigarette ends and joyous festival pee.

Had we been a modest yacht or motor cruiser we could have gone through a small lock (max dimensions 20 m x 4 m) and passed through Regensburg on the old river route. There are boat clubs close to the city offering moorings to visitors, where a yacht could moor disturbed only by the strong current.

We walked into town past the stalls set up by the footpaths. Some were organised by pressure groups associated with one good cause or another. An exhibition of pictures of the Danube was dedicated to preventing the construction of two more locks and barrages that would regulate the flow. The pictures selected were highly emotive. The entrance of an existing lock had been photographed with false perspective to give an impression of unending concrete quay, which we knew was wrong; we have said how beautiful we found the Altmühl. Bill asked why they were not concerned with improving the navigation. They found us a pleasant young student of architecture who spoke good English and we had a friendly argument pointing out that if the navigation were not improved, another *autobahn* would be necessary. 'Only a small one,' he said.

Laurel quoted Marryat's nurse apologising for her illegitimate baby: 'If you please, ma'am, it's only a little one.'

The student laughed. He said the problem of transport was the most difficult for the Greens to solve, and we parted amicably. We can only go on repeating to all who will listen, that water transport is the most environmentally friendly of all ways of moving goods. One medium barge equals 40 trucks, uses less fuel, makes less noise, and never kills anyone but the bargee or his family.

Since the opening in September 1992 of the Rhein–Main–Donau Kanal (RMDK) linking Rhine and Danube, river traffic in Regensburg has increased more than tenfold. It is still (in 1995) being inhibited by the Jugoslav crisis but further expansion can be forecast.

Forgive us for putting in a couple of interesting tables. The first shows the growth of river traffic at Regensburg:

Calendar year	Tonnes
1991	250 000
1992	500 000
1993	2 200 000
1994	3 300 000

The second table explains why this is a good thing. It is a comparison by environmental consultants of the environmental costs of road against rail, against canal/river.

	Pollution	Accidents	Noise
Road	2.36	1.78	0.87
Rail	0.33	0.12	0.70
Barge	0.34	0.01	0.01

The figures are based on data in Germany and allow for the fact that the railways run mainly on hydro-electricity.

We crossed a footbridge over one arm of the river which split into several branches through the town, and made our way to the Steinerne Brücke. Like everyone else we leant over the bridge parapet to watch the water swirling through the arches. Navigation is directed through the two arches at the city end; 7.70 m wide, and a clearance height for the downstream-going arch of only 3.72 m at highest water. It was still close to that, with the quaysides almost under water along the handsome promenade.

Could we wait for calmer times? Bill had been to consult the lock-master, and two Dutch bargemasters. The rain had been intense, they said, and the snows were still melting. This could go on for a long time. It was an unusually bad year, with unusually bad navigation; one must grin and bear it.

The river experiences two types of flood: 'white floods' caused by melting snows, occurring every spring, and 'green floods' caused by heavy rain in the flatlands drained by River Danube and its tributaries, which happen throughout winter and occasionally after heavy thunderstorms in summer. This spring we had had the two together, and both had been worse than normal.

Never mind, we were in Regensburg to enjoy the Bürgerfest. Laurel had steeled herself for some serious walking, for the whole of the city centre had been pedestrianised for the occasion.

The streets were crowded, and lined with stalls, and here in the centre they were mostly selling food of one sort or another, for a German's thoughts are never far from his digestion, and the Bürgerfest must feed 100,000 people over the weekend. We sampled mountain ham, and some Javanese seafood.

There were booths everywhere, from huge charities to kids selling last year's toys on a blanket, from the well-organised beerstalls able to cope with the 100,000, down to one man with a cauldron over a fire of sticks, selling portions of vegetarian stew. There were floating balloons pegging down children with painted faces, clowns, cats, birds, or just fantasy, and it wasn't long before the hat madness got you. You could see how it began, the Bavarian felt hat lends itself to having things pinned on it, and the festive atmosphere ensured that this happened: flowers, fruit, small toys, kitchen implements, up to fully fledged windmills and similar flights of genius. Laurel, having spotted the trend before leaving the boat, had decorated a bargee's cap with a fanciful rose and some veiling, and was getting approving nods. Any of Bill's hats were quite festive enough.

About 300 different bands were in town, everything from Rock to

Baroque, and Mambo to Madrigal. Music or theatre spilled from every doorway. On almost every street corner was a band of some sort. Sensibly, Rock-n-Roll had been confined to the *Rock Zipfel* (the Rock Corner) but here were swing bands, New Orleans jazz bands, folk groups, zither bands, drum bands, and Anciaunt Musick. As the sound of one disappeared round a corner the sound of the next could be heard, implying some clever location work to avoid a cacophonous mix. Drums summoned us to the main square to support the Grampian Police Pipe Band, another of the UK's contributions to the music. They were popular; it was hard to find standing room. Resplendent in black and silver, with the Black Strachan tartan and the police black-and-white checked band under their towering headdresses, they knocked your eye out and assaulted your eardrums simultaneously. As they marched forth with the pipes skirling the crowd discovered that two of them, a drummer and the Drum Major, were women, and voiced uproarious delight. Oh, weren't they wonderful!

After that we needed a drink and a seat, and found a square full of tables and benches ruled by beer and a Bavarian oompah band in embroidered *lederhosen*. Five Deutschmarks deposit on the glass! No wonder people were walking around carefully carrying them. You got a huge pretzel, too. As for eating: as you walked about the city you could eat Turkish, Japanese, Polish, Indian, Thai, Chinese, Tyrolean, Italian, anything from a light breakfast to a plate the size of a cart-wheel. There had been an ox roast, but now at teatime there was little left but a lattice of stripped rib bones. They would roast another tomorrow. At the fish roasting stall the cooks had tried to find a peaked Breton cap like Laurel's, but we were a long way from the sea, and they succeeded only in looking like policemen.

On our way back, the last group of the evening were playing at the *Zipfel*. They were punk. They were appalling. The crowd, refusing to accept that a capacity to shock replaces talent, were drifting away along the riverside paths. Alongside the paths down the sloping river banks couples writhed discreetly.

Plugging up the Main had taken more fuel than we expected, so early Sunday morning the Bunkerboat was alongside. He could give us drinking water, he'd got filters, paint brushes, a whole chandler's shop and some staple foodstuffs on board. We took on 500 litres of fuel, bought rope, lubricating and hydraulic oil and filters. The loading on board of heavy drums was easier this way, but payment was a pain, he took no credit cards – Deutschmark über alles.

We were finding it difficult to get currency in Germany, a country that considers it epitomises all that is good about banking. It wants to run the European Bank and control European currency. God help us if they do, for German banks, as we experienced them, are hopeless from the point of view of monetary transactions. Credit or charge cards are virtually useless. We were not able to charge anything during our stay in Germany, in contrast to Britain, France, Italy, or even Turkey. It makes Germany a third world country, financially speaking.

The Bunkerman looked admiringly at our boat and asked how many tons we were, saying that we would make a good bunkerboat. No, we said, it's our house, we don't wannabe a bunkerboat.

Off went the Bunkerboat, having given us a 25-year anniversary mug ('Bunkerservice'), an Esso flag, a beer opener, and a ballpoint pen that didn't work.

Bill was happier. We now had about 2100 litres in the bunkers which included 600 for the generator, and so had enough to take us downstream 2000 kilometres to the sea.

We were moved twice more as barges came and went, and ended up alongside our old friend *Böhmerwald*, who had been to Rotterdam and back since we last saw them. They were not leaving till 0600 Monday, which enabled us to dive into the Bürgerfest once more that evening and sample the Street Theatre, huge fantastic beasts on tall stilts, very imaginative, swooping at the crowd with 20 foot arms stretched out, and trailing long nets and ribbons as light as cobwebs. Part of the team were drummers, expert crowd managers, holding back or guiding the crowd, so that the stilt monsters had enough space to perform.

The ladies of the night had also joined in the *fest*. Out of our festival programme dropped a burgundy coloured card, lettered in gold:

'SEX, CHAOS and ENERGY,
TEST IT!' (they suggested)
'THE RED LIGHT LADIES' TEMPLE':
A sensual and bizarre experience, forbidden to under 18s

We thought we would probably pass up on that.

• 15 •
SHIP CRASH
Geisling

It was 26 June but you wouldn't have known it by the weather. We left Regensburg at 0600, because *Böhmerwald* had said he would be leaving then to go through the sluice; he wasn't stirring yet, but we slipped away without bothering anyone. A Romanian tug and barge took our place at once. We used only one engine as the current was enough to give a good speed over the ground.

On the outskirts we passed a cluster of Romanian barges against the bank, which looked as if they had been there long enough to take root; there were chicken huts on the hatch covers, rabbit cages, and vegetables growing in boxes. Nobody was about. They could have been dormitories for foreign workers.

This was the stretch of the Danube below Regensburg where King Ludwig, he of the Kanal, built Walhalla, a Grecian temple perched in the forest. It is a Pantheon to German culture and contains statues and busts of famous artists, sculptors, composers and writers, all glorifying the Germany of his time, 1830–40. There it was, huge on the hill, perfect but incredibly wrong without the wash of Greek sunshine, honeycoloured stone, and the blue Aegean sky. It looked cold, white, and plastic, lost in this northern forest.

A big pusher-tow coming towards us turned out to be the first we'd seen from Ismail, in the Ukraine; he had clearly come through Jugoslavia. We were getting into deeper and stranger waters. Just below Walhalla were the first barges we had seen anchored, swinging to the stream. Romanian ones again. The thought that the stream was wide enough to anchor pleased us. We were used to anchoring in the Greek Islands: it is peaceful, and we wouldn't have to give place to others as we must at limited mooring on the banks.

These ancient and decrepit barges from Romania would rather spoil the tourist photographs of Walhalla unless you thought them romantic. We were getting to know the new flags of Eastern Europe, Ukraine, Bulgaria, Romania, which had changed in the turmoil of the last few years.

On our left the forested hills receded into the distance, blue and purple, with rays of light from the clouds highlighting a copse here, a field there as the early sun and cloud played hide and seek over the countryside.

At 0745 we were at Geisling lock.

Geisling is the start of a difficult bit, where the Greens are holding up construction of two locks that would make navigation much easier. The Danube would then be navigable in normal conditions (and these are alarming enough) by barges up to 180 metres long, and 8 metres broad, and drawing 2.5 metres. At the moment the minimum standard depth on the stretch from Geisling downstream to Deggendorf is only 1.7 metres, and even little *Hosanna* draws 1.5 metres. This level is indicated by the figure 298 on the Pfelling *pegel* and is the present limiting danger. There would still be only 2 metres on the stretch below Deggendorf to Vilshofen, but that is a whole foot deeper.

We were not worried about depth after the floods. Should be a piece of *torte*.

We had to wait an hour for Geisling lock while a Dutch-crewed barge with Luxembourg flag left downstream ahead of us. The keeper was friendly, but our exchanges were limited as his English was no better than Bill's German. We left the lock at about 0900, and were just leaving the sheltered water to rejoin the main river after it came over the spectacular weir. We planned to leave a channel-marking red buoy to our right, according to the convention, when a voice came over the VHF radio and without preamble started shouting along these lines:

'Hosanna, Hosanna, Rechts fahren. Rechts fahren, Right go, Rechts fahren...' in a crescendo of volume and agitation. Bill hoisted in that we should go to the right, and urgently.

'That would mean leaving the buoy on the wrong side?' Bill had a query in his voice, but no time to answer his own question. We could not talk to the lockmaster, who was still broadcasting and so unable to hear our transmission. It was obviously urgent. Bill made the decision that we were being warned the buoy was out of position and he swung to the right. Almost immediately we struck rocks and came to a noisy, grinding stop.

We couldn't back off against a current that was pushing us forward. Bill put the rudder over so that the current spun us on the rock that pinned her, and we swung towards the channel we had left. He ran the engines at full ahead. *Hosanna* graunched, grumbled, and ground over the rocks, bouncing and heaving painfully, as we inched forward into deeper water, got back to the channel side of the buoy (clearly NOT out of position), and with three engines and a sluicing current ran away downstream at speed.

Our first action was a thorough inspection of all bilges to see if we were holed. Had we started rivets, were we taking in water? The river here was narrower and shallower, the navigation more dangerous, and we were going much faster in the strongest current yet encountered. Laurel reported all well below, and Bill relieved his feelings with some gentle swearing. In a crisis there is no time for the luxury of bad language. The crisis, unknown to us, was not over.

What had the lock-keeper been trying to convey? He had been very agitated, and there had been a serious misunderstanding. The VHF had been silent since he lost sight of us. Now we heard him talking volubly on channel 22 to another barge.

'Never mind,' said Bill. 'Thank the Lord for a strong boat, but I am beginning to disenjoy this voyage.'

Then we heard the lock-keeper again. 'Hosanna! Hosanna!' his voice was more measured.

'Here Hosanna,' answered Bill, the Germans seeming to like sentences being spoken backwards.

'Hosanna, to the right,' began the voice.

'Not again! This man has a fixation,' Bill murmured to himself.

'To the right. Iron. Iron.' He pronounced the word with heavy emphasis on the R, EYE RON, rolling it like a Parisian. 'To the right, iron,' adding the key words: 'Halt. Make fest.'

About 500 metres ahead of us to our right we discerned 3 large steel piles, dolphins, 5 metres from the bank. Bill assumed that we were being ordered to make fast to them. It would have been impossible to stop alongside them pointing the way we were going, with the current at about 18 km/hr, about 10 knots. Bill thought of telling the lock-keeper to get lost; we were being told to do something difficult and dangerous, and we had already had one unfortunate experience obeying his instructions. But something in the man's manner told us that there was a serious problem; Bill's earlier impression had been of a competent man in a crisis, and all of us with a language problem. He decided to do again as we were bidden.

The only hope of mooring to the piles was to turn and point upstream before reaching them, and so approach them with the ship going forward through the water, but backwards over the ground. It would be complicated because the river was narrow and the water surface was a mass of swirling whirlpools. This would be a difficult ship-handling manoeuvre with scope, but no room, for misjudgement. Bill started to turn short in the narrow river, which was about 120 metres wide, shallow at the edges, telling Laurel to go forward on the port side with a heavy rope loop and lasso the pile as we went past it: an old Norfolk joke, thought Laurel, a trifle bitterly.

Such was the current that we were only three parts round when we came to the first pile. Laurel had no hope of getting that one, but Bill got our bows between numbers 1 and 2, and as *Hosanna*'s port shoulder hit number 2 with a thunderous clang, Laurel got her rope on and rapidly turned it up on our bitts. Well done, and a good job too, because the rebound took us clear of the third pile. Bill's manoeuvring had been inelegant, but adequate. We now rode to a long, strong rope out to the middle pile, and it was simple to adjust the rudder so that our bows nestled against the third pile, on to which Bill made fast another rope. We switched off engines and Bill reported to the lockmaster that we were 'fest to the Eye Ron'.

'Gut.' The relief was palpable. 'Ist ein ship crash. Vait.' We relaxed and vaited for further instructions. Relaxed? Bill was in no state to relax. He went dangerously quiet and moody, until an English-speaking voice over the VHF reported that the Luxembourger had run aground 10 kilometres further down at Kp 2340, and was completely blocking the river. The current was so strong it would be ages before he was free, and there was nowhere else to wait. If we had not succeeded in stopping at the Eye Ron, we would inevitably have crashed into the grounded barge at some speed. It appeared that the news had reached the lockmaster just as we were leaving Geisling lock, and he had been attempting to recall us to the quay on the right of the lock approach before we got into the stream again. Moments earlier and we might have got the message before leaving the lock. This was the cause of the misunderstanding.

The news cheered Bill up, not the misery of the unfortunate Luxembourger, but the explanation. Nothing could be done until we were permitted to proceed. So we declared a Sunday.

All traffic ceased, both ways; we could hear the lock-keeper at Geisling berthing the barges as they piled up. We were marooned in the Danube to our dolphins, all alone. We were quite happy; it was like being at anchor, cut off from the world except for the VHF, maybe for days. It was more peaceful than any berth we'd had recently, especially having been moored next to the Rock Festival at Regensburg. We needed a little time like this.

In order to sleep well we contacted the lock: 'Is everything still closed? Do we overnight here?' is what we thought we'd said. Traffic will start about midnight, he said (we think). Then he went into total panic and called us back, 'Hosanna, you must *nicht*, *nicht*, *nicht*, *nachtfahren*!' We told him we had no intention of *nachtfahring*, all we wanted was a good nacht's schlaf; but he got very excited and repeated it several times; he was afraid we would cast off in the night and tangle with a huge rush of big barges in both directions. Poor man, we tried to tell him that we wouldn't dream of navigating by night in the circumstances. He calmed down, so we think he got the message.

We were there all day and all night. We barbecued some pork chops, coated them with a mixture of cream, mustard, and grated cheese, and browned their tops with a blow-lamp, as we had been taught to do by a French chef. Pork chops Avesnoise. Delicious. We ate on our verandah, basking in silence except for the singing of the land birds, and the chirruping of the water birds, and the rustle of the swift flowing river.

At about 2030 a Wasserschutzamt convoy came by. It contained a large floating crane: the breakdown gang. Then the midges came out and drove us below. The day had been physically and mentally exhausting; bath and an early bed were welcome.

• 16 •

AUF WIEDERSEHN
Deggendorf and Passau

Nothing came through overnight, which was one of the most peaceful we'd had for a long time. At 1000 the hotel boats *Calypso* and *Wilhelm Tell* came downstream. Hotel boats have a much-resented priority to maintain tight schedules. We heard over VHF what we thought was a prohibition of anything over 2.3 metres draught: the water level had fallen by 30 cm. We are shallow draughted and if we could follow another craft life would be easier. When the laden barge *Tina* went past we asked permission to follow, and received a go-ahead, so we cast off hastily, turned and followed *Tina* down to Straubing lock. We called Geisling once more to thank them for their help; communication was limited, but appreciated. Goodwill is important.

To start with, the navigation round sharp and shallow bends, and through the *strudeln* was extremely difficult, even following *Tina*. Many of the buoys had been swept away. Passing was difficult, and we clearly offended a Hungarian pusher whom we met on a bend, who thought we had not left him enough room. By gestures he indicated we should radio ahead to give notice of approach to that bend. Some of the bends had signs, like road signs, indicating that a toot on the siren as well as warning on VHF was obligatory. We had scrupulously obeyed these, but we now understood that convention obliged us to do the same thing at other unmarked places. But how to know these places before getting to them? Obviously this was part of the Donaupatent, that hard-to-get licence to drive commercial ships.

We passed the bend where the Luxembourger had blocked the stream, and his grounding did not surprise us. There were tremendous twists in the Danube at that point, the usual sandbanks being augmented by shoals in unexpected places caused by floods bringing down extra silt, and the huge barges are carried down by the current practically out of control. This is the stretch that the Greens are campaigning about, where works are projected to make it less dangerous, and the Greens, forsooth, are against it. After our experiences yesterday and today, we thought: bother the Greens!

The Wasserschutzamt were about, indicating where the deeper water was, and we waved thanks as we passed as slowly as the Danube allowed.

Tina also guided us past a dredger on a bend, going inside close to the bank where we had not expected to go. We had a 2 metre depth there, and *Tina*'s 100 metre length had difficulty getting round. Thereafter she streaked ahead fast and we couldn't keep up. We missed her when undecided which way to pass a spit: we left it to port, and came to no harm, but with problems like that we didn't see much scenery. Five hundred metres on we were held up at Straubing where, because of the blockage, barges had been delayed, and the lock was full. We had to wait 90 minutes while four commercial barges did the whole cycle. We locked through with the empty barge *Donau*, empties having low priority just above ourselves, and reached Deggendorf at 1630.

The Guidebook said to moor in the off-river *Schutzhafen*, so we swung round and entered by the narrow channel. Small craft were moored end on to the bank on the landward side of the long narrow basin, but the gear was too light for us, even if there had been space. The workboats of the Wasserschutzamt occupied the end of the basin, and that left the spit of land that separated it from the river. According to the map, this should have been quayed on the inside. There were bollards on the top of the sloping bank, but why no boats?

Bill is cautious, and he approached the bank delicately until Laurel, looking over the bows, called urgently: 'Back Off!' He responds instantly to that tone of voice; it was 'Full Astern!' and no questions. Laurel had seen the leaves of a bush sticking out of the water a yard or so out from the bank. This tells you something.

We closed up again, very slowly, sounding with a quant-pole, and found a ledge about a metre under the surface. Poking about a bit more, we found bollards on it. The situation clarified, though the water didn't. The river was still in flood, the quay was a metre under water, and we had again overlooked the *pegels*.

It is time for a word about these beasties, who are not folklorical fairies or hobgoblins, but are signs put on the bank to help navigators assess the depth in that reach. The river is surveyed exactly to a datum. The datum is then related to the lowest water level at which the fairway has a certain depth. This level is known not by its German name, though that is the language of navigators in the upper Danube (though not the lower), but is named in either Russian, which is the language of the lower Danube, or in French, which few on the Danube comprehend at all. (We will come across many language problems in this polyglot river.)

In French the lowest level of safe navigation is called the Etiage Navigable et de Regularisation (ENR), and the datum above which the ENR is measured is mean sea level, but a different mean sea level in different parts of the river. They don't make it easy. In Germany, it is related to the mean sea level in the North Sea. In Austria it's the Adriatic.

The *pegels*, which are black boards on which are hung white numbers like a cricket scoreboard, show the level of the water, the date the board was last changed, and the difference since yesterday. The *pegels* give the figure as above mean sea level, so it is necessary to know the ENR to be able to calculate the depth of water. If you think all that is confusing, try sorting it out on the hoof, so to speak, in a mixture of French, Russian and German, spoken by a Slovakian tugmaster.

It is little wonder we had been careless with our *pegels*. The whole last day or two had been fraught with enormous difficulties. You could say we were out of our depth, and literally so at Deggendorf.

Bill sounded all along the side of the ship and traced the outline of the quay, where small bollards would have punched neat holes in our bottom if we had moored over them and then experienced a fall in river level. Fortunately, *Hosanna* has vertical sides, and we had a few stout planks of about 2.5 metres length that we use as staging to paint the side. Bill rigged these vertically down from the gunwale so that we could not ride over the quay, even if the river rose by a half metre, which was unlikely as the level, we knew, was falling. He manoeuvred the bows close to the quay and tried to deposit Laurel on the shore, but she could not face the jump required and he had to jump himself, leaving her to manoeuvre the ship while he scrambled up the grassy bank to make fast to the bollards on top. It had taken 90 minutes, and in the later stages a largish motor cruiser, *White Friar*, flying the red ensign, came in, and on our advice held off while we finished making fast, when we invited them to berth on us. It is unlikely they would have had the equipment to fend themselves off under water.

Ken and Eva Bain, and their little daughter Janet, were fighting their way upstream, having a faster boat than we had. They were the first red ensign we had met since St Omer. They had been living in Bratislava for some time, and were now returning to Britain. We picked each other's brains as seamen do everywhere, and got some useful information about Bratislava as well as being invited to tea and *apfelstrudel*.

The following day was a day of rest, purchasing new gas bottles, changing oil, and getting our hair cut.

Opposite the berth, on the Motor Boot Club side of the basin was a little Biergarten which turned out to be Greek. Homesick for Island Greece, left two years before on our voyage round southern Europe, we went for a meal, remembering enough of the language to qualify for double ouzos on the house to go with our *pikelias* (mixed hors d'oeuvres), a copious helping of *paidakia* (grilled lamb chops), all to the accompaniment of Mikis Theodorakis' music on tape. To add pleasure to our evening, we sat in the open air just opposite our own ship. *White Friar* had left on her way upstream, so Bill had an uninterrupted view of *Hosanna*; the loveliest view in the world.

After untangling the moorings and planking, we left early next morning. The water level had fallen a few centimetres but the current was a little less strong; about 8 km/hr. The river was wider, and bridges less frequent.

There was an intriguing 'green' ferry. A high wire was strung across the Danube with a pulley-block threaded on it, and from this depended a pendant to which the ferry-boat was attached. By using its rudder the boat was turned at an angle to the current whose force pushed it across the river without the use of any fuel whatsoever. Running costs: nil.

While ambling along quietly, a hotel boat overtook us. Knowing he would have priority at the lock ahead, we tried to keep up to avoid a long wait, starting all engines and giving chase. We couldn't match his speed, but were well in sight of the lock by the time he got in, and a kindly lockmaster held the gates for us. After the lock *Hosanna* berthed at the town quay in Passau.

Passau is checking-out point for Germany into Austria. Pounced on by the *Wasserschutzpolizei*, we were told that berthing on the town quay was for work-ships only. Bill produced our *Schiffsattest* stating we were an *arbeitschiff*. After a moment's thought Authority came up with: 'Even so the quay is only for ships attending to the customs, and overnighting is only permitted if the customs are closed.'

'OK,' said Bill, 'what time do the customs close?'

'They do not close.' The policeman smiled triumphantly. It looked as if he were winning. He and his colleague went through our papers with great care, even asking to see Laurel's helmsman's certificate, the only time we ever had to produce it. Our passports must be taken to the office, they said, and once cleared we must leave within two hours.

Hang on, said Bill. We want to see your beautiful town. (They were mellowing by now.) Where can we moor for a couple of days?

Not here.

No, but where? There must be somewhere for tourists? They looked a little shy.

In theory, yes. In practice, no.

But they were definitely softening. We expressed our surprise at having our passports checked; was this not the EU? And was not Austria also in the EU? Now they were smiling. *Hier wie lassen Europa*, they say; Here you are leaving Europe. *Ho Ho! Here, at Passau, the Balkans begin*! They were falling about now.

They suggested that we moor next to the art-ship, about 700 metres down, on the opposite side.

We are allowed to moor there? we asked.

No.

But the art-ship?

The art-ship has *erlaubnis* – permission. Light dawns. Anything in Germany that is not expressly forbidden needs permission? That's about it, they agree, but we tell you it's much worse in Austria!

We cast off, and rather than turn twice, once downstream and once up in this busy rapid river, Bill did the 700 metres backwards, or, as he called it, a forward-moving sternboard. No one seemed surprised, indeed later we saw several huge hotel ships do the same thing when changing berth. Bill had happened, by commonsense, on a ploy used by experienced captains with local knowledge.

We moored just downstream of the art-ship, which was occupying rather more quay than it should, and tucked in behind it. Our stern projected past the end of the quay, but that mattered little in a strong stream when our position could be controlled by lashing the rudder to exactly the necessary angle.

We contemplated the art-ship, an exuberant floating sculpture on an open barge of about 22 metres length. Bill growled 'Tate Gallery,' which damned it in his eyes, but for Laurel it was saved by its fantasy and humour and a refreshing lack of grandiose self-importance. Somebody had obviously spent a lot of money on it. It was difficult to imagine a purpose for it, but that begs the question of whether art has to have a purpose. Somebody loved it. Bill did not.

The water level had come down about a metre from its high point, but was obviously still very high; it was lapping the quay and the mooring rings were underwater. We had observed the *pegel* and now had time to do the sums: the river was 2.25 metres above normal.

We were in a splendid spot; sheltered by high stone walls from the thundering highway above, and the only access to the tucked-away quay was a subway under the road. Few people used it. We had a superb view of the magnificent Passau waterfront: Passau, yet another Venice of Bavaria; Passau, town of the three rivers, seat of the Prince-Bishops whose domain once spread as far as Budapest. Passau, where Kriemhild of the Nibelungs married Attila the Hun, to further a terrible revenge. Opposite us was the Rathaus, from whose tower the biggest Glockenspiel in Bavaria rang out across the river to our delighted ears.

• 17 •
HERE THE BALKANS BEGIN
Passau to Linz

Passau of the Three Rivers drapes herself with studied elegance over the confluence of Rivers Danube, Inn, and Ilz. The houses and churches in the old town look edible, in sweetie colours, gingerbread and marzipan and sugar icing.

The old city stands on the peninsula between the Danube and the Inn, which is predominantly low-lying. We were on the other, high and hilly, side of the Danube, upstream of the Luitpold Bridge, under the fortress of Oberhaus. *Hosanna* was a tourist attraction both to anyone on the bridge, and the passengers of the tour boats, which passed up and down the river every minute, embarking and spewing out their chattering hordes at the quays opposite. Some were huge hotel boats, with Ukrainian and Romanian flags, cashing in on the fat cats of the West wanting to glide in luxury from Strasbourg to Budapest. The smaller boats did an hour-and-a-half Three Rivers Run. The day was hot, and all the boats were packed with passengers, at least half of whom had camcorders, and *Hosanna* was filmed so often that Laurel dared not hang out the washing for fear of her smalls appearing on hundreds of holiday videos.

We walked across the bridge and went sightseeing, after a different band of police had called and asked to see the only document that remained uninspected: our radio licence. They left saying that they hadn't seen us, which we took as an indication that we could stay on our mooring, undisturbed.

We wanted to look at the Dom, which was about to close for another organ concert. We sneaked in attached to a French tour group, who were being allowed a quick peep as long as they didn't talk.

Asking the French not to talk is about as optimistic as asking Germans to forego lunch.

The Dom is exceptionally baroque, full of hundreds of white sugar saints in wildly theatrical poses, wriggling and writhing over every inch of architecture, and only freezing into statues when you look directly into their mad but holy eyes for a moment. Then, quickly, we were swept out again to make way for the *orgelkoncert*. We were hot and thirsty, and the exuberant saints had exhausted us. Bill was desperate for a drink, so in the shadow of the cool and ancient Ratskeller, under walls jewelled with mediaeval paintings of Passau's Age of Chivalry, we took immense pleasure in a tankard of beer and a glass of *gespritz*, wine and soda mixed for a hot summer day, and a view of our boat across the water. Perfect.

The view from our boat was also lovely, so much so that we decided to enjoy Passau from our verandah for the afternoon. There was plenty of activity on the river. An empty tourist boat arrived to tow the art-ship away, looking as embarrassed as a schoolboy whose mother's hat is too flamboyant. After making fast alongside the art-ship, they cast off and towed it out into midstream, going slow ahead, and falling backwards downstream (as we had done the day before) till they reached the confluence with the Inn. Bill was gratified to find the manoeuvre used locally, for it can confuse people who are not accustomed to it. He should have known that river men are superb ship-handlers and use every trick in the trade.

The art-ship was starting its Season, improbably staging an avant-garde spectacle of music and dance at all important cities downriver in the interests of Peace in the Balkans. Very worthy, peace. We enjoyed it all afternoon.

In the evening we walked across the peninsula to the frontage of River Inn, the quieter side of Passau, where they had taken the art-ship. Because there were no mooring facilities, they had made her fast to a mediaeval tower at her upstream end (which obviously takes the strain), and the downstream end was tied to a lamp-post. Somehow, this suggested Mediterranean insouciance rather than German efficiency.

We dined in front of the Rathaus, where a man in a dark suit played the jolly oompah-pah tunes, inseparable in our minds from Bavaria, on a synthesizer: no plump and sweating brass band here. The flood marks on the Rathaus wall, going back centuries, indicated that it was a damfool place to build a Rathaus, for the higher marks were several metres up. We ate our favourite zander, on a beautiful evening. The atmosphere was good, the waitress friendly, and the view of our boat across the river scored many points.

We had two lovely days in Passau before the weather broke on our last night, with thunderstorms and rain.

Next morning, early, Bill took the long walk into the town to Customs and Immigration. Austria being in the European Union, we expected to be simply nodded through, as we have grown accustomed at other European borders.

Oh no. Not in Austria. Here there were forms to fill in, passports to stamp.

'Why?' Bill asked the German immigration officer.

'Don't worry,' a Dutch barge skipper who had been waiting some time interrupted, 'the Austrians are just Germans with no brains.' This prompted a lot of jokes in German which Bill did not understand, but at which all laughed immoderately.

The Austrian officer was worried that we did not have a *Fahrterlaubnisdonau*, a permit to navigate. The Dutch skipper (the Dutch are a most helpful race) said surely it was unnecessary for a pleasure boat. Bill loudly hoped not to be delayed. The Dutchman

The Rathaus, Passau

supported him. Quite right, he said, one had to press on. At last the worried officer said we were to report to the Ober-something-or-other who would be upstairs in the control tower at Aschach lock. Bill promised to do this when he got there. The bureaucracy was at least efficient, and *Hosanna* was under way at 0730.

As we turned downstream and followed the hotel ship *Mozart* we looked back at the lovely city of pink, soft yellow, pistachio and almond green, with five swans bobbing at the quay, and realised that we were sorry to leave.

Aufweidersehn, Germany. Despite your restrictions and regulations, and your passion for tidying everything into pigeonholes, we enjoyed your country; we found your people disciplined and contented, the land calm and peaceful to journey through, apart from our adventures on the river.

We came to the confluence where Rivers Danube, Inn, and Ilz all flowed together. From now on there would be more river, more water, more volume. We could see the difference in colour between the Inn and the Donau: the Inn was chalky, and the Donau was flood-brown, the dividing line was clear.

The Inn was flowing very strongly. It is a bigger river here than the Danube, to which it is a tributary. It has a greater volume of water flowing in it. Why is it a tributary when it is the bigger river? Why the Blue Danube, and not the Blue Inn? Geographers do not always use the volume of water as a criterion. In this case they invoke something called apperception. Because the combined river is more nearly in line with the Danube, and the Inn joins at an angle, the river that flows the straightest is 'perceived' to be the continuing stream. No, we don't find it very convincing, either.

The word Danube is the Latinised version of the river's original name; the letter B replaces V in Italian, English and French. The central Europeans use a name based on Donau or Duna, or Dunav, and this word appears to come from an old Slavonic word for water. Rivers sometimes unite the lands on each side, but a really big river is divisive. We presume the Donau got its name in the downstream part, where it is a gigantic piece of water completely separating the countries on each side.

Perhaps the name spread westward with the emigrating tribes from Eastern Europe, so that the Danube was named upwards, not downwards. This is supported by the fact that no-one can agree on the source of the Danube. There are three separate claimants, of which that at Donaueschingen is most vociferously advertised, the town being the wealthiest of the three sites. They have a monumental fountain marking the source so they must be right. This upper part of the Danube is not navigable, so we do not feel justified in going deeply into these shallow streams. Claudio Magris discusses the sources in his excellent book *The Danube*, which hardly mentions navigation, but like ourselves and the river itself, wanders about in all directions.

The current was strong, but later eased a little to 7 km/hr. The river was wider but winding. Wooded cliffs towered up on either side of the river, disappearing into the mist, which wreathed halfway down the forest clad hills. The sky glowed pink and yellow ahead, promising better weather later in the day. We were learning to advertise our presence, with these blind corners and fast hotel ships, and followed the practice of giving our name and kilometre post over the VHF at intervals: '*Hosanna* bei vierzehn, talfarht.' (*Hosanna* at Kpxx14, going downstream.)

We were heading for Linz in Austria. The bank on our right became Austrian, and though the bank on our left was still German, we had been told that it was *verboten* to visit Germany again now that we had checked out. We took down our German courtesy ensign and for the time being did not fly the Austrian, not wishing to show partiality.

On the German side the cliffs were steep and almost unclimbable, while the Austrian side looked like a little Switzerland, with chalets, onion domes, green slanting fields, and domestic vignettes.

The chief navigational problem was a crowd of canoeists, hundreds of them, paddling downstream on this Sunday morning. Those that did not dash, cheerful and heartstopping, across our bows had an upsetting habit of wearing red or green lifejackets, and hovering at the river's edge impersonating buoys. No one would have thought, seeing them, that we had done some of this journey since Regensburg with our hearts in our mouths. They seemed to take the Danube entirely for granted. They had known it from birth, they presumably knew its ins and its outs, and its ups and its downs; and had no fear of it. Just, we hoped, a very healthy respect.

There was also a tiny little boat drifting downstream with two sweeps and an outboard motor. On it, someone was playing the zither in the rain.

Obenzell was another attractive little town, the pastel coloured chalets with geraniums on their balconies, the church with two towers, and a sugar-shaker dome, picked out in soft yellows and whites. The exterior murals are beautiful in this part of the world, lovingly painted. What kind of paint do they use, we wondered, matt surfaced, rather like tempera, that stands up so well to snow and rain?

On the approach to the lock at Jochenstein, the last one in Germany, we had to give the canoes a toot, they were everywhere, some rafting up together in little groups. In the end we all locked through together; *Hosanna*, and about a hundred canoes. We had to wait for them. They streamed back two kilometres, and the stragglers were a long time catching up. As it was raining, the lock blossomed with colour as the canoeists opened umbrellas and oilskins, until the entire water surface became a canoe garden. They had been told to be at the lock by 0940, and at 0940 exactly the gates closed; anyone who missed it had to portage past the lock, overland.

Chat was exchanged: where were we going? Where were they going? They were no Sunday outing, but an International Canoe Club; there were canoes from Slovakia, Holland, Germany, and Austria, going downstream and camping at night on the bank; some would be stopping at Bratislava, others might be going further on. We should meet them again.

At Aschach lock, as promised, Bill climbed flights of concrete steps and disturbed the Ober-something-or-other who had been watching television, and asked about our *erlaubnis*. He telephoned head office, but got no reply. Finally he sighed and said, 'You go to Slovakia, yes? Well, go.' Evidently we could do without the mystical document. No-one ever asked for it anyway.

At Ottensheim lock, the last of the day, we waited in the lock chamber for 20 minutes while the back gates remained open until two coxed rowing fours arrived. On leaving there was a stunning view ahead of us; hills with little fields of tawny gold and green, forest copses of pinewoods, and little villages dotted about here and there – a miniature patchwork quite different from the sombre forest gorges we had come through earlier.

Linz is known, apart from its raspberry tart, as an industrial city. The iron and steel industry expanded here during the war, and is still in production. There is a lot of barge traffic, and the barge-building yards are active.

We had hoped to berth at the town quay but were disappointed. We passed through the city, entered the old *winterhafn* and requested permission to berth at the elegant, empty pontoon of the Motorboot Club of the Nibelungens. A squad of boatmen came down from the clubhouse and helped us, making us fast at our suggestion, not to the pontoon, but to the bank behind it. We then made the pontoon fast to us. This nicety, which seems a tautological reciprocity, may be lost on some, but it is significant in avoiding doing damage when you are a large boat at a small pontoon. We took up the whole of it, and had the impression that they had never seen anything quite like us before.

The clubhouse bar was comfortable and we had a few beers. There was another heavy thunderstorm in the night, followed by a stormy day. Bill started to walk to town, as a visit to the Post Office and Bank had become imperative, but it turned out to be too far and there was no bus. The Nibelungs of the Motorboot Club were rich and had splendid cars, but they were not chummy. We got on better with the boatman and the bartender, who told us that someone from the club workshop would be going into town later and would give Laurel a lift to do some shopping.

We were both tired, but there were chores to do; couplings to tighten, shafts to grease, galley to be given its weekly clean-out, bedding to be washed and dried. While we were thus engaged the Slovakian tug *Polana* was brought in to the shipyard opposite by workboats of the Austrian fire brigade. She had grounded, ripped a hole in her hull and sunk in the river about 2 kilometres downstream. Fifty men and all the pumps they could muster were in use. That and the Luxembourger near Geisling meant we had encountered two accidents to solid-looking boats in a fairly short period. It made us think.

While Laurel was watching this cabaret a man came down to our pontoon and began to shout at her, saying that we were too big, and demanding, it seemed, what the hell we thought we were doing breaking up the pontoon. She pointed to our ropes going ashore in approved fashion, and not to the pontoon at all. She said that we had paid our dues to the Club and that all was in order: 'Alles in ordnung'. At this point Bill realised that his wife was being browbeaten, and came behind her and loomed. Bill can be a very effective loomer. The man shambled off, muttering disbelievingly, 'Alles in ordnung!' Adolf Hitler, born in Austria, wanted to retire to Linz in old age. His spirit lives on, it seems.

We do not hear much nowadays of the part played by Austria in setting up the Nazi Party and devising its policies. It is all blamed on Germany, but in fact some of the worst manifestations of Nazism took place in Austria. Though the Nazis first took power in Germany, the Austrians responded eagerly to their invitation to join in, and welcomed the German troops marching into Austria in 1938.

The Hauptplatz, Linz

At mid-morning a car stopped by our boat, Laurel made going to town signs, the occupant nodded, she got in gratefully. His name was Hans, he spoke a little English, and was a retired engineer. As he drove he chatted, interested in our boat and our voyage, but suddenly broke off and pointed to a van ahead with a Czech registration plate, towing a car-transporting trailer. 'He's come to steal a Mercedes,' said Hans bitterly, 'A new one, of course. He has already chosen it to order, and will have forged the papers.'

Everywhere we went, it was the adjacent country who was suspect, thieves, cheats and robbers, to a man.

Hans took Laurel to a shopping mall, where she got the posting done. It was registered and expensive, so Hans lent her sixty schillings till she could get to the bank. 'There is no bank here,' said Hans. 'I take you, but first I must tell my wife where I am.' His flat overlooked the Danube. Laurel said 'Come and look at the boat and bring your wife.' 'This afternoon,' he said. 'Come to tea,' said Laurel.

She was back on board, all commissions executed, by midday. One of the boatmen drove by, slowed down and hooted. 'All done, thank you,' we said, and he waved and drove on.

Hans and Heidi and their dog all came to tea. We talked about boats, and engines, and the Danube. Hans' working life had been spent at the shipyard opposite. Not here at the Motorboot Club? 'No, I have not friends here, they are very...' he made the universal gesture of lifting the end of the nose, meaning snooty. 'Not even in the workshop?' Laurel faltered. 'No. I came to look at the *Polana*. The Captain had been drinking you know.'

It dawned on Laurel that she had hijacked an innocent and

unsuspecting retired Engineer, and forced him at the point of a loaded smile to take her to the Post Office and the Bank. She explained her mistake, and our tea and buns ended in gusts of laughter. Heidi was beautiful, thick black hair in a plait down to her waist. She talked adoringly to the cats, the dog was impeccably behaved, and Hans had been a perfect gentleman. We were glad they had come to tea.

Later that evening a strange and piratical passenger craft kept coming by as if we were a thing of some interest. She was called *Fitzcarald*o, and was of an original, if not downright odd, design. So was her extravagantly bearded and extrovert skipper, Bernhard. He stopped close to our ship and asked questions, as his passengers were interested in us, inviting us to join the tour group, which turned out to be the local Architectural Association. After the tour Bernhard took us all to the commercial harbour to look at the repair ship that he had just bought. The interior seemed to be about the size of the Albert Hall, though the only decoration was the tattered remains of calendars of the type found in engineering premises. What should he do with it? he asked us. That was the problem: he had now to remove it from the commercial harbour.

Ideas from the architects were forthcoming; restaurant, dance hall, exhibition hall. Bill suggested a Youth Hostel: they rather liked that idea. Then they all came to see *Hosanna*, and ten architects prowled round our boat poking into corners and admiring the effective use of space, their questions indicating that they may have absorbed some ideas. They were impressed. New houses in Linz were going to have a nautical look for the next year or so. Look out for a new Austrian school of architecture, not Bauhaus, but Bargehaus.

Before leaving we filled our tanks with fresh water. We have a plumbing system not dissimilar to that of a house, except that we have neither a roof tank, nor a water-main. Most boat-dwellers have to compound with a quasi-permanent shortage of potable water, their supply being limited to what their boat can carry. Barges are built for load carrying, and we had had to ballast *Hosanna* before converting her. It seemed sensible to install large water tanks in the bottom of the ship and make part of the ballast work for a living. We carry 5 tonnes of water. Instead of the header tank in the roof, we have a pressurised system which switches a pump on whenever a tap is opened. It works well. We do not waste water because we have to pay a comparatively high price for it. Without stinting, but with sensible economy, we use about 1½ tonnes a month. We were aware that Austria was perhaps the last country where we might be wholly confident about the quality of the water. The mooring charge was steep, but water was included, so we made the most of it and filled right up.

• 18 •
NOSE TO THE GREINSTONE
Linz to Marbach

Wednesday 5 July was cloudy and the view past Linz steelworks was not inspiring. We passed the point where the *Polana* had been wrecked but could see no obvious reason why, except that it had been at the height of the floods. As we passed, the river was some 1.30 metres above ENR and the barrages were open to drain the upper reaches, for snow in the Alps was still melting and coming down the Inn, giving us a current of 8½ km/hr. During the war it was a sinister reach; Mauthausen, on our left, 3 kilometres below Linz, was the site of one of the nastiest Nazi death camps, where Jews and Gypsies were worked to death in the quarries. The Gypsies' deaths are not much mourned: is this because Gypsies, unlike Jews, make no works of art; they sing, play and dance, but compose no music; tell stories but write no books? They are colourfully paintable, but paint no pictures. Their arts are as ephemeral as their unregulated way of life, their deaths by the million as unregarded as those of butterflies.

The river widened and the current eased. For the first time since the Straits of Dover, we used the autopilot for short stretches, which helped to relieve the tension. One could sit down, but the Mini obscured vision. Bill could see over it when standing, but had to crane his neck when sitting; Laurel, barely five feet tall, had either to peer through the car rear window and windscreen, which gave her a distorted view of the way ahead, or else walk from side to side of the wheelhouse in order to see round it.

We had been using an excellent guide for the German part of the Danube, but had now to change to a loose-leaf book published by the Motorboot-sportverband für Österreich. This had adequate charts, but otherwise consisted of a list of marinas too small to accommodate us. With these books, we had some confidence in our ability to navigate the river. The snag remained Jugoslavia. But we had become less nervous about that too, as we talked to more tugmasters. The BBC reported that Croatia appeared ready for an offensive against the Serb enclave. Would that affect the Danube? We planned to visit embassies and consulates in Vienna. They would surely know something this close to the Jugoslav border.

We were in picturesque country with romantic castles on crags overhanging the water; it seemed as if there was always at least one in sight. The river narrowed and flowed faster, cutting through a range of hills.

We now approached one of the most difficult stretches in the whole river, near Grein, where the current accelerates to its fastest and there are dangerous whirlpools. There is an elaborate system of traffic lights described in the Austrian guide, but only in German. These had seemed simple, but on re-reading as we approached Tiefenbach, hidden meanings and doubts appeared. The instructions, magically entitled *Schiffahrtsbeschränkungen bei Struden*, contained coloured illustrations of a signal light system with a huge display resembling an inverted Christmas tree. We were desperately trying to decypher it as the current increased and we gathered speed, hurtling towards the point of decision: would we have the right of way or not? The chances were that we would; downstream boats normally have precedence because it is so difficult to stop, but we could not be sure.

We hoped the lockmaster at Wallsee, 12 kilometres above the light display at Kp 2095, would keep the controller of this stretch informed as *talfahrt* boats left his lock. We were still working out the different classes of vessel, each with different priority, when we rounded a narrow bend with a current under us exceeding 15 km/hr, with no hope of stopping, and suddenly confronted the light display. For readers of German, we give a summary of the instructions:

Die linke signalhälfte, gilt für den Strudenkanal.
Die rechte signalhälfte, gilt für den Hössgang.
Die obere signalhälfte, gilt für Einzelfahrer.
Die untere signalhälfte, gilt für Verbände.

The lights were shown in the book like this:

```
RG          RG
  RG      RG
    RG  RG
     RG RG
RGRG          RGRG
  RGRG      RGRG
    RGRG  RGRG
     RGRG RGRG
```

Linke and *rechte* were obviously left and right, and Struden and Hössgang are villages either side of a small island that obstructs the narrow channel. But our small German-English dictionary gave *verbänd* as a bandage, association, or political party (the publishers of our guide were a *verbänd*). *Einzelfahrer* did not appear at all, but aware that Germans agglomerate words, we took *ein* as our clue. We decided, as we flashed past the brilliantly illuminated sign-board, that an *einzelfahrer* was a boat on its own, and that the *verbände* must be those tied together. It was logical that single craft and multiple tows should be treated differently. We sighed with relief and then looked at each other with horror: neither of us had noticed whether the board was lit up *linke* or *rechte* or *unter* or *ober*. Lit up it certainly was, no mistaking that.

'Anyway,' Bill observed struggling to keep *Hosanna* on course in the first big whirlpool, 'there was no way we could have stopped.'

Laurel had time to think. 'I'm sure there were more green lights than red.' she said, helpfully.

'Well, keep an ear on VHF. I'm sure we are being watched. If the enemy opens fire, drop to the deck.'

Laurel broadcast on Channel 10 that there was an English ship *talfahrer bei Grein* and got no response. Good. The bend at Grein is sharp, and the water rough. There was supposed to be a mooring at Grein, but if so we went past too fast to see it. We were both very tense, not enjoying ourselves. Immediately after Grein is an overhanging cliff which forms another sharp corner at Schwalleck. Before barrages and locks were built, this part of the river often became impassable because of rapids and whirlpools. At Schwalleck the current was deflected by a rocky cliff, and before being able to resume its journey downstream it formed a violent whirlpool and carried many a craft onto the rock face.

The name Grein is supposed to be onomatopoeic with the cry of a drowning sailor, and tradition had it that a man who fell overboard here was left to his fate as a propitiation to the gods, who might then spare the rest of the crew. Ships were often lashed together like catamarans to achieve better stability in the turbulent waters, and usually they had warps to the bank to help the pilots negotiate the corner. It could take a team of 50 horses to pull a boat upstream, as the graphic models in the ship museum at Regensburg showed. When the current was extra strong navigation was suspended in both directions, and the goods transported overland.

During the last two centuries, tons of high explosives have been used to ease the sharpness of the turn and reduce the whirlpools. Even so, most boats until recently stopped (somehow!) to take on a special pilot for this reach. Nowadays, with a barrage and lock at Wallsee, and another downstream at Ybbs-Persenbeug, it is merely horrifying, where it used to be death-dealing. With the river at its narrowest, the gradient is more than twice the average. The whirlpools are dangerous only during floods, but the channel is so narrow that when the river is in spate, the level can rise by 15 metres, which must dampen the spirits in the cellars of riverside holiday houses.

The river was high, but not quite overflowing its banks, and the passage was officially navigable. There were secondary traffic lights on the little island of Wörth, by Struden, directing us into the right-hand channel. We just had time to conform, mainly because we were expecting them. As we rejoined the river it narrowed further by the village of St Nikola, and in the bend by the end of the village we met a Ukrainian tug with two big barges, motoring ahead but stopped geographically. The skipper leant out of his wheelhouse and made a gesture that was difficult to interpret. It was not obviously hostile;

nor was it a friendly wave. Laurel interpreted it as 'Move over', while Bill saw it as 'For God's sake get a move on, I don't want to wait here all day.'

'Did you see the Black Monk?' asked Bill.

'No.' said Laurel.

'Thank God for that.'

The Black Monk reputedly lived in a tower overhanging the Hausstein rapids, and those who saw him faced disaster and death. Any idiot casting his eyes up the cliff for Black Monks when they should have been steering through rapids deserves disaster and death.

We shot past Sarmingstein, the river widened again, the current eased, and we could take time for a bite to eat.

In his book, *Danube*, Claudio Magris says that 'At Grein there are no longer the whirlpools... which terrified travellers... Skilful works... have turned this into a tranquil stretch of the Danube.' Tranquil indeed! Well, well! His very readable book, a glorious name-dropping commentary on intellectuals and politicians of Eastern Europe, is set round and about the Danube, but we do wonder if he ever actually travelled *on* it. Other eminent academics, moored to their dreaming spires, pontificate on nautical matters with such ignorance that one marvels they are considered scholars at all. They pride themselves on researching their subjects, on checking sources and references, but we never see them at Greenwich, let alone at sea, where they might be genuinely enlightened.

Grein may be a fraction of the terror that it once was, but it is still a beast when the river wills, and we experienced a little beastliness that day.

We settled on a village stop for the night. The map showed two *yachthafns* at Marbach, and we headed there. We were unable to enter either of them. There was, however, a concrete quay near the village centre, about 3 metres long with no bollards. We snuggled up against it and put out a strong headrope to a stunted tree to take the main strain of the 5 km/hr current, not so strong as we were used to, for the river had become wider and deeper. We put out other ropes to a weak-looking wooden jetty, which looked in need of repair. 'It'll need still more repairs when we go,' Bill observed cheerfully. 'Let's go into the big city for a beer.'

There was a supermarket conveniently close. For yachties, it is often better to shop in villages, even if it is more expensive, because of the problems of getting heavy goods back to the boat. Everything is centralised in a village; in town, you need a car to shop in mega-stores on the outskirts.

While cooking supper on board, the main generator failed. There was no cooling water. Bill tried cleaning the filters, but that was not the problem. After the whirlpools at Grein we did not need this. He shelved it until the morrow, and supper was cooked by gas.

• 19 •
GOODNIGHT VIENNA!
Through Austria

The generator fault was a disintegrated impeller in the pump. Not serious if you have a spare, and you should have because this is the weakest part in any marine diesel engine, and it is sad that nobody has yet invented a more reliable pumping mechanism. It is as if a vital part of Concorde's engines were dependent on elastic bands. Of course we had a spare.

Didn't we? The generator was new. It had been ordered with a spares kit.

There was no impeller in the spares kit. But was this the spares kit for the other generator and (senility rules) had we got mixed up? If so, where was the other spares kit? The search continued off and on all day, with more or less hopeful, despairing, or acrimonious discussions. One of the problems of having a big boat is that there are more places to lose things, and Bill is an expert misplacer. In *Hosanna* he has the ideal field for full expression of this expertise. Laurel usually finds what Bill has mislaid. Not this time. (We found the other spares kit 4 months later.)

Thursday 6 July, and this ought to be halfway day. In distance that is. Timewise we hoped we were further than halfway; we hoped it would not take as long again to get to Constanţa on the Black Sea. We would stop for a few days and enjoy the delights of Vienna, be sophisticated tourists, treat ourselves to some Kultur and Kugelhopf. After three months travelling, we deserved it. More, we *needed* to go to Vienna. We wanted to get our visas for the downriver countries. After much expensive phoning, it seemed the visas available in London before we left would have expired before we got to the borders, a penalty of slow travel. One could get visas at the borders by paying double the fee. We hoped to save those fees in Vienna.

Very early in the morning the river was in pinky pearly oystergrey mood, the hills a bluer and fainter grey, and the sugar-shaker tops of the churches were silhouetted grey against grey. Nothing monotonous about it, though; it was a vibrant grey, alive with colour. We came to Melk lock against the early morning light, like a cut-out theatre set in monochrome. The lock was the darkest shade, charcoal grey, and behind it were cardboard cut-outs of castles and towers the colour of storm clouds, and behind those a row of hills and more hills, sharply defined in receding shades of grey – pigeon to distant dove.

The Donau is too wide here to be bridged, so every now and then were ferries taking two or three cars, probably the only way to get across till you reached Vienna. On the wall of a factory over which the sun, as Bill pointed out poetically, was rising, was a long, long mural of the history of the Danube, beautifully done. There were the Crusaders, the salt trade, horses and Knights, Bishops and castles; a work of art, and visible only from the river, on which most of the people in this country seem to turn their backs. The Gasthofs are perhaps an exception; they provide pontoons for customers, but on the whole the Danube here is regarded as more of a nuisance than an asset. It can't be crossed except by ferry, and it floods inconveniently. It has small tourist potential; trips are available on the hotel barges or the day-tour boats, but there is no thought of waterway cruising, holidaying in your own boat as in England and Holland and France. That simply cannot be done; if you have a boat at all here it's a small fast one, and you zip up maybe 20 kilometres to the next lock, and that's it, back for tea.

We kept well clear of Schönbühel rock, towered over by Schönbühel castle. Here in the river gorges lives the Noek, who is a bit like the Drac who inhabits the Rhône river luring mariners to their death. The Noek is a giant half-man half-fish, and does the same thing. It seems to be necessary to great rivers to have entities like this to explain the disasters and difficulties of navigating them.

Every few kilometres another castle perched on a projecting spur of rock like a fairy picturebook. There is a long history of feudal landowners building fortresses which they garrisoned with men able to extract a toll from any passer-by. It is very spectacular, and we felt glad these robber barons were no longer able to exact any payment. They would have rubbed their hands at the prospect of a yacht. Yachts are regarded as fair game by those thinking of making money. Non-yachtsmen see yachtsmen as being in three categories: rich, very rich and mega-rich, which may once have been true. It is these three categories that are conspicuous at holiday resorts, but nowadays there is another: those with a love of the sea who spend, often unwisely, their modest income on this love, and live in a boat. We too should be counted.

We passed Willendorf, home of the Willendorf Venus, a Neolithic statue which bears about as much resemblance to a Cranach Venus as an elephant god. She is topshaped, and has exaggerated sexual characteristics. Laurel looked forward to making her acquaintance in the Museum at Vienna.

And then we were at Dürnstein, and beetling in silhouette above us was the gaunt and craggy castle where Richard Lionheart was imprisoned for two years, at the top of a high, forested hill. Here his minstrel Blondel found him after singing round Europe at every castle wall until he heard his master's voice singing the refrain with him, and knew that here Richard was imprisoned.

Under Dürnstein castle, on the river bank, is the village, with an Alice Blue church decorated with white icing. The mediaeval villages of Stein und Krems were our geographical halfway mark; there were 2000 kilometres behind us, give or take a couple. For the seagulls overhead it was only 400 or so as the seagull flies down through Jugoslavia to the Adriatic Sea, but no outlet there for us, riverbound. We had 2000 kilometres to go and we were 200 metres above sea-level. *Hosanna* was as far from the sea as she would ever be.

All this time we were observing *pegels*, calculating water levels, and passing through locks. The *pegel* for Wien (Vienna), which was repeated higher up the river, showed 351 cm; the 'normal' is 95, so the water was 256 cm higher. At Keinstock the level was 232 higher than normal. As we approached Vienna the current increased.

We ran out of kilometre posts; the banks were churned up by bull-dozers and the posts were hidden in the sand. This led to missing our destination at Klosterneuburg by half a kilometre, and having to claw slowly back against the current by the water's edge. Heikell's guide recommends this marina above Vienna on the right bank as being hospitable and helpful. We had been disillusioned with most Danube marinas, so being anxious to stop at Vienna we had sought reassur-ance from some Austrian pleasure-boaters who said we would surely get a berth there, so as we turned with great difficulty into the creek in late afternoon we had high hopes.

Wrong, wrong. Men came running down to the pontoons, jumping up and down and waving their arms like the man at Linz, shouting 'Go away'. There was plenty of room, and we could see in this quiet backwater off the river that the pontoons were well able to take us. But there is no staying where one is not welcome. We went a short way up the arm and turned, impeccably as usual, just to show them how to do it, but they'd quickly filled the pontoon with little boats by then and waved us off, shouting '1919', which we took to be the kilo-metre post of the *winterhafn*, a lot further on. We left feeling bruised by Austrian inhospitality.

Worse followed. The current was carrying us fast down through a Vienna that, from the Danube, was one vast construction site, the left bank all sand, tracked by bulldozers, and on the right, the city itself invisible behind house-high concrete, newly poured, bristling with re-inforcing rods like witches' whiskers. New bridges not on our chart and a lack of kilometre posts made navigation appalling. The only mooring pontoons were full of hotel and restaurant boats. There was nowhere to stop. We flashed past the centre of Vienna having seen nothing except building materials and a coloured glass monstrosity, the IBM building, erected on the site where Strauss wrote some of his waltzes.

'We're catching up those barges ahead,' Laurel said. 'They've stopped.' This is rare, they usually go too fast for us. What was the obstruction?

'Dear God,' she said, 'there's two red lights!' 'I can't stop,' said Bill, 'the current's too strong.' But by reversing everything we managed to slow down after passing the first barge tug *Ybbs* and reach a near stationary position.

'It's a lock!' said Laurel. 'They've built a bloody lock!' What they had not yet completed was the barrage to carry the water-flow to one side, and leave the lock approach in slack water. Somehow we held our place, and when the lights went green we waved *Ybbs* past us, as was proper. The Romanian tow ahead of us, hindered by the current, took an hour entering the lock. We finally got in alongside *Ybbs*, and sought information. The new lock and barrage is part of the scheme for refurbishing the river banks throughout Vienna, and at the same time reducing the strong current past the city.

'This lock is not on our chart,' we said to the Captain.

'It's been open only ten days,' he said. 'Nothing works properly, and there are long delays.' They had difficulty closing the gates, which were of a rotating type, rolling up from the depths. From underneath the surface came rumblings and groanings as if one of the old Danube dragons, maybe the Noek himself, had been shut down there, afflicted by too many Viennese pastries.

'Where can we overnight?' we asked him.

'Just after the lock, immediately on the right, there is the old *winterhafn*. It is being rebuilt, like everywhere else, but you should find a corner. Be careful: when you leave the lock everyone will be blue-flagging, so tell the boats waiting that you must cross their bows, otherwise you will miss the entrance.' It turned out to be good advice. He kindly broadcast on VHF that a little Englander was crossing over, and we had only to make the appropriate sound signal and the big tows positioned themselves to let us by. There is much goodwill among river people irrespective of nationality. We try hard to keep to the standards, and if we fail occasionally it is through ignorance rather than wilfulness.

The quays in the *winterhafn*, now renamed the Freudenau Hafn just to confuse us further, were still unfinished. They were about 10 metres high, and there were no bollards. However, several bits of steel reinforcing, and holes in the sheet steel piling allowed us to make a precarious mooring away from the current. Overhead we could hear the lorries and diggers lorrying and digging till midnight, but the noise mostly passed over us, which is more than one can say for the mud which rained down in sloshy splashes every time we heard the roar of a large diesel above us. There was no ladder to climb the 10 metre wall above us, and no possibility of getting ashore from here.

Goodnight, Vienna!

In the morning we rose, cleaned the mud splashes off the deck and windows and left Vienna early and thankfully, giving up on visas, Venuses, and venal Wiener Schnitzel.

One checks out of Austria 36 kilometres further on at Hainburg, the frontier post at Kp 1884. We had been warned by The Captains that the pontoon was a killer. Turn first, The Captains said, and drop back onto the pontoon. Built for administrative convenience, but to the great peril of mariners, on the outside of a narrow bend at the exact point where the current is fastest and strongest, the pontoon was a big one, floating on huge cylindrical tanks, and having a superstructure of steel girders against which it was impossible to fender oneself. Boats have been lost attempting to stop as regulations require, and people have been killed.

The pontoon was on the right bank of a left-hand curve, so one had to turn round to starboard. Halfway round we virtually stopped turning because the current varied, and we started going rapidly sideways towards Slovakia. Bill cursed whoever had chosen such a bad spot for a frontier post; it couldn't possibly have been worse placed. We got round just in time for Laurel to lasso a bollard (she's much better than a cowboy; she can do it with a rope as thick as her wrist), and we swung hard against the pontoon with a crash that rattled the crockery. We bounced there for a bit doing minor damage, while two uniformed men appeared and inspected our passports. They were handed back and Bill told Laurel to let go.

'Your ship's papers...' shouted one of the officers.

'Sorry,' Bill shouted back as *Hosanna* moved rapidly off the quay, 'we cannot get back, the current's too strong.' He shot off downstream murmuring: 'We'd have been wrecked if we had stayed there.' Laurel agreed that we could not have stayed on a pontoon so badly placed, even for barges twenty times our weight. We were soon out of pistol shot and could relax.

Now we approached Slovakia, and our first contact with ex-Iron Curtain countries. We searched anxiously for the Slovak frontier post. If the Austrians had been difficult, what would ex-communists be like?

• 20 •

MILAN'S TREFF

Bratislava to Komarno

We were in Slovakia before we realised it. 'A customs launch will escort you to a mooring,' said the River Guide. No launch appeared. The customs post on the bank was deserted. 'Good,' said Bill, 'the Slovakians have the right idea about the liberty of the individual.'

We had been advised by The Captains to berth in the old Bassin Petrolu, downstream of Bratislava. We passed under the Bridge of the Slovakian Uprising, now mercifully called the New Bridge, which has a restaurant at the top of an exuberant suspending pillar, like the Post Office Tower in London. We kept to the left, the city side, turned, and fought the current into the first harbour entrance only to be tooted by a barge coming out. By the time we'd avoided him and got back into what appeared to be the Bassin Petrolu judging by the oil tanks, we'd had enough, and moored alongside a friendly Dutch barge for elevenses.

It was a big basin and barges were loading or discharging. The Dutch are usually helpful, so we put our mooring problem to them. They called their Slovakian agent, who called the Harbour-master, and we were told to go back into the river and into the last basin. We could not miss it.

We didn't miss it because we didn't get there. Nervous about our ability to return if we overshot, we again turned too soon. Into the New Basin, we found later. It had a shipyard on one side with nobody working, and on the other, men were repairing an old barge. Feeling unwanted, we moored to a derelict barge out of everyone's way, but with no access to the shore. When in doubt, have lunch.

A speedboat came alongside to chat. With little common language we conveyed our situation, and bless them! they produced a photocopy of a large scale plan of the river and showed us exactly how to find our basin. Bill asked if he could make a photocopy of their photocopy, we being now without any charts except the inadequate ones in Heikell's guide, so they gave it to us. They would be able to take a copy from the original, they said. What a welcome!

After lunch we felt strong enough to go slowly down river close to the bank. The water level here was only a metre above normal. Close to the high, stone-lined bank we saw an entrance going back at a very acute angle, far sharper than we could turn under rudder only. The current was enough to cause a whirlpool in the basin entrance churning a mixture of tree branches and plastic bags. Bill turned *Hosanna* sharply, using engines, dodged the débris, entered the still, green water of the creek, and went up to the end. With only a foot or two to spare we turned in our own length under the astonished gaze of a few late-lunchers at the two restaurants-cum-marinas. Their pontoons had no space for us, but someone indicated the one adjacent, and moved a small boat already alongside it. This pontoon was rusty and in a poor state of repair but we made fast with great relief.

It being Friday afternoon it was lucky we got there before the weekend rush of Germans and Austrians in their speedboats. Milan's Treff, with the apostrophe in the right place (more than one could expect in England), was the name of the restaurant immediately next to us. (Treff means a dive or joint: an informal meeting place). Milan had provided everything visiting boats would want; moorings, power, water, showers, and non-stop beer and food at incredibly low prices from breakfast to midnight. As little boats arrived, their owners manhandled them stern-first into the mooring, got out their cables, and plugged into power like a row of electric irons. We threw a cable across the gap between the pontoons and got plugged in too, a great relief since our generator still wasn't working.

Vienna is only half an hour away by speedboat, and a huge beer here costs half what a small one does in Vienna; you can see the attraction. We went to Milan's for several evening drinks, a meal, and a bottle of wine: the whole lot came to £12 for two. We were in clover. We spoke to some of the Austrians who were there at the restaurant. 'Did you enjoy Vienna?' they asked. 'No,' we said shortly. 'Vienna had the builders in.'

The old Bassin Petrolu was a narrow creek, with high sides to allow for floods. The banks were clad with big trees, little breeze got down, and a heatwave had just begun.

Cold Slovakian beer was like nectar to Bill during the hot days that followed (though the Slovaks mourned that the best beer came from the Czech part of old Czecho-Slovakia), while Laurel was sufficiently dry to add soda water to good Slovakian white wine. We ate at Milan's almost every evening, and sometimes lunchtime as well. While we learnt about Slovakia, in Slovak or German, as Milan had no English, we watched his cheerful cook literally sweating over his hot stove. The place filled up, most people sitting informally and good- humouredly on benches at simple tables. The fare on offer was new to us, and the presentation elementary. We encountered for the first time, but far from the last, the Eastern European salad, which is not fresh lettuce but pickled vegetables, sometimes with shredded cabbage and peppers, and the cold plate of mixed meats and salame. Wiener Schnitzel was always to be had; the customers expected it.

Josef, Milan's cook, was a good humoured, well-covered young man, as cooks should be. He wore a white baseball cap back to front, (the *dernier cri* in Bratislava) with his white T-shirt and trousers, over which he tied a printed tablecloth, apronwise; a different one every day. He was a dab hand at *Palatschinken*, a kind of pancake, and did a savoury one containing goulash that was his own idea. We also enjoyed *vyprazany ostiepok*: ham wrapped in sheep's cheese and fried. If there were enough people coming Milan roasted a big roll of meat on the spit: a Donau kebab, we called it, but he didn't see the joke. To him the river was the Dunaj, and Turkish cooking a mystery. On the other hand, Hungary was not far. You could tell; the cruets had an extra place for the paprika.

The best thing was the company. Everyone wanted to talk to us, even if they spoke no English. We met Oleg and Sabina; Andrea, Maros and Vlado, and Konstantin. We learned *Dakujem*, for thank you, and *pivo*, for beer, and got used to *Ano* for yes. As we relaxed under the awning we felt better than we had since Passau, as if we were cruising again, and worries could take care of themselves; we had landed among hospitable people who wanted to be friends. Suddenly the journey ahead, which had been causing us more and more concern (the Serbs had just taken Srebrenica after fierce fighting) took on a different shape. We would eat it, Serbs and all, and spit out the pips.

We went into tourist mode, and looked about us.

Our pontoon was typical of those we would find all the way down to the Black Sea. There would be few moorings for any vessels except pontoons which could rise and fall several metres according to river level. They were held off by two huge spars, each about 20 metres long, and connected to the shore by a brow, or gangway. In our case the brow was derelict, its floor reinforced with an uninspiring patchwork of chipboard, linoleum, and cardboard which effectively disguised the state of the girders underneath.

The pontoon itself was about 30 metres long by 8 broad. At either end was a cabin about 5 metres by 4, and an open space between. Some have this open space covered with a roof with fretted valancing, and those which serve as passenger boat terminals have seats and potted plants. There is a faint suggestion of the old village railway stations we knew in pre-Beeching days. In Milan's Treff, one cabin was the kitchen and stores, the centre part under an awning was for diners, and the other cabin formed a bar with a few indoor tables.

Milan's Treff pontoon was in a better state than ours, well painted, and guarded by a silly, good-natured dog. There was no telephone, and for the first time on the journey our GSM phone no longer worked. After the weekend Bill walked 400 metres to the Motor Boat Club to phone an order for our urgently needed spare parts, which were promised by courier.

Milan produced a visitors' book with the names of cruising boats that had preceded us. Some of the entries were nicely done, so Laurel asked permission to take the book to *Hosanna* so she could give full vent to graphic design. Most of the boats that had passed on long voyages had been either British or Dutch. Many had subsequently turned back.

Milan's Treff, Bratislava

We taxied (summoned by VHF) into the city next morning at little cost, about 50 pence, passing through dreary suburbs. All the buildings seemed identical, finished in drab concrete formed by rough wood shuttering, and were black-streaked by rainwater which had found its own route, marking it clearly so the next rainstorm could follow.

Top of our list in town was sending a fax to confirm our order for spare parts. We tramped shabby streets to find the only hotel in Bratislava with a fax machine: it took some time and research. Same problem with the British Embassy, where we wanted to ask what information they had about conditions further down the Danube. We had telephoned London for its address: it had moved. No comment!

In the old city, picturesque and well kept, we found the British Council in a lovely, well fortified building. The British Council concerns itself with Culture with a capital C; and navigation, even on the Danube which passes close by, is not considered to be culture at all, even with a small c. Indeed anything that can be defined, described factually, calculated, or has any practical use, has no part in British Council thinking. But they were courteous people and we got off to a good start when they found we were writers. Their interest faded a bit when they discovered we write travel books and not poetry, and faded further on discovering that our books were mostly about sea or river travel. The sea is *awfully* uncultured. But they continued to be unfailingly polite and helpful about the city. They knew where the Embassy and Consulate had gone. We hied ourselves there.

The Embassy remained hard to find because it had a large Turkish flag outside it. It was on the fifth floor, the Turks occupying the first.

This is a highly dubious security position; Turkish consulates and offices were currently being blown up round Europe by disaffected Kurds, and it seemed quite likely that Britons and Turks might well be forcibly united in the basement. The building had a scruffy foyer decorated, like the entrance to a Labour Exchange in the thirties, with green and cream paint that was worn through in places, and greasily dirty elsewhere. Stone stairs led laboriously up.

In the entrance lobby on the fifth floor, we conducted our business through a sliding window just big enough to allow intercourse between two hamsters, and placed at such a low level that Bill could not see the person on the other side unless he dropped to his knees. Perhaps that was the idea. Having established some sort of credentials, a door opened and we were ushered into a waiting room with posters of hunted-looking Guardsmen, Big Ben at an angle reminiscent of the tower of Pisa, double-decker buses and other British scenery, a notice board about accommodation available, small items of furniture stacked in the corner, and bundles of magazines tied up with string. Someone was hanging up curtains, after the recent move. It must be rather difficult moving an Embassy; it did not look as if they were yet ready for customers.

Nothing could have been further from the truth. After a couple of false starts we found ourselves with Nigel Baker, Deputy Head of Mission. He apologised for the inconvenience associated with moving, and we hit it off very well. He had been only a short time in Bratislava after a long spell in Prague, and confessed to knowing almost nothing about the Danube, but wanted to learn. Mr Baker had appointments that morning, so we invited him down to see us in the Bassin Petrolu, an area hitherto unknown to him, and we left. He had recommended a cheap and cheerful spot for lunch round the corner, U Petra, where we ate mixed turkey and pork, with a peppery sauce.

K-mart, the supermarket, fascinated Laurel as a first glimpse of what was available in Eastern Europe. It was an odd mix. There were expensive luxuries in tins, crisps and appetizers, but little variety or quality in not-very-fresh vegetables, meat, and charcuterie. We had got used to the absence of lamb: that had started in Germany. Pork and turkey were cheap, chicken was dear, and for special occasions. Beef looked iffey. There were no fresh pork sausages, only smoked ones or salami, and they were soft and pasty looking. There was a total absence of mosquito repellent, sorely needed as the Bassin Petrolu was alive with them. Laurel noted the Slovakian plural as *-y*: as in *dressingy* (mayonnaise and salad oils) *syropy* (soft drinks), and wondered what they did about more than one *whisky* (or would that be catfood?), and delighted in the discovery that *dzem rohliky* were jam rolls.

We stayed on in Bratislava, enjoying the break. We painted ship, talked to friendly people, and always ended up at the Treff with a party, usually musical. One night there was an accordionist, whose bald pate was so attractive to the mosquitoes that the music was punctuated by slaps and curses until someone produced a repellent, probably bought in Vienna. We had combed all the rare pharmacists in the city and found them to be sad 'Central Office' places looking as if they were still state-run, with a few drab-looking bottles and faded packets on lonely shelves. Repellent was unknown, and the concept of a shiny drugstore that makes huge profits on beauty products, health foods and toilet accessories had not arrived in Bratislava.

Nigel Baker, the diplomat, called on us one morning, immaculately dressed, and found our pontoon gangway a bit difficult. We removed the cats' cushion from the best chair, and spent the rest of the morning in stimulating conversation.

Our spare parts arrived within two days and were brought to Milan's Treff by the courier with a customs officer in the passenger seat. We had forgotten about customs, being so long in the Common Market. He required 50% import duty on the value of the spares. We did not have it in cash.

'Never mind,' said the customs officer through a friendly passer-by who translated. 'I see that you need urgently these parts, so take them, and I come back for the duty tomorrow.' *Never* in all our wanderings through almost 40 different countries have we found such a sensible and co-operative attitude. We were very grateful, and Bill installed the water pump impeller straight away. Next day we went to the city to change a Eurocheque and to try to find the Chief Executive of the Slovakian River Transport Authority, to whom we had a letter of introduction. Unfortunately he was away in England, and we ended up with the Harbour-master who obligingly gave us more river chart photocopies, and sold us a copy of the *Indicateur Kilométrique du Danube*, a most valuable reference book published in Russian and French (extra-ordinary, the latter; we saw no sign of the least French influence anywhere along the Danube). It was only later that we found a printing error which deprived us of about 100 kilometres of data.

We did some tourist-style sightseeing in the old part of the city, including the heavy dark stone cathedral of St Martin's which made one think of fortresses, as probably the early cathedrals hereabout were. When the Turks in the days of the Ottoman Empire passed this way to besiege Vienna, they had to remain on the south side of the Danube, as it was in spate, so Bratislava was spared. The siege of Vienna was unsuccessful, and it marked the limit of Turkish conquests in Middle Europe.

The central Post Office in Bratislava was a magnificent building, though the service was less so. The central hall is near-elegant, with its high square clerestory of curved glass, decorated in a style that Bill described as Burnsey-Jonesy Art Nouveau. Laurel thinks she knows what he means; she had been parked in a café as the walk was too far.

Unlike the old city, beetled over by the Castle, where the mediaeval and Renaissance buildings were majestic and manicured, there were beautiful 19th century buildings in the rest of the town but no money for their upkeep. They were shabby and neglected, their ornament damaged, the paint fading and cracking. Their worth shone through the peeling plaster like a Duchess on income support.

Nigel and his fiancée Sasha invited us to dinner, and took us to a country restaurant run by Hungarians. We drove past what must be one of the biggest council housing developments ever. We have forgotten how many thousands of dwellings it contained, but unlike many similar but smaller developments in England and France, say, it has been a most successful estate, perhaps because it accommodates people of all economic and cultural classes. Some MPs live on it as well as doctors, actors, lawyers, bricklayers, factory workers, and so on. It seems that by mixing, an acceptable standard of general good manners is maintained.

The restaurant was by a lake, and on this hot evening we ate outside on the terrace. Repellent was not needed as the terrace was covered with a gigantic mosquito net. It was a good meal; lamb, well cooked, and the conversation enjoyable, ranging far wider than the Danube and its history.

Back at the Treff, it continued unbearably hot. Splashing each other with cold water was only partially effective. Friday was a day to do nothing, though Andrea and Maros, reporters for PRÁÇA, came to interview us, and Vlado took the photographs for it. It became sultry, brooding thunder.

Konstantin visited in the afternoon and found us shutting hatches as black clouds stormed up. He thought the storm would miss us, but we persuaded him to put his bicycle in one of the derelict cabins. Just as well; the storm hit with a tremendous crash and a cloudburst. Between thunder claps Konstantin told us of the Russians who settled on the opposite side of the Danube in September 1968, after the Prague Spring. They had a big military camp there, he said. 'On the riverside there was latrines and showers and everything and we went this side of the river to see them; we are watching what they are doing, and water level doubled overnight, about two metres higher overnight, and next day there was no one Russian!'

'It's marshy over there?' asked Bill.

'Low land, yes,' said Konstantin. 'Used to be forest, but in 1968 it was open area. It was very funny. Made us very happy: Danube is working with us!'

No, the Slovaks do not love the Russians.

Vlado brought down the photos he had taken and a copy of PRAÇA with the article about us in it. There was also an account of the thunderstorm: 38 mm of rain fell in 45 minutes, and there were pictures of cars with water up to the wheel hubs in flooded streets and damage done by the violent winds that had also brought down a tree across our pontoon gangway. Bill had to get the chainsaw out so that Konstantin could get his bicycle through.

Vlado also gave Laurel a copy of a book of works by a Slovakian artist, Albin Brunowsky, a man of talent unknown to her. Vlado, too, was an artist, trapped into a press photographer's job. He gazed at

Laurel soulfully as she communicated her pleasure at the gift, and wrote in it: 'To Mrs Laurel,' and kissed her hand.

After almost a fortnight, on Sunday 16 July we prepared to leave. Bratislava, with its hospitality and friendliness, was a high point of our journey. Milan and Josef waved us goodbye from the floating restaurant, where we had eaten so well and so cheaply, as we slipped downstream on a fine warm morning. The current was running at 8 km/hr, and we were soon at the spot where the river flows off to the right (Hungarian) side, while the navigable channel follows an artificial cut. The cut is part of the Gabçikovo Project, the great barrage and dam that was to have provided hydro-electricity and control the Danube in a joint effort between the Czechoslovaks and the Hungarians under Communist rule, but the Hungarians have pulled out, and the Slovaks have been left to carry out their portion of it by themselves. It is now the cause of a serious dispute between the two countries.

The Slovakian part is finished, but the Hungarians have not only abandoned the project, but have started to demolish what they had already built. This has caused the Slovaks major inconvenience, and considerable extra expense. We have received two different accounts of the squabble, which is almost certain to end in the International Court at the Hague.

Navigation is easy along the cut, which extends 39 kilometres from Kp 1850 down to 1811, and contains a huge lock. The first part, down to Kp 1819, is straight and above the level of the flat countryside.

We had to wait at the lock and made fast to a fine quay and watched while other vessels arrived and waited their turn. There was a light westerly breeze, which Bill had decided was not strong enough to worry about, but close to the quay it raised a surprisingly sharp slop in the water. It was as well it was no stronger.

The lock is at the south-eastern end of a 31 kilometre straight channel which is about 150 metres wide. Unfortunately, strong winds here are predominantly north-westerlies, and these blow exactly along the axis of this channel, raising big waves by the time they get to the lock. Worse, there is no spending ramp at the lock, so the waves are reflected back. A spending ramp, usually a beach, should be placed at the end of stretches like this to absorb wave energy. The omission here is hard to understand, as the result is that the waves build up a static harmonic system, known as *clapotage*. Such waves are short, high, steep, and dangerous.

It was here that Nick Sanders, waiting at the lock, was caught in just these conditions, and his butty was overwhelmed while turning and sank in the channel. By all accounts the Slovakian authorities were first class. They salvaged the barge (we understand they did this free of charge), the incident featured large on Slovakian television, and Nick, after a bad experience, was well looked after.

We strongly advise (endorsed by the Tug Captains) all small craft *not to attempt this cut downwind with a north-west wind of force 4 or over*. That is not a strong wind, so there is a measure of caution in that advice, the sort of caution which has kept us alive in a lifetime of small boat cruising. It allows for the probability (Murphy's Law) that the wind will freshen in the two hour passage, and for the probability that if the boat has to wait (there is nowhere to stop on the way) she may have to turn broadside to the waves near the lock at the very worst possible place. It would not be a penance to wait at Bratislava for the right day, or to anchor at the entrance to the cut. One should try to contact the lockmaster (Russian or German is needed) on VHF Channel 78, and time arrival to minimise waiting outside the lock if there is any north-westing in the wind. This book is not a Navigational Guide, but this advice appears nowhere else at the moment, and we think it important.

Bill watched the Romanian barges entering the lock, spellbound. An ancient tug was towing three 1000 tonne barges behind it on a loose tow rope. Bill speculated what a devil of a job her master would have entering the lock and then stopping with a strong wind behind him. Bill was once a tugmaster; he would not have enjoyed it.

After the lock the river widened; the fairway snaked from one side to the other and smart buoy spotting became necessary. We were also on the lookout for upcoming traffic that might want to pass on the wrong side as they sought the least current, our eyes skinned for the flashing light that indicated blue-flagging. The traffic was changing. There were big Romanian tows, the occasional Dutchman still going strong and spanking smart compared with the Romanians, and quite a few Hungarians. It was all commercial, except for a few speedboats. Every now and then a voice came over the VHF saying something about the Anglitski, or Angulol, which was us. We hoped they were telling their colleagues where we were because we hadn't a prayer of learning Hungarian.

The photocopied plans we got from the port office at Bratislava were very helpful. The originals had been marked in German 'Do not copy'. Lucky we can't read German.

On the Hungarian side of the river people were swimming from the beaches in the hot sun and barbecueing under shady umbrellas. So these were Hungarians!

At 1700 we arrived at Komarno, the Slovakian frontier post on the left bank. There were two pontoons, one either side of the bridge which spans the river. A Romanian tug, *Medias*, was just making fast. This was the first tug from the lower Danube that we had had a chance to lie alongside. We had been repeatedly warned by Slovakian, Austrian, and Dutch masters that we should on no account tangle with the Romanians who had the reputation of stealing the vest from under your shirt. Bill was hungry for information, and thought potential thievery was a modest price to pay for it. He turned short and put *Hosanna* neatly alongside the big tug, but he sent Laurel, as First Mate, ashore to complete the formalities because he might have to lay off if *Medias* wanted to leave. Also he would be better able to keep an eye on any

Romanian schleppers *in Gabçikovo Lock*

light-fingered Romanian. This turned out to be quite a wise move, but not for these reasons.

Medias was large and ancient, about 56 metres long (twice our length) with a low profile and drop-down stern. She had once been painted with a black hull and buff upperworks, like all tugs in the state-owned service NAVROM, but it had been a long time since she had been tickled with a paintbrush. She was indescribably untidy, her decks littered with what appeared to be old furniture and fridges, though a glance through her open doorways showed clean living quarters. She had a well-set-up, taut-spread, tent-like awning over her wheelhouse. She seemed at first sight to be crewed by a crowd of disreputable brigands, wearing the oldest and tattiest clothing imaginable. Her builder's plate showed she had been built longer ago than *Hosanna*. With the exception of the neat awning which would only be noticed by a seaman of the older school, she inspired a confidence rating marginally above zero.

We were to grow very fond of this nautical horror story, and her rakish crew.

• 21 •
GREEN DYNAMITE
Esztergom and Budapest

Laurel had difficulty clambering over *Medias*. With all the junk on deck it was a hazardous exploit, involving ladders up to the bridge and down the other side. The crew were very welcoming, and though they looked as if they would slit a throat for sixpence, a lady crossing their decks brought out the romantic in them; they moved things to help her, and placed a wooden box to assist her over the bulwarks. People were performing their ablutions in open doorways in the heat, a man peered in a mirror through a mask of shaving soap. He was still shaving when she returned half an hour later.

She made it to the pontoon and then up long flights of rough concrete steps to the top of the flood wall. The frontier post was on the road by the end of the bridge, for the river here was the border between Slovakia and Hungary, and the bridge the only crossing in a long way.

The official looked at the ship's papers and said something that included the word *raport*. Laurel was in trouble, no official spoke any of the four languages she is fluent in. Fortunately, standing in the doorway was a tall thin young man with long black locks and a black beard wearing an embroidered velvet waistcoat over a neat white shirt. He spoke English.

'He wants to know where is the *raport*?'

'What *raport*?' said Laurel.

We should have a *raport*. We should have been given one in Bratislava. She told them that we were passed by the police every day for nine days in Bratislava, and no one mentioned a *raport*. We had, of course, never officially checked into Slovakia, and it might have been very difficult to check out, had it not been for Blackbeard. His name was Relu, he was second in command of *Medias* and was very helpful, knowing all about Eastern European Bureaucracy. He had a pad of blank *raports*, and wrote one out for *Hosanna*, purporting to be from Bratislava, which was then stamped, and he then filled in another one which would do for tomorrow, he said. The customs man, a little bemused, seemed to accept this, but now needed *Hosanna*'s ship's stamp on the *raport*. Laurel decided that if Relu had displayed creativity regarding documents, so could she. 'The Captain has it, I must go back to the ship.'
'Yes, you must, because the Captain must also sign the document.'

Back she went, across the *Medias*, more ups and downs, and more stairs, past the man shaving again. Having no stamp, we invented one, the Royal Naval Crown, an old-fashioned wooden typeset block that we had found second-hand in Carcassonne. It looked fearfully authentic, and we used it at all stations thereafter, probably illegally. Relu, who was checking *Medias* out of Slovakia, accompanied Laurel to the soldiers on the bridge where there was another customs post, and they stamped our passports. The last time we had our passports stamped was in mainland China, and that was three travelling years ago. We had got used to crossing borders without all this fuss.

Laurel asked Relu what happened when they went back to Romania through ex-Jugoslavia. He said there was no problem except for the transit tax. 'It is too much money. For the tug and 6 *schleppers*, that's the barges, it is 12,000 dollars'. It wasn't clear whether the tax was by tonnage or length, or the whim of the soldier with the gun. Laurel asked the authorities for permission to stay overnight in the industrial *hafen*. Impossible. This word was another thing we were not used to. We could spend the night on the next pontoon if we paid 100 kroner (about £2) but we MUST NOT GO ASHORE. Relu said that *Medias* could not afford that, and would go off to anchor. Relu whispered: 'You give him a bottle of white wine and there will be no problem about going ashore.' We learned that Relu's favourite phrase was No Problem.

The other pontoon was different to most; it was an old barge with her hold covered in. Her tatty wooden wheelhouse remained at one end. The hull was covered in tar, hung about with huge tractor tyres, but there were bitts for mooring. We were tired and hot, so we stayed on board and had Indonesian fried rice, and enjoyed it.

Just before we began our meal a man who had been fishing when we arrived at the pontoon dashed up with a paper bag full of apricots, and wouldn't stay to be thanked. Everywhere you go you meet kind people.

Next day, Monday 17 July, Bill walked across the bridge to Hungary, to enter, but got his knuckles rapped. He was told very sharply to go back and bring his ship over to the right bank. So we got a reluctant Tansy out of the derelict wheelhouse of the pontoon, where she'd found a comfortable pile of sacks, left the Slovakian side, and crossed over. By now all the frontier people were at the railway station, and Bill had to go in search of them. He found them, but was told to wait at their office. He waited. Bill is not very good at waiting.

When his turn came, he was asked why Laurel was not present? Bring your crew at once. Bill mimed a bad hip. The office was 600 metres from *Hosanna*, and the activity of the previous afternoon had done Laurel's dislocated hip no good at all. The Hungarian officials could not see how anybody in the crew of a ship could be unable to walk half a kilometre. The Dutch skipper of the barge *Martina* helped with translation, and after much hostile tooth-sucking, a party of officers mustered and trooped down to *Hosanna*. Instantly their mood changed. Nobody has ever seen anything like *Hosanna* before, but this time the wonder was poly-evident. They gazed round our comfortable wheelhouse, whistling.

'How many motors?' asked the boss. 'Three? Jesus Maria!' Our library impressed him. We admitted to being writers, it often helps to explain our eccentricities. One of our books had a flamingo on the cover. Ah, Professor Biologica, nodded the officer, sagely, and Bill accepted that designation as being a more innocuous profession in these countries than Retired Naval Officer.

The formalities were done with speed. Laurel asked what Thank You is in Hungarian, the officer was taken with that idea, and wrote it down in six languages, four of them Eastern European, and kissed her hand as he took his leave. A soldier brought back the ship's stamp which Bill had left in their office.

Despite our early start it was mid-morning before we got away, something we were going to have to get used to at almost every stop. We were in Hungary, though the left bank was still Slovakia for a while. We changed the courtesy ensign from red white and blue and the Slav cross, to red white and green, horizontal stripes. To make up time, we used all three engines, but realised we would not reach Budapest that evening as we had hoped.

Fifteen kilometres into Hungary our digital phone 'clocked on' again. We were travelling fast. The left or Slovak bank was low level plain, sparsely populated. The Hungarian side was hilly, with a cliff at the river's edge. One could see which side of the river suffers more from floods, and why Hungary had less to gain from the barrage/dam project. A road ran along the bank on the Hungarian shore, with all that road transport brings; villages, churches, industry, and sandy shores where people could walk and bathe. We decided to stop at the historic city of Esztergom.

Esztergom is unmistakable. You know you are there. The immense cathedral, built on Castle Hill, towers over the Danube Bend, and dominates the country from horizon to horizon. Unfortunately, it presents its worst profile to the Danube; the dome looks far too large for the marble box it sits on, and there is an absence of harmony. The proportions are better seen from landwards, where two wings can be seen to flank the central box, minimising the dome.

After poking our nose into a neat creek that would have been ideal for us, but was blocked by a badly moored boat, we made fast to a pontoon belonging to the Hungarian State Shipping Line. Tourist and hotel boats come to Esztergom, and it is well supplied with pontoons.

Bill went for a walk along an elegant waterfront which formed a treed and grassy park below the high stone walls of the city. He crossed a small bridge which spanned a tributary of the Danube, and found the agent's office. He had more or less to drag the gentleman in to pay our bill, which was not very much. The amount seemed to be debatable, so they debated it.

When he returned he found Laurel had been reading guide books

The cathedral at Esztergom, Hungary

and was determined to walk up to the cathedral. It was a long climb up the hill even to reach it, punctuated by several beers. Halfway up Castle Hill, hiding behind a stone rampart, we found a Saint, sitting on a bench and holding what we thought at first was an accordion. You could sit on the bench next to him and chat if you felt like it. Laurel did. The accordion turned out to be a model of a church, and both the Saint and the bench were made of sunwarmed stone.

Inside the church, built in 1846 on the site of previous churches for a thousand years, one had an oddly secular feeling, as of a huge marble bathroom. No soaring ribs or columns to carry the eye upwards and take your spirit through lacy vaulting to heaven awaiting. This was a pink stone box with the lid firmly on.

The best thing in it was a side altar to St Istvan (Stephen), born and crowned Hungary's first king, here in Esztergom. His skull, without its bottom jaw, rested comfortably as a kitten on a cushion in a glass-fronted box, with an arm bone leisurely draped in front of it. The box had two clips, one on each side, for carrying purposes probably; they looked like little hands beckoning you eagerly forward. The carpet in front of the skull was spread with coins. We added a few.

We climbed and counted 403 steps to the top of one of the biggest cathedrals in southern Europe. It was a hard climb and the last bit was a stone spiral staircase, well controlled to limit the number of people at any one time, but increasingly giddymaking. The controllers looked at Laurel's walking stick, and looked at her, and we could see them imagining how to get her down if she failed to make it. She managed, with determination. The view at the top over the Danube Bend, where the great river turns majestically from East to South, and the hills of the Magyar Massif rolled away into infinity on the Slovakian shore, was immense and worth the effort.

There was so little room on the parapet that the guide had a chair outside it, back legs sawn short to accommodate the slope of the roof, perched above a sickening drop to tiny rooftops and dinky cars in the streets below. Laurel had to stop looking down, and concentrate on the horizon. East Anglians are not used to heights.

We then ate at a fish restaurant, the Szalma Czarda, sitting outside on forms at rustic tables, our evening enlivened by an atrocious Magyar threepiece; zither and two violins, one old, one young, both untalented. The old fiddler had swivelling eyes, until they fixed on a couple of dogs knotted under a tree, and stayed there. His playing style was acrobatic but untuneful; he played his instrument upside down, on its back, and the right way round, and with a tempo that varied with the activities of the dogs. The young one did the fast bits, missing half the notes and landing on wrong ones like a cat on hot cinders.

The food was new to us. We had bean soup; everyone eats soup even in summer, as in Slovakia. Laurel ate carp. Forget the day's catch fresh from the Danube, it was frozen. In one form or another it is the staple fish of the river throughout its navigable length. Bill indulged himself on roast boar with mushrooms, chestnuts and cream. Everything had paprika in it; you learn to like it. We drank a white Tokay. The bill was 1650 Forints (at that time 192 Fts ≡ £1).

We went to town early next morning. Bill badly needed a chart, the ones provided by the Bratislavs having finished at Komarno. Essentially we were now driving blind, depending on our reactions to the channel markers. These were not always reliable as the channel meandered about the river bed, and the method of marking is idiosyncratic to the Danube. The buoyage system is normal, that is to say one passes green conical buoys to port when going downstream, and leaves the red can shapes to starboard. The buoys consist of small shapes about half a metre high, mounted on small boat-shaped floats.

They are widely spaced, and looking up sun in the morning, for example, can be very hard to spot.

Other channel markers are on the banks. There are the kilometre posts, the *pegels*, and other posts indicating 'the channel is on this side', or 'here it crosses to the other side'. Sometimes there is a solitary leading mark on which to steer. In sea-going channels, these consist of two posts, each with a different topmark, and one has to keep them in line. In the Danube there is only one post, and it can only be effective if one starts off in the right place. If you miss a post, you can be in trouble. *And* one does miss posts, *and* one is usually unaware of the fact, for the posts are not large and are set back from the water's edge, and by summer they are generally overgrown by a rich burgeon of flora. Another hazard is that many of the posts are erected with a topmark that is only differentiable when abreast of it. Thus you reach the post on which you have been steering only to find that it is in fact a kilometre post. Fortunately the river level was still about a metre above datum so we did not take the ground in Hungary, but that was more a question of good luck and quick reactions than good navigation. One had to maintain a high standard of alertness.

In Esztergom the 'boat shop' was closed. It said on the door that it would open at 0830, but by 0930 was still closed.

No maps.

The shops were more interesting and well furnished than those in Slovakia; we found the mosquito repellent we needed. A virulent and powerful lotion is essential in the Danube valley. You can put up all the mosquito screens you like, but they still form up in phalanxes and batter their way through in their desperate thirst for human blood.

There was a cheerful market with fresh fruit and vegetables; for the first time for ages we found soft fruit, gooseberries, apricots, raspberries and redcurrants.

We left Esztergom and passed the junction with the Ipoly river. Here Slovakia ended, and both banks became Hungarian. We mustered all the data we could on Nagymarós (the g is soft, and the s is pronounced as sh), the Hungarian end of the Slovakian barrage/dam at Gabçikovo. When the Communist regime fell the projects continued until the first free elections in Hungary, and the emergence of a Green party.

We believe in hydro-electricity as a renewable, continuous, non-polluting source of power that is inestimably preferable to burning hydrocarbons, or splitting atoms, which are at the moment the only viable alternatives. Nagymarós is on a sharp S-bend in the river where there are extensive sandbanks. The proposal did not involve flooding vast quantities of land; it would have raised the river level above the dam only as far as the flood level. The scheme was expensive, the Greens held a balance of power and were against it, and those in charge of the new Hungary pulled out of it to buy votes. Now it seems they are regretting it. They will get no hydro-electric power, and must pay a huge indemnity to the Austrian contractors. Worse, the Hungarians are demolishing their part at Nagymarós. Everything was being blown up with dynamite. We had to let them know we were coming so they could suspend the explosions while we passed; demolition was in full swing.

The Captains had advised us to radio ahead on channel 16 when we reached Kp 1705, and warn Nagymarós Control we were an English ship on the way down. The light at Kp 1700, near Dömös, would give us a red or green signal. We must be careful, the explosions were substantial.

The lights were red, visible a good way away. We went astern to remain geographically stopped. The current was not strong, 6 km/hr. We called up Nagymarós radio, who spoke only German and Hungarian (the most useful phrase in our book was 'I do not speak much Hungarian') and were not easy to understand, but they finally noted our 'pozitzion', and just as Bill began to get frustrated enough to creep round the corner and have a look (it was a blind corner but the river was still wide here) the lights changed to green. Instant full ahead.

We hoped we would not be blown up if we proceeded. That would have been a shame, because it was a beautiful morning, and the hills and scenery recalled the Wachau in Austria.

The river round the corner appeared almost completely blocked. The area involved in the demolition was that of a small town. Buoys led us via a tortuous channel that must have been a nightmare for big barges. The bottleneck dramatically increased the current; suddenly we were belting along with 15 km/hr or thereabouts (there was no opportunity to measure) and Bill reduced our engines to slow. There were huge works and concrete everywhere. We got through the worst part, waved to the control tower, passed a hotel ship, and had time to look back and contemplate what was going on.

Green lunacy can hardly go further than this, one would think; after having constructed all that, to be now blowing it up, and doubling the disturbance, cannot be sensible. If it were based on the preservation of the natural environment, on habitats for this or that bird or animal, or on peace and quiet: whatever the justification for originally opposing the scheme, there could be no possible justification for its dismantling. The damage to the environment had already been done, the destruction was compounding the damage, making it worse, prolonging the agony, when the best solution must have been to finish it quickly and restore the land as fast as possible while enjoying cheap, clean power.

We neared Budapest, and the river became populated with canoeists. Holiday homes climbed the banks, and a horse was up to its hocks in water, happy on this hot day. On little beaches under the shade of trees where speedboats had drawn up, people were having picnics. Hungary has no coastline, and this is their only opportunity to get on the water, apart from Lake Balaton.

We passed Szentendrei-sziget (St Andrew's island) and the old town of Szentendre, an artists' colony. The basins marked 'yacht marina' that we passed seemed empty and deserted. We had been advised at Esztergom to try a marina on the entry into Budapest, so on the approach we shot under Arpadhid (Arpad's Bridge), turned sharp right on to a reverse course, and approached a very unlikely looking marina in a narrow channel inside Hajógyari-sziget. Our reception was lukewarm, but they moved an American yacht to make us a space, shore power was forthcoming, and they promised to crane out the Mini the next day. There was a bar on shore inside an enormous wooden barrel and we went along for cold draught beer, and some dreadful wine in a plastic cup.

The marina boss's son had been recently in Belgrade, taking part in an international wet-bike championship. This contrasted oddly with the news on BBC that the UN were demanding that the Serbs account for 13,000 missing refugees. If the Serbs were wet-biking they might not be killing anyone, at least not on the river. It made the Danube sound pleasantly normal. This championship was the first indication that UN sanctions against Serbia were far from effective.

• 22 •
JUST LOOKING
Budapest to Dunaföldvar

The Mini was craned out. It looked odd 40 feet above our heads, but the quay was over 30 feet high, a precaution against floods. The battery was flat, but we put that right, removed the spiders' webs, and drove into the city; not that easy, as the road following the right bank of the river has few turnings. We headed towards the famous Adam Clark iron bridge, erected 150 years ago when Scots engineering led the world. Mr Clark's skill is still commemmorated in the square that bears his name.

Failing to get on the Clark bridge, we crossed by the next one down after dashing the wrong way down a one-way street which went unnoticed. We suspect nobody pays attention to one-way streets in Budapest. Our destination was the British Embassy. Budapest is the capital city of the country adjacent to Serbia, from which sanctions against Serbia were administered. As much trade passes on the river, they must know what is going on.

Bratislava restored our faith in those who represent our country abroad: the Embassy at Budapest removed it. Whereas we had felt in Bratislava that the building was dodgy, it was clear that a Security Officer with manic dedication had been at work in Budapest. Everyone we wanted to talk to was unavailable. We were put in a waiting room and could converse with staff only by telephone, as if we had some unspeakable disease. To whom could we give our information on the Danube, in return for some of theirs? There was massive disinterest. They thought perhaps someone from the Military Attaché's office.

We were asked to discuss information about river traffic and sanctions, which ought to have been classified, with a Flight-Sergeant in the Royal Air Force, over a telephone labelled 'This is not a secure telephone'. It was soon apparent anyway that he was not even clear that the Danube actually flowed through Hungary and on to Serbia.

Bill challenged him directly: 'You know nothing about this subject, do you?' He admitted that as it was not his brief, no, not a lot. 'Well, find someone who does,' Bill ordered, putting on his military voice. He was at last allowed to speak (on the same insecure phone) to a lady from the consular department. She knew where the Danube was; and told us that a year had passed since the last report of Serbian piracy, by either the New Byzantium or the White Rose groups, and gave us some names in the European Union Sanctions Control at Mohács who would certainly know more.

We never got further than a hot, claustrophobic waiting room so small that its height was the most substantial dimension, its biggest door being that of a safe, while a television camera had its beady eye on our every shuffle and fidget.

We cooled down with iced coffee in the square at Gerbeaud Cukraszda, a patisserie as famous as Harry's Bar in Venice. Its *fin-de-siècle* décor had a run-down air, and the service was poor, but the coffee was good. We drove back, managing it with the Mini intact, which was no mean feat. The increase in traffic volume has greatly outgrown Hungarian traffic engineering, or, put another way, a large number of Hungarians had become prosperous enough to own a car, but in their enthusiasm had not learned how to drive.

We drove next day some 200 kilometres down to Mohács on the Jugoslav border to see for ourselves what traffic was going through. Driving out of Budapest is not easy. We had to cross the entire city, and roadsigns were absent or invisible among the advertisements. In the countryside dipped headlights must be used even in daylight, but with the way Hungarians drive even this measure cannot make much contribution to road safety. With a few false turns we found the right road through deerhaunted woods and later the plains of the Pustza over on our left, beyond the cornfields and plantations of sunflowers.

Having discovered that there were some British Customs Officers attached to the Sanctions team, we hoped to pick their brains. This would be the nearest we could get without actually crossing the border. There were signs that the quiet period which had interrupted the fighting in Jugoslavia had come to an end. We listened to every news broadcast in the BBC World Service, marvelling that with so much apparent fighting, there were so few factual reports, and so much second-hand opinion relayed from cities far from the action. It is only when faced oneself with the firing line that one becomes acutely perceptive of such nuances.

At Mohács it took us a while running to earth the two officers of HM Customs and Excise attached to the Danube Mission; one was out examining a barge and the other was preparing to return to Britain, time expired. When our man was finally off duty, he turned out to be a gem of a fellow. Over a beer he reassured us that there was considerable traffic going through. Of course he did not know what conditions were actually like further down, but all this talk of barges with windows covered with armour plate and ships being boarded by pirates was nonsense. Of course the Serbs boarded the convoys and tried to buy diesel. It was the UN's job to prevent them, but they all knew that evasion took place. He outlined the procedure we would have to follow at Mohács when we arrived in *Hosanna*, introduced us to the officers in charge of the operation (for the UN: a friendly Dane, and for the Western European Union, who did all the dirty work, a preoccupied, but not unfriendly, German).

The visit had been worthwhile, but when we returned to the Mini, parked in the shade of a tree while we had a pleasant riverside lunch, we found we'd left our headlamps on and the battery was flat.

We had jump leads with us (it's that sort of car). Bill tried to solicit a boost from a passing pickup, but not speaking much Hungarian he found he had accosted some sort of breakdown gang. One that causes them, not cures them. One thin villain with carboned hands, and a fat one with a black beard. They lifted the bonnet lid, and made a half-hearted attempt to start us with the jump leads. The engine fired, but did not take. Big mistake, Sandor, how dreadful, we nearly succeeded. They signed to Bill to get in and try to start, and the moment he did so one of them ripped out a bunch of wires, saying triumphantly 'Starter kaput'.

Bill got out and slammed the bonnet shut. He then invited them to leave, though those were not the words he used, since he was now faced with a horrifying mess of electrical spaghetti without a circuit diagram. He tried empirically to re-connect the torn out wires, but with only a basic knowledge of the principles, he could not reconstruct the wiring harness. It would be necessary to find someone who had enough knowledge to eliminate obviously wrong connections.

Our British Customs Officer had gone back on duty, and was out of reach. Laurel recalled the Bank Manager who had changed a Eurocheque before lunch and spoke some English. She went to ask his advice. He was distressed by our experience, allowed Bill to wash his hands in the bank washroom and made a few phone calls after consulting his chief clerk. A taxi was summoned. It took us two kilometres to a scruffy garage, doors open but deserted. There was an old bus seat on the floor. Laurel sat on it and we waited.

When two young and grubby men came, Bill was able to indicate the problem by sign language and drawings. After a pause all of us piled into a Citröen with torn upholstery and regained the car park. They worked on the Mini's innards like surgeons, talking quietly and testing as they went. It took an hour of thorough, conscientious, logical work to sort out and re-connect the wires, the mechanic tutting away steadily. Bill went to buy a new battery from a motoring discount shop nearby, and vroom! away she went. Starter kaput, my eye! Our benefactors charged us only 1000Fts (£5), for an hour's work for two men.

We paused to thank the Bank Manager; smiles all round, and we set off, too late to be back in Budapest in daylight, so Bill was faced with finding his way through poorly lit suburbs in the dark.

Dusk came when we were well short of Budapest. It seemed that every Hungarian car had its headlights adjusted to illuminate the drivers of on-coming vehicles, something that did not matter so much in daylight, but was lethal in the dark.

We stopped for an evening meal at a *csárda* by the roadside, and were fascinated by a swallow which had built its nest indoors in a corner of the restaurant. Through a fellow diner we asked about it as we watched it fly in and out of the window or round the room, its mouth full of mosquitos on the return journey, and crawl into its mud nest of peeping nestlings. 'Yes, it comes every year, and we have to

The Calvinist Church, Budapest

leave the window open for it. It keeps the room free of mosquitos. I do not know what we would do without it.' We got home late after getting lost, as expected, in the suburbs.

We did little next day except running repairs, and Bill talked to the marina owner who turned up in his large new Mercedes. He had himself been down to Belgrade for the wet-bike festival. The traffic on the Danube, which had been kept over to one side of the channel during the championships, had seemed normal. The Serbs, he said, were OK, if left to solve their problems their way.

We did not take to him. He was thickset, bronzed, blond and brushcut, and drove his enormous speedboat past us at 30 knots in the narrow creek, making a punishing wash, which is bad boat manners, and we are wary of anyone who messes with wet-bikes. We rested. With the temperature at 33°C, we had barely enough energy to think up a wet-bike repellent that wouldn't land us in jail.

Next day we had a hot, exhausting shopping drive towards the city. We found only a shabby supermarket. It had things that we wanted which we knew would not be obtainable further down, but the fruit and vegetables were too withered to be worth buying.

We wanted to dine out in Budapest which all the guide books praise for food, atmosphere, and value. Various Hungarian boat owners recommended the Casino in the city centre. Bill did not want to drive again in Budapest, especially after a good meal, so we went by taxi. We dined well, accompanied this time by a first class Magyar band. The return taxi driver was a pirate. They have you over a barrel on your return from a restaurant; the alcohol limit for driving is 0%.

We had now reached a point in the journey where bridge clearances were higher, and we could start replacing such things as radar aerials, which we had demounted for the low bridges on the French canals, and had kept demounted because clearances on the RMD Kanal and upper Danube had been reduced by the floods. Bill also started getting our new mast in order, and adapting and checking the arrangements for stepping it, for it was still where it had been man-handled before starting our journey, and the temporary absence of the Mini made it easier to get at.

Laurel was groggy the next day, 25 July, so Bill drove into the city to draw money. It was difficult to find a bank which would cash Eurocheques, though there were private change bureaux, who would do it at an exorbitant price. It meant queuing at the bank, but it was safest. Travellers in Eastern Europe should know that banking transactions are accompanied by wicked commissions that appear on one's home bank statement months later. The best form of travellers' cheques are dollar bills in lowish denominations, higher denominations being suspect because there are many forgeries about. Deutschmarks are good currency, too, but not pounds, francs or guilders etc, they being too rarely handled to be freely convertible.

The Hungarians we met were, with notable exceptions, the most bad-tempered, bad-mannered, greedy and commercially corrupt Europeans we came across. The Budapest exceptions, most of whom we met at The Barrel, stood out a mile. There were few in-betweeners.

We had generally been unable to communicate much. We speak English, French and Italian, and a smattering of Greek and Spanish, but any Hungarian with a foreign language at all, and there were few, usually spoke German. We had one interesting afternoon sitting by The Barrel, talking to an Hungaro-German, Ferenc, who had much information and gossip about the way Hungary was going since the fall of communism. Not much change, we gathered, except that the ordinary people were worse off, while the ex-communist officials could exercise their cupidity openly and to a greater extent than ever before. True, there were signs of prosperity about, but the people who were succeeding at the moment were self-employed in businesses that involved little capital investment with high cash turnover. The site of the marina we were in, for instance, was the old state shipyard which had been auctioned off for private development. And are you surprised, said Ferenc bitterly, that the successful buyer had been a senior official of the old party? Certainly the gentleman had become prosperous, with his Mercedes and his speedboat, and dealerships in waterskiing and wet-bikes, and a blatant and vulgar display of wealth. No wonder those not in posts to enable them to jockey for power and feather their nests before and during the change were generally discontented. We sensed the dormant seeds of future trouble.

Hungary, once the great imperial power of Europe, has lost much land after the last few wars. There are substantial populations of Hungarian speakers in Slovakia, Romania, and in Jugoslavia. There is a strong political will to 'bring home' these folk, who are not always well-treated by their foster countries. It would not surprise us if trouble in Hungary (or Romania, which we come to later) succeeds that in Jugoslavia. Western Europe, and particularly the European Union, should distance itself politically, if not from a humanitarian viewpoint, from Eastern Europe until they have sorted out their sub-surface problems. History shows us that we are bound to back the wrong side. We always do.

The young Hungarian girls were startlingly attractive. We had read in a guide book that Westerners might be astonished at the readiness with which the young exchanged minor body fluids in public. Given the way the girls dressed in the hot weather, perhaps we should not have been surprised. Not only did they dress provocatively, but they moved in an uninhibited consciously feminine way. Bill hadn't seen anything like it for years.

The mail arrived, freeing us to move on.

We re-loaded the Mini. The blond boss charged us for the use of the crane. He was the only one in the whole voyage to do so.

We sailed at 0830 on Wednesday 26 July on the last leg before the border with Serbia. Laurel had been attacked by qualms, and began to hide valuables. The blond boss's flaunting of gold chains and Rolex was clearly resented by his underlings. We did not have such things, but we did have some attractive boat equipment and, since *Hosanna* is our home, some valued possessions. A low and modest profile seemed in order among peoples envious of the West.

We sailed through Budapest, past the Hungarian parliament building like a multi-coloured wedding cake, and under elegant bridges. Budapest has some lovely buildings, a few awful ones, but its position athwart the river forces the assembly into a whole whose effect is strikingly beautiful.

Apart from the marina, we could have stopped at one of several private pontoons in the town, all probably better and cheaper, for the marina over-charged for the moderate facilities it provided. However, we could not have landed the Mini over a pontoon.

At Kp 1645, downstream of Szabadsaghid, the fourth bridge after Arpadhid (a double cantilever modestly resembling the Forth Bridge) a pontoon on the left permits a short free stop to visit the market. Somebody must stay on board to move if a priority boat arrives, so Laurel braved the raging traffic, crossed the road and disappeared alone into wildest Budapest.

She spent an hour at the market and returned flushed with success. It had been an excellent market, and the traders were honest: she had carelessly left behind at one stall the change from a huge note, worth about £50, and on her despairing return to the stall there was no trouble, the money had been put aside for her.

We slipped straight away and went downstream with two engines, making good 15 km/hr, which indicated a current of 6 km/hr. It was an uneventful, quiet day in rather a dull stretch of river.

At 1500 we entered the basin at the new port of Donaujvàros and circled round it, but it turned out to be a loading quay for chemicals and grain; and the noise, smell and dust persuaded us to move on.

Our expensive Hungarian charts, bought at the Budapest marina, showed a yacht mooring at Dunaföldvar, at Kp 1561. If it ever existed, there was no sign of it now, but there was a converted barge moored as if it were a pontoon. We sidled up to it and made ourselves fast at about teatime. Tousled young heads popped out of portholes, and after a short period during which reasoning and perception slowly returned to their sleepy brains they made us welcome. It was only then that we realised we had moored next to a night-club belonging, apparently, to a Hungarian version of the Club 18–30.

The sleepyheads at 1630 were explained; clearly they stayed up all night, and would undoubtedly play disco music at a decibel count off our scale of tolerance. Could we face it? Bill decided it was better than trying to find somewhere else. If the noise became unbearable during the night, we could cast off and anchor as the river was getting wider, and other barges were moored in trots here and there close to the banks.

We walked ashore and found a grim war memorial, with many names on it; First World War, judging by the bayonets. It was very different from the memorials beloved by England and France, typically an angel trying to sheathe a sword while supporting a quietly dying soldier. Here were men with contorted and savage faces, there was no pulling back from the horror of war, no victory, no glory, no angels.

And, dear God, we would soon be in Serbia, after a stop at the border, Mohács. The news from Bosnia worsened every day: Bihac was under attack by the Serbs, and ethnic cleansing was rife. Still, Bihac was 250 kilometres from the Danube. Would Londoners feel an immediate threat from a bombardment in Sheffield?

We distracted ourselves from gloomy thoughts by eating at a fish restaurant close by. We ate zander, as usual, but cooked in batter. It was cheap and satisfactory.

We discovered with pleasure that the night-club would be closed that night. There were a few youngsters having a drink in the cavernous interior which was decorated in matt black and lit by pulsating spotlights that created a most disturbing sensation. The young people themselves were well-mannered and pleasant, and we passed a peaceful night.

We had difficulty finding Tansy in the morning; she had found a delightful bush. This delayed a planned early start, but we were under way by 0740, up sun, as always. The channel is winding here, and it required two of us, one steering while the other peered ahead through our naval binoculars, which are fitted with graded sunfilters, looking for buoys and marks. Difficulties eased as the sun climbed. Markers seemed to become haphazard after Budapest; maintenance had been skimped since the Jugoslav problem had reduced traffic, and some kilometre posts were missing. A flashing light ahead frightened us till we realised that it was the sun glinting off the buckets of a dredger.

'Just after the next buoy there should be a kilometre post,' said Bill. 'See it?'

Nude sunbathers shouldn't sit near kilometre posts if they don't want to be surprised by a pair of binoculars. 'There it is,' said Laurel. 'Move over, madam... it's 1548'.

At Kp 1506, by Fajsz, a voice came over VHF channel 16 calling: '*Hosanna*! Güte Reisen!' This heartwarming message must have come from a dredger moored on the opposite shore, since no one else was in sight. We waved a response, and Laurel broadcast a 'Danke schön'.

We were on the last lap before the Serbian border. Good wishes were desperately welcome.

• 23 •

WAITING FOR *REVISION*
Mohács to Bezdan

It was turning out better than we hoped. As we approached Mohács, we saw our old friend *Medias* moored a kilometre above the town, and we went alongside them. They were poised to take eight *schleppers* to Romania. Relu was delighted to see us again, and we were glad to see him. 'You join our convoy through Jugoslavia,' said Relu. 'No problem.' They were awaiting orders, so we could lie alongside them. One of our cats jumped on board the tug: 'Cat is welcome,' said Relu. 'We have mouse.'

Medias was on the right, Mohács bank, and the *schleppers* were anchored on the other side. The crew asked us to stand off while she went over to give them their orders. We would be going tomorrow, Friday, it seemed, after police, customs, immigration and the Sanctions inspection team had all checked us, a process known and dreaded as *REVISION*. We stood off and waited.

Relu, coming back from the town with a tin of Coke, waved us back alongside again, quite cross. We should have waited until HE said. He drives the ship, he wasn't there, so how could the ship go without him? There is something odd here. The Captain almost never appears, and rarely drives. Relu, First Mate, does everything, and seems to make all the decisions. He is maybe 24, and knows his trade, but has one more examination to take before he is a Master.

After several more false alarms *Medias* stayed put, and Relu went over on the ferry with the orders.

Later the Monitor and Relu came to look at *Hosanna*. The Monitor is a relic from the political agent (the Kommissar) that all ships used to carry. He wore respectable clothes, sometimes a smart suit. His job now was to see sanctions respected and the company's money well spent, if it was spent at all; Relu said ruefully there was no cash for paint, which explained the shabbiness of Romanian tugs.

Relu loved our boat. On $6 a day pay, and newly married, he was saving up to buy a cargo boat; he fancied a Dutch one; and then he would trade up and down the 1000 km of the Romanian Danube. There was plenty of work for such a boat, and he would see his new wife oftener than on these long journeys up to Vienna. Sometimes he was away for two to three months. The Monitor also spoke English, and between them they gave us the lowdown on Jugoslavia. They told us the truth about the diesel pirates. We learned how to cope with the bureaucrats and the military. The information was contrary to the official version, and partly at variance with what we could glean from news sources, and was to prove accurate and invaluable. In the BBC coverage of war-torn-Jugoslavia, no one seemed to bother about the Danube, its traffic, and its sailors, which left a distorted view.

Relu explained the convoy system. They had gathered two tows of eight *schleppers* each, laden with 16,000 tonnes of grain from Germany, Hungary and Austria, bound for Syria. It was agreed to be a sensible precaution to go down the river in their company. They would drive from 0500 until 2100, and we should follow. Then they would turn the tow and anchor for some sleep. There would be no need for us to anchor, we could lie alongside *Medias*. Bill worried whether we could keep up. 'Oh, sure,' said the Monitor. 'We go only 10 kph.'

'At Kp 1202 the Serb *Nafta* boats will come,' said Relu. They would demand diesel, sometimes, we had heard, with threats, because of sanctions. Relu wrote down the Serb for 'Sorry, friend, no diesel.' *Nemo nafta, Kuskrie.*

'There will be no problem,' he said. Not with the 20 brown and hefty lads on this convoy, villainous looking thugs all, though with us they were gentle as kittens.

We rang our daughter.

'You're going on then?' she said.

'Yes, our feelings are very positive, there shouldn't be any problems as far as we can tell; we thought we'd let you know, just before you fly to Paris and on to Montserrat.'

'Oh-umm,' she said, 'I might not go to Montserrat, the volcano there has just erupted. But we'll go to Paris, anyway.'

'After that terrorist bomb on the Paris Metro?' we said.

'Yes, well--'

'And you're worried about *us* going through Jugoslavia?'

'What it is to have irresponsible parents!' she wailed, but she was laughing. 'Do be careful.'

How often we had said that to our children. We had had to hold our breaths while they rode motorbikes, went through a commune phase, skated lightly over the drug scene, and in one case crossed the Atlantic in a light aircraft.

'Don't worry,' we said. (And how often had the children said that to us?) 'If anything should happen, like your volcano erupting, you're not to blame. We are over eighteen, and this is our motorbike. We've done our homework. All will be well.'

Our young also forget that once we were children in a dangerous place: Britain in wartime, and that unless one was away fighting, or being bombed, almost everything else was normal, or became so. You accepted it. Shortages were normal. Carrying your gasmask was normal. One egg a week was normal. Going down to the air-raid shelter when the siren went was normal. People were born, got married and died in bed. Laurel got measles, her brother had his appendix out. Life goes on in wartime. Even on the Danube.

It's very much a waiting game, this *REVISION*. We are up at 0630 for Bill to tighten the auxiliary machinery belts. Tansy is absent again, but turns up for breakfast just before 'colours' at 0800. We are in no hurry, but *Medias* has again to go out to visit her *schleppers*, so *Hosanna* moves out to let her go at 1035. We transfer to the customs pontoon to start formalities. *Medias* will meet us there and we will all go through *REVISION*: the papers, customs, police and sanctions checks; together. It is Friday 28 July. Croat and Bosnian forces have cut the Serb supply line to Krajina.

Bill hates starting any great enterprise on a Friday.

We wait, ignored by authority, despite camping at the office, where Laurel has learnt to commandeer one of the few chairs, since no one will offer her one. During the day three large, laden Ukrainian convoys cleared through upstream, and we have to re-berth outside a Bulgarian tug, the *Stara Planina*. It is evident we are low priority.

At noon we see the friendly Customs Officer, and ask him what usually happens. 'Oh, it takes forever,' he says. 'It takes ages for *Medias* to move her barges over here, then we'll be a long time giving them the rummaging to make sure they aren't breaking sanctions; it all takes a lot of time.'

Medias moves her barges backwards down the Danube a kilometre and anchors them about 200 yards astern of us, a tricky manoeuvre, and we wait for her to come and clear.

By 1700 nothing has happened. We expect to go if done by 1900; there would still be enough daylight to get to the anchorage near the border post.

Waiting, waiting, waiting. And the adrenalin running a bit high. By 1800, the inspection team have taken two hours on each of the first two Ukrainian tows. We collar our friend when he comes off the second one and say 'What's going on? Have you done *Medias* yet?' And he says, 'No, we're doing the Ukrainians. It's not our job to make the roster list, the Hungarians do that. We just follow what they tell us.' We suspect that the Ukrainian agent went this morning with a present for the Hungarians, so the Ukrainians have bought priority.

It is becoming clear that by the time *Medias*'s tow has been rummaged it will be too late to go, so we get permission to leave the pontoon and lie alongside one *of Medias*'s *schleppers*. We are made to understand that by associating with the Romanians, we are considered mad, criminal, or both. No one in their right mind goes near the Romanians.

We dine on pork and beans, watching and listening to the barge-tow. There are eight *schleppers*, each occupied by a couple of crew, or a family. Their plating is dented and rusty. On deck there's an assortment of driftwood and old wire and rope that mustn't be thrown away. There are chicken coops, and the trundle for cutting firewood, and rabbit hutches, and old boats and furniture and all sorts of come-in-handy things, like a bathtub. There's a wheelhouse aft because they steer even though they have no engines; and they each have an anchor and windlass. There's an array of six stovepipe chimneys on each barge. Four are domestic (central and eastern Europe can be icy in winter) and the others are for generators which no longer work because they can't get the spares, so the barges are lit by flickering oil-lamps at night.

At the front of some wheelhouses is a veritable kitchen garden, with vines growing up to shade it. We came to realise how difficult it was for them to get ashore to shops when they were almost always at anchor, and that the goods in Hungary, Austria and Germany were in any case beyond their means. When they went ashore they were diligent pickers-up of abandoned trifles, some of them slightly before abandonment, hence their reputation.

The river is wide by Mohács, over 500 metres in places, especially to the southern end of the town. It is shallow, but deep enough to provide anchorages and turning room for the large tow-convoys waiting there. Upstream of the town there are grain silos and loading quays, for we are in the fertile plains of Hungary. The town has an elegant frontage, though most of it is hidden from the river by flood walls. There is a hotel, with a large stork's nest, still occupied by five storklings, on top of its chimney. As the nest took only four birds, the fifth sat on the H in 'Hotel'. This hotel was occupied by UN and WEU personnel, present in great numbers. A steep ramp for a busy car-ferry ran down to the river, and a pleasant restaurant-bar with a raised terrace overlooked it. There were customs posts, and police offices. At one time the Jugoslav customs office had been here to speed up proceedings, but since Sanctions, the Jugoslavs had retired behind their own borders, and the WEU were occupying their building. On the waterfront was a humming textile factory.

Ashore, the town was clean, well-kept, and mostly newly-built with some architectural flair. There was evidence of prosperity. It did not take much probing to discover that there were a great many newly enriched inhabitants of Mohács and district, whose wealth had no evident explanation. It was the centre of a substantial sanctions-busting industry.

There were sanctions not only against Serbia, which are the better known, but also against Croatia. The recent Jugoslav problem erupted into open slaughter after Germany, against the advice of her European partners, recognised the break-away Croatian republic. There are historical reasons why she did so, and it was the revival of this history that fuelled old hatreds which might otherwise have stayed buried, or at least quiescent.

When Germany invaded Jugoslavia during the Second World War, the Catholic Croatians were their allies against the Orthodox Serbs. It was often the Croatians who committed the atrocities against their fellow-countrymen, or who betrayed them; they were the quislings of southern Europe. It is to Josep Broz Tito's credit that he forbade

Mohács – centre

reprisals after the war and worked towards reconciliation, and tragic that his works have been undone.

There is thus common ground between Croatia and Germany, as well as an old alliance between Germany and Hungary. It was probable, or at least possible, that Germany was supplying arms and material to Croatia to support the push that the Croatians were about to make in the Krajina. Where else did the materials come from? Some evidence was there to be seen, and given that the sanctions team was German led, and German manned to about 50%, we feel that Germany has some explaining to do. Bill, who has some experience of fighting terrorism, and of enforcing blockades, spent some spare time ferreting about. It was not difficult; sanctions were held in such contempt locally that much cross-border evasion was being openly carried on.

On the river, however, all traffic must be inspected to make sure that no strategic materials were entering Jugoslav waters. The inspection was rigorous, and included an estimate of how much diesel fuel was on board the ship. Documents were prepared under seal, and had to be re-presented at Kalafat, across the far Jugoslavian border. There the ship's contents would be checked against the sealed manifest, an allowance made for the fuel used in transit, and the ship, provided there were no anomalies, cleared for onward passage. It was a lengthy and apparently foolproof system; we discovered later that it was ineffective.

Before one could be inspected one had to wait because not many vessels could be processed in one day. The Hungarian authorities were officially in charge, because this was their territory after all, the

WEU being there as reinforcements. It became clear that the Hungarians resented all these foreigners on their territory. Co-operation seemed to be at a formal, rather than a friendly level. The Hungarians did the paperwork according to whim (or bribery) rather than by logic or chronological order. As soon as their border paperwork was done for a particular vessel or convoy, the WEU team leapt into action: about a dozen uniformed or overalled men and women, most carrying side-arms or sub-machine guns, boarded the two German customs launches which had been loaned to the team, and sped out to inspect, making a lot of wash as they did so. As soon as the *REVISION* was over, there would be a short wait while the manifest was given its gold seal, and then one left.

There is nobody to impart the routine to passing ships; one finds it out as best one can, and as it is impossible to do much delving from a ship at anchor, we were extremely grateful for the help we received from the British Customs Officer. He was circumspect, because his position demanded that he should be, but he saw to it that we were not disadvantaged by our lack of knowledge of the system, nor our inability to leave a ship's officer on shore to keep up the pressure on the Hungarians who decided the order of passage. He counselled us against offering an inducement to them; he said it was evident that this was the way it was done, but that unless one knew just how, when, and how much, the potential problems were not worth it. In this his advice fitted our own policy acquired over many years of dealing with levantine and oriental officials. Wait until the bribee clearly indicates that he is ready to receive. Query: is a country with openly bribable officials suitable for membership of the European Union?

We spent a quiet night alongside our Romanian friends until dawn, when bedlam broke out as cocks crowed, cats howled and dogs barked aboard the *schleppers*.

At 0700 we return to the pontoon and restart the *REVISION* process. We are told at 0755 to expect *REVISION* in half an hour. At 1130 we are still waiting. At 1150 the MAHART agent, who is responsible for the pontoon, comes down to protest that we are alongside the pontoon for too long. This precipitates a lively discussion with Bill, who is not over-impressed by having to hang about waiting for officials who ought to be more efficient. Reinforcements arrive on the MAHART side, men go off to talk to other men, and by a bit of firmness a decision is reached: our *REVISION* will be at 1300.

We go along to the restaurant for lunch. One of the British officers sees us and asks if we have our visas. We reply no, that we had been told by the Jugoslavs in London that visas for crews of boats in transit could be got at the border posts. He is doubtful. He thinks it might be different now, but it is not his business and he does not know for sure. It's too late to go and re-check.

Promptly at 1300, twelve men and a uniformed lady, all except the Scot armed to the teeth, carrying crowbars, jemmies, axes and clipboards, come on board, their heavy boots clumping about the steel

Romanian tow awaiting REVISION, *Mohács*

decks. We are thoroughly searched, though we think much of this was curiosity about our lifestyle rather than any intention to poke into corners. There are difficulties measuring our stock of diesel oil. Our tanks do not have dipsticks; we estimate their contents by sight glasses, but unfortunately one cannot see the whole of the tanks at one time, nor are the sight glasses calibrated in units of volume. Bill just knows when we need more fuel, and that is enough. They have to take our word for the size of the two tanks or pull the whole boat to pieces, and in the end they accept that we have about 1500 litres of diesel oil on board; they estimate that we may use 600 litres on the 400 kilometres to cross Jugoslavia (double that if going upstream). We receive our papers and are told to go and anchor, but not alongside the *Medias*, who has not yet been inspected, and await final permission. We haul off, come to our bower anchor, and then watch while *Medias*'s tow, anchored nearby, starts to drag anchor. The current has been getting stronger, and the Romanian barges, who have difficulty working their heavy anchors and cables with ancient equipment, had anchored last night with insufficient cable. We alert *Medias* and the tow by hoots on our siren, and they call us on VHF to say thank you.

According to the BBC things are quiet on the fighting fronts. We cheer up. Now we only have to wait for *Medias*.

At 1545, the Customs launch comes by to tell us that we must leave at once.

But we are in convoy with *Medias*, we say.

No good, Go.

Now is the time to panic!

Their decision has been taken: the Hungarian Water Police say once we've been stamped out we must go, whether *Medias* comes or not.

This strict interpretation of the rules is rare and unnecessary, but we are not in Europe, this is the Balkans. We had not bribed.

So goodbye to our shoddy bodyguard, and our hopes of protection. They may catch us up later. In the meantime, it's over the top with dry mouths. Twenty kilometres to go to the border post of Bezdan in Serbia, and now the moment has arrived our hearts are failing us a little. We feel alone, small and vulnerable.

We leave, since we have no choice. The actual border is 13 kilometres downstream of the town and the German patrol boat comes with us; they say they have to make an inspection of the border twice a day, but it feels as if we are being escorted off the premises.

This part of the river is almost totally deserted. It is quite wide, and meanders between thickly wooded banks with beaches here and there. On some of these there are incongruous groups of campers in gay tents. There are shallows, and navigation is tricky. Our watch-dogs on board the patrol boat bid us farewell as the inconspicuous border marker comes in sight (a goonbox in a forest clearing), and 15 minutes later we round a sweeping S-bend where the river narrows a little and come to the Serbian border post of Bezdan. It is 1700.

Bezdan is on the steep left bank, just before a high level bridge. An old barge serves as a pontoon, and we turn and make fast to it, watched by a sentry in a tower. Adjoining the big pontoon is a smaller one at which a patrol boat lies. No one comes near us. Laurel goes ashore, climbing a metal staircase up the cliff to see what the form is. The sentry directs her across a football field, long unused to judge from the yellow dry grass, to a barrack building 200 metres from the river. A star has been roughly removed from its pediment.

Bill waits for 30 minutes, and then goes in search. With some difficulty he runs her to earth in a room at the front of the barracks. Laurel is sitting in front of a desk, fairly relaxed, filling in forms with two men, one in uniform. Next door, more men are glued to a black and white TV. Saturday afternoon means football, even in war-torn-Jugoslavia.

The uniformed man regrets politely, but we have to pay the transit tax. The rumour had always been that it was exacted at the whim of any Serb you met, that it was demanded with menaces, that no receipt would be given. The reality is somewhat different. Pistols remain in their holsters, we are sitting down and given coffee, and all business is transacted with one ear on the latest score.

Laurel does not know the relationship between horsepower and kilowatts. A formula is applied to craft not carrying cargo, based on engine power multiplied by the distance to be travelled in Jugoslavian waters. It is calculated on a computer programme and works out at $216. The official apologises for having to charge it. He explains that navigation is supposed to be free for all by international treaty; that Britain, together with others, has abrogated that treaty and restricted navigation to Serbia's disadvantage. Serbia feels justified in retaliation. It is the small guy who pays when politicians mess things up.

It takes time to make out the forms. They let us see the log book showing the pleasure craft that have passed this way before us, 8 so far in 1995, and 8 in 1994. These include a party of canoeists who have paddled through Jugoslavia. Of the remainder, 4 of the 15 entries were British yachts, two of these belonging to the Royal Naval Sailing Association, showing that our retired naval sailors still get about where few others care to wander. There are two entries for Nick Sanders and his narrow boats, one up and one down. Among the others, we note Dutch and German.

Along the passage, we run into trouble with the immigration officer. Our friend in Mohács is right: the rules have changed since we were in London. No visas are available at the border. The young soldier is not unpleasant; he telephones superior officers, but there is no remedy, we cannot be allowed to transit. We must return to Mohács and get visas there. There is an agent in Mohács, they tell us.

We return to the first room, undo the transit tax documents and our dollars are returned. It is now quite late, so Bill asks if we may remain at the pontoon for the night and leave at 0700 the next morning. There is a short discussion with the immigration officer and they decide this is reasonable, but would we please anchor off. We return on board, groggy with conflicting thoughts. Should we abandon the project; is it an omen? In any case we must return to Mohács.

• 24 •
AN UNCIVIL SERVANT
Budapest

Return we did, motoring against a 6 km/hr current back to Mohács and, with tails between our legs, checked back into Hungary, apologising to the WEU, the Hungarians, Uncle Tom Cobleigh and all. Everybody was sympathetic. We were questioned closely on what our reception had been like (after all, it was a bit like going beyond the grave, not many people came back, especially yachts, so they got no feedback from people who passed through). We wrote a short paper for the WEU team, describing the procedure at Bezdan, and suggested they advise yachts what exactly would happen to them. They thanked us, and agreed it was a good idea. We were going to be around for a few more days.

Mohács, not the most attractive nor the largest riverside city, was our most significant stop. Historically, it has enormous significance. Since leaving Vienna the right bank was land which once formed part of the Ottoman Empire. The Turks had long held the lower Danube, but at the Battle of Mohács in 1526 the Turks overwhelmed the rag-tag army of Louis II, and ruled over this part of the Danubian plain for over 150 years. One must see the history of Eastern Europe in terms of its subjection to Ottoman rule and be glad the Turks did not get past Vienna. The Turkish Empire was one of the largest ever, and was obtained by military conquest. Military strategy and tactics as we understand them were virtually unknown in mediaeval times. Battles were more a question of the opposing armies being ranged face to face and slogging it out in brutal hand-to-hand combat.

The best of the Turkish army was organised into units of men who had been brought up especially to be soldiers. Many of them were taken as babies from the subordinated races as a sort of tax. Thoroughly indoctrinated, these Janisseries would fight like demons with no regard for their personal survival. If they lived they remained with their units and were given valuable privileges as craftsmen, thus creating over time a powerful *esprit de corps* (a military asset unregarded by our present day politicians). Battles were noted for heavy slaughter, and the Turkish army was good at that. It was only when Ottoman leaders weakened through over-indulgence and over-confidence, when the Janissery troops became themselves corrupt and luxury-hungry, that Europe was able to turn the tables.

Up to that time the only successes against Turkey had been isolated single victories, though Vlad the Impaler from Romania had had considerable success, outdoing the cruelty of the Janisseries by impaling his prisoners.

Guess what? There was no longer a Serbian consul at Mohács. We would have to go back to Budapest for our visas. We contemplated returning 200 kilometres upstream with misgiving. The current was no longer as strong as it had been, but it would still be a tough problem. Jimmy, our friendly Customs and Excise Officer, said a WEU minibus going to Budapest the following morning might take us.

There wasn't much doubt about which of us was to go. During the next few hours we had to shift berth twice, and it was evident that someone capable of doing that on their own had to stay on board. Bill was the only candidate, so Laurel would go to Budapest. The senior officer at WEU pondered whether it would be an abuse of official transport to give her a lift, decided that in the circumstances it was reasonable and gave permission. We celebrated by going out to the *Harfa* restaurant to eat. 'Harfa' means Harp. The proprietor's wife and attractive daughter did the cooking, then Josef Strauss (yes, really) having seen to his customers' needs, picked up his harp and played, as he had played in most of the great liners and cruise ships of the world. His ability to improvise and arrange the music to suit both his international guests from WEU and local Hungarians was outstanding.

On talking to the sanctions team we discovered that each person was individually accredited to the Corps Diplomatique, and technically attached to their countries' Embassies in Budapest. This seemed a good arrangement for most countries; the French, Dutch and Italians were content, but the British officers complained bitterly about being let down by the British Embassy in Budapest. There had been a parade in Mohács to mark the Hungarian national day, and the Commission's officers had sent for their best uniforms to parade in. They were sent by diplomatic bag. The British uniforms did not arrive at Mohács in time, and they were discovered in the Embassy, where they had lain for over three weeks. Personal mail, documents and other matter were not sent on promptly. In several months, the Mohács team had been visited only once by someone from the Embassy, who had spent most of the visit alone in the restaurant having a good lunch. Teams from other countries had frequent visits by officials wanting to know how things were going. All these grumbles reinforced our opinion that our Embassy in Budapest was functioning below acceptable standards.

Bill got up at 0320 to see Laurel away in the minibus at 0400. At 0830 she was outside the Jugoslav Embassy, alarmed to see that there was a queue. As the Embassy didn't open till 1000, this bode very ill. The concrete flower beds on the pavement were broken from desperate sitting, so she found a shady portion of the stone wall that fronted the building and sat there. At 0900 a hardfaced man came out. Everyone flocked about him, waving papers. If he approved the papers you got a number. Laurel joined the flock.

She hadn't got the right papers. We thought a visa was personal, so she had not taken the ship's papers, which were essential. He was quite adamant. Proof of your means of passage was required; your train ticket, your car documents – in our case the ship's papers.

She went to the British Consulate. In the Visa section they were very helpful, ringing up the Jugoslav Consulate and extracting the admission that they would accept a fax of the document, provided it arrived by midday, and making an appointment for the Jugoslav Consul to see her at noon. Laurel phoned Bill to fax the papers. He was out at anchor, but said he would see what he could do.

Laurel went back to the Jugoslav Consulate. Every time she took a taxi from one Consulate to the other (only a kilometre) the price seemed to double. This time, after a long wait, she got to speak to the Consul, Mr Bisiç. Through a little guichet in the waiting room. To stop her killing him.

Twenty or thirty other people were waiting, listening with ears agog. There were not enough seats – and those were covered with torn plastic. Mr Bisiç was hostile and unpleasant. Why cannot your husband bring the papers? Why could he not leave the boat? Why are you causing so much trouble? Laurel tried to explain the set-up at Mohács, only one pontoon and the comings and goings of a busy river at a border post. He didn't listen, he was enjoying baiting her too much.

'The fax of the ship's papers should be here now,' said Laurel, hoping to distract him. He exploded with rage.

'How dare you use my fax? How dare you DREAM of sending a fax to the Jugoslav Consulate?' He denied all knowledge, and said it hadn't arrived. As Laurel could not be certain that Bill had succeeded in sending it she couldn't argue.

'Now you will have to go back to your luxury hotel, have your English tea, and wait, like everyone else,' crowed Bisiç.

'Now, I have a four hour bus ride back to Mohács, and no bloody tea,' retorted Laurel, unwontedly indignant.

Meanwhile, back in *Hosanna*, Bill was also having an eventful day. At the time of Laurel's phone call everyone was holding off while our dear friend the art-ship from Passau appeared, towed by a Hungarian tug, and was slotted in between the two pontoons, one strictly for patrol boats, and the other for all other craft. Three more ships came and went on the public pontoon. Being the smaller vessel *Hosanna* had always to be on the outside, which suited Bill in a way because he was out of view of the MAHART man who ran the pontoon, and who was not over-friendly. The pontoon was only free if you were awaiting *REVISION*, otherwise he would demand exorbitant mooring fees, hundreds of dollars.

The art-ship, with its title of *Donau Tropfen* (Danube Drops) had brought its Message of Peace down the Danube, giving performances on the way. Most of the town came to look as coils of electric cables were run out, and adjustments made to the sculptures, which were huge man-driven mobiles. The troupe of artistes, camped in the ship beneath the extra-ordinary sculptures, had decided that this would be their last stop. They would give a performance tonight, but did not feel they could take their vessel, symbolising Peace and Goodwill among mankind, down river to war-torn-Jugoslavia, where it was obviously desperately needed; which says something about their faith in what they were doing. They had decided to go as far as the Jugoslav border tomorrow and give a symbolic performance there; what a pity the border was somewhere in the wilds 13 kilometres away, so there would be no audience, and no Serbs or Croats would actually see this uplifting piece of Peace.

Bill had to manoeuvre *Hosanna* single-handed for almost two hours on end, receiving Laurel's request for a fax to the Jugoslav Consulate in Budapest in the middle of it. It was an hour before he was back outside another ship on the pontoon. The WEU office decided, not unreasonably, that they could not let him use their fax machine. It took time to track down another, and send the fax. A fax confirms that it has been received at the other end, and at what time. Despite the delay, there was no doubt that it had arrived before noon.

With three other ships alongside, all moving frequently, Bill felt unable to keep an adequate eye on the cats, who had developed wanderlusts of their own, provoked no doubt by generous cooks in various tugs. The cats are Laurel's pets. To have one missing in these circumstances when we were both heavily stressed and tired out would be intolerable. He decided to anchor off again. Before doing so, the yacht *Rainbow* arrived, containing Jean and Jerry from Zimbabwe, very tired after a weary journey from Holland, and much information was exchanged.

There was a violent thunderstorm at 1720, with fierce winds. He shut all hatches and windows, furled all awnings, secured all loose gear and kept a watch in case *Hosanna*, or anyone nearby, dragged anchor. At 1815, which was the time the minibus was expected to return, he moved alongside the tug that had brought the art-ship. They were interested in *Hosanna* and he showed them round. He discovered the art-ship was to give a performance at 2000. The long gangway leading from shore to pontoon, down which Laurel would have to come from the bus, would be ideal to watch from.

Crowds gathered. The performance was late starting and there was some whistling, but it got under way at 2020, just as Laurel returned. She was tired almost to tears, not only unsuccessful, but shocked by rudeness, abuse and obstruction at the hands of the Jugoslav Consul, and rapacious demands from Budapest taxi drivers.

Laurel comes from a theatrical family, and the show, with music by Markus Stockhausen, was a welcome distraction. The sculptures were moved, rather jerkily, by figures in gold leotards who also played instruments, and uttered sharp cries. A man walked a tightrope from the main masterpiece to the mizzen masterpiece. Bits of sculpture swung, and balanced. The people of Mohács watched in puzzled silence. It was certainly original, and ought from its theme to have

The art-ship Donau Tropfen *(Danube Drops)*

been emotionally moving. We are sorry to say that after a particularly prolonged and tremulous fart on the trombone, we managed to get below decks in *Hosanna* before giving way to helpless laughter.

Laurel was far too tired to contemplate another 0400 start, so she rested, and we thought it over. Should she go at all? Was this another omen? Wouldn't it be better to admit defeat and go back? The news from Jugoslavia was not encouraging. The BBC correspondents there were unanimously gloomy from their 'forward positions at the front' (in the Belgrade Hilton, we suspected).

Medias was still here, unprocessed; something was wrong with the documentation of their wheat. Somehow sheer busy-work kept us going. Its momentum was inexorable. Once started, an enterprise like this is hard to stop. There was much to sort out before Laurel went to Budapest again, there were documents to photocopy, never easy in small places in Eastern Europe. Having succeeded, a small victory in itself, we went off to anchor for a bit of peace.

Bill restored morale somewhat by raising the mizzen mast. It is smaller than the others, only about 8 metres above water level. It could be useful for lowering our dinghy in order to avoid the constant shuttling of the day before. By a careful study of the *Indicateur Kilométrique*, he had concluded that we could get under all the remaining bridges downstream with the mizzenmast raised. We like to have the masts up. Not only is it easier to move about the decks, but it also makes the ship feel more of a ship. One only, and the shortest one at that, was not much, but we needed a boost.

The news from Jugoslavia continued to be disquieting, and everyone was getting nervous. Relu called to say they had got their papers straight at last and would be leaving. If we could not come yet, then their sister ship would be following, and had been told to look after us. It was a nice thought, but it would not be the same; we had become fond of the crew of the *Medias*: almost every one of them had found a few words of English to chat to us.

We went in to berth alongside the art-ship where no one else wanted to be, knowing we would not have to move till morning. We went to the *busz* station to get a ticket, passing on the way an imposing flight of steps leading up to a plinth with nothing on it. It had been the Russian war memorial, destroyed to the last stone when Communism fell. The rage is understandable, but as at Saverne, men dying in battle deserve a memorial.

We had a drink at the *Harfa*, nearby. Laurel girded herself for the foray the following day, she made us a good supper of spare ribs, and then, in spite of our fatigue, we had to be sociable to the crew of the tug alongside us. These crews can be of enormous help, and it is worth keeping up the goodwill.

At 0415 Bill escorted Laurel to the *busz* station through the dark streets, after which he took *Hosanna* to anchor off the pier.

Soon he was asked to move by the Hungarian police as he was in their way. He was at least 100 metres off the police pontoon and their boat was a very small easily-manoeuvrable craft; this was obviously a bit of bloody-mindedness, but one cannot do other than obey. He moved right over to the other side, confident that Laurel could not be back for some hours. About 30 minutes before her bus was due, he went alongside a tug at the pontoon. He had checked that the MAHART man went off duty before this, and anyway *Hosanna* was virtually hidden behind the big Bulgarian tug.

Laurel returned, cheerfully successful, but very tired. This time the taxi from the *busz* station to the Jugoslav Consulate had tried to charge her 4500 Forints (£23) for a ten minute journey, which should have cost about 800 (£4.50) and in Mohács would have been 200. In reply to her protests the driver merely said: 'But I am *Privat* taxi, Madame'. Laurel had wisely emptied her purse of large notes, and put them elsewhere. 'This is all I have,' she said, indignation giving her strength to lie with conviction. 'You had better call the *rendörséget*, the police, and arrest me.' This did not suit him at all, of course. He emptied her purse, containing about 2500 Forints, including every last little coin, leaving her, as far as he knew, without a penny, at 0830 in the morning, outside the Jugoslav Consulate.

This time she got her number, eleven, without which you cannot enter those hallowed halls, and then only at a given time. At 1100 she presented herself, and Bisiç very nearly won again. The form clearly stated that the money for visas was payable in dollars or Deutchmarks. When Laurel produced dollars, he said triumphantly: 'Today, only Deutchmarks'. His face fell when she produced Deutchmarks, it was his last chance of obstruction. Shrugging discontentedly, he stamped the visas, grudgingly handed them over, and after another four hour bus ride, Laurel was back in Mohács.

Bill had had a frustrating day, very much on edge, and had been unable to settle to anything constructive. As soon as Laurel was on board, we slipped and went over to the other side of the river, above the ferry, and anchored well out of everyone's way (we thought). We had a quiet evening together, barbecuing some pork chops, until chased below by mosquitos, then a quiet night. Morale was a little better, but Bill was not sleeping well.

We were chased off even this berth in the early morning by a tow that wanted to anchor. We went alongside the pontoon in order to pound the door of the Hungarian Customs Office so that we could check out again. One or other of us played sentry the whole day outside the office, but they would not see us. There was only one Customs man on duty and he had not time to do all the barge tows and us as well (he said), so we waited a whole long day, from 0830. In early evening the big hotel ship *Donau Star*, Romanian flag, berthed inside us. She would be staying the night and her captain made us welcome alongside him. This meant we could safely go ashore. We did, to the *Harfa* again.

It was a good meal in good company, with most of the WEU contingent there too, celebrating the imminent departure of one of their number. We knew most of them by now and joined the party. Josef played everything from *J'attendrai* to *Danny Boy*, and *Autumn Leaves* and *Roll out the Barrel* in both Hungarian and English. The latter tune had revolutionary connotations, and was very popular in Hungary. We spent a convivial evening which did a lot to restore morale.

'Are you going tomorrow morning?' asked one of the officers. We hoped so, we said.

'No problem with your visas?'

'Not now, but they will probably find something else.'

'We have to make new papers for you. Tomorrow then, at eight?'

We also got a message that the Hungarian Customs promised to see us at 0600 next day, 4 August.

At daybreak Laurel duly walks past the storks' nest for the hundredth time with all the papers.

Nobody there. Door locked.

The UN Team, already at work in the building across the yard, laugh heartily at her optimism. 'Oh, the Hungarians won't be there till 0700,' they say. At 0615 the Customs man *is* there, but sucks his teeth and tells her exasperatedly to come back at 0700. He's too busy, he says, he's got too much work.

The relentless process begins at 0710. First the Customs documents, then the police check the passports, then the border police look at them, then fill in forms and stamp them, then we stamp and sign them too. Next we wait for the *REVISION*, which is the Team, the 12, now well known to us, heavily armed, with clipboards. At 0800 *REVISION* is under way. This time it is a cheerful party that stomps over *Hosanna* in spite of all the weapons and heavy boots. We think they have by now abandoned all suspicion of our activities; most officials do, but it takes time. Our way of life is not usual, and people have to adjust to the fact that eccentricity is not criminal. We have quite an emotional leave-taking, and they all wish us luck and bon voyage. Once checked out, we try to stop for a cup of coffee, and hear the BBC news, but again we are chased away by the Hungarian police boat: 'Go, go, go,' is the clear message.

We did not expect after the long weary hours, even days, of waiting, to be hustled so indecently fast. We did not want to go this early in the day. Jugoslav formalities would take a few hours we now knew, but we were unwilling to quit the comparative safety of the Bezdan border post to spend the night, where? Vukovar, among the ghosts of the massacred? No thank you.

But we have no option. The Hungarian police are quite nasty about it. Go we must. We weigh anchor, and head downstream, as slowly as possible. Bill decides that he is damned if he will be bullied. We do *not* want an early arrival at Bezdan. He runs on one engine only at dead slow ahead, 2 km/hr, though with the current we are moving faster over the ground. What causes him much amusement is the fact that the Hungarians, who are this time our escort to the border in a smart speedboat, cannot go slow enough to keep station on us. He is almost childishly pleased about that; there isn't much else to laugh at.

We listen to the news, this Friday 4 August 1995.

Never sail on Friday, sailors say, with good statistical cause.

Croatia, said the BBC, had this day invaded Serb-held territory at Knin. No wonder the Sanctions Team wished us luck.

• 25 •
OPERATION STORM
Vukovar, Novi Sad

We listened to the news with mounting horror as we dawdled towards Bezdan and our date with the Serbs. The Croats had this morning invaded Krajina, that part of the old federation which the Serbs had taken from them at the start of hostilities. This territory extended to the Danube, which once had been the border between Serbia and Croatia. The Serbs had thrown the Croats out from alongside the Danube (directly opposite Bezdan, even), massacring as they went. The worst of these atrocities were the sackings of the cities of Vukovar, through which we would pass, and Osijek, just off the river. The Croats were emotional about this part of the country, and though the BBC spoke mainly of fighting nearer the coast, we knew that events 'occur' only where their reporters happen to be. As the TV news people say: 'No pix, no news'. We also knew that the term Krajina meant different areas to different people. There were those to whom it included the territory up to River Danube. The news bulletin, while it might have satisfied most people in the world, left us with more questions than information. Soon we would be at Bezdan. We had already left Hungary, and in the circumstances it was doubtful we would be welcome back a second time. We passed Kp 1433, the frontier, almost without noticing it. The Hungarian police launch peeled off, revved up, and disappeared northwards in a cloud of spray.

To our surprise, we felt better now that indecision had committed us. We settled down to muster the advice we'd been given. The other Romanian tow had left Mohács at first light, so we'd missed him. Relu, still struggling with his documentation, had been particular that one did not leave Bezdan (Kp 1425.5) other than at first light. Then we should go full speed and stop overnight at Kp 1202, where the big tows anchor. Even if the Romanians were not there, there would certainly be other barges, and there is safety in numbers.

The Serb government had suppressed amateur terrorist groups such as the White Rose, and New Byzantium; the dollars that the passage of cargo barges generated was badly needed, and traffic was not to be discouraged. Now the only problem was diesel pirates. We would almost certainly be accosted by boats asking for diesel. For small amounts, they would pay us in fresh fish, always welcome to a crew on passage, but larger amounts would be paid for in dollars. There was a fair, fixed price: 5 litres per kilo of fish, $400 per tonne. They understood the need for a refusal and there would be no problems. There was an etiquette in the trade, and there would be little likelihood of theft; the Serbs had realised they got more by being correct than they got by crime, because so many of the barge people were both poor and sympathetic to their cause. No one liked the Croatians, and the Bulgars and Ukrainians in particular identified with the Serbs. Of course we might meet an exception, especially because we were British, but unlikely if we kept with the crowd. It was quite like the old times after the war to be British and unpopular. Going through Serbia, it would have been worse to be German.

With 223 kilometres to go next day, we needed to stop at Bezdan overnight. There were no tows in evidence there. We did not then know that they were 3 kilometres further on, round the next bend.

We were recognised and welcomed back at Bezdan, though some of the personnel had changed. Inspection of our documents went smoothly. Five copies of everything were made, with carbon paper and a heavily wielded Biro. We went to the police first this time, and our visas were OK. But Laurel was doing the business, and again the kilowatt confused her, and that is what they base the transit tax on. They wanted more dollars than they'd asked for last week. Bill, fetched, was able to show on our registration that the kilowatts were just the same as they were last week and there was no need to change the tax from the $216 that they had wanted then. They regretted, but $222 was what the computer had coughed up this time. We paid, and got our receipt. The Customs Officers came to the ship and didn't board but asked a few questions. They were very correct and pleasant. The thin Customs man gave us a long talk about the political situation. We understood very little but place names, but hoped our body language was sympathetic. He spoke more in sorrow than in anger, even when he kept throttling himself to demonstrate what Sanctions are doing to his country; the transit tax, he indicated apologetically, was the only response available to them.

They asked us if we had heard the news, and we asked what were the implications. We'd looked at the map again to refresh our memory, though in fact the trouble spots were already branded there, Bihac, Banja Luka, Tuzla, Knin, all the distance from Surrey to Yorkshire away from the Danube. They said the Croats were moving towards the river, but had not got far and were being held.

With bated breath we asked: Could we stay the night here? Yes, but not alongside, go a few hundred metres upstream and anchor within sight of the observation post. With great relief we did so and anchored in 30 feet. The bottom was rocky, but the anchor held well.

And now at anchor we sit in the evening quiet. The crows call, the cormorants fly past and the anchor cable chafes and grumbles among its rocks. On this side, thickly willowed, the town is 3 kilometres away and invisible. There's just the building across the dried up football field. It is a barracks with peeling paint, central office furniture rather the worse for wear, and mosquito screens in the open windows. Built out from the shore is a gantry with alarming tilting steps to cope with different heights of the Danube, down to the old barges which act as border post pontoons. Half a kilometre away across the river in Serb-held Croatia is a wooded cliff. Under it is a hamlet with a church and a little strand from which the splashes and shouts of paddling children come. Dogs bark, cocks crow, voices carry across. You could tell what they're saying if you spoke Serbo-Croat. On top of the cliff is a tall pillar, and on top of that is one of those statues beloved of Eastern regimes, a mythical female with billowing draperies with one arm above her head, holding what might be a torch. She faces across the Danube and could be waving to the Serbian side, but the gesture seems more derisory than amicable.

On our side, this peaceful evening, the only disturbing thing is that the patrol boat is being covered with camouflage netting.

We are up at 0445, Saturday 5 August, but it is foggy and too dark to see the navigation marks. This is a difficult stretch of the river and we have no charts from now on. We ran aground yesterday on a 5-foot patch in mid-river, not seriously, because we were going slowly. We wait until 0510, when Bill decides conditions are acceptable. He looked down river a couple of kilometres last night, and felt that with conditions improving, he would be able to see the markers. We are soon going at full speed.

We do not know how far the Croats have advanced during the night. Last evening at 1800, the Serbs admitted they had been taken by surprise and were falling back. Have the Croats reached the river? Are isolated bands of Croats, who might have been left behind in the original evacuation, now re-activating themselves in guerilla form? Are the Serbs on the opposite bank calm, or will some of them be jumpy? We have no idea. We discuss it at length, but are no wiser, and the BBC is no help. They only get news where they have reporters, and they have been taken by surprise as much as the Serbs.

Bill calls Laurel over soon after the start, while we are on a straightish stretch.

He says: 'The river is about 400 yards wide. I shall try to keep as near the centre as the channel will allow, about 200 yards from each bank. Your ordinary soldier is not so good at moving targets at that range. It's the best I can do.'

He pauses to turn a sharp bend.

He goes on: 'I shall try to keep an eye on the banks. If I say DOWN! then get down below and sit on the deck. You will be almost entirely below the waterline, and anyway behind 8 mm steel.'

Says Laurel: 'What about you?'

'Someone must drive. Most of me will be behind 4 mm steel. That won't stop the hard stuff, but it will absorb much of its kinetic energy. The important thing is that one of us should be unharmed to get the hell out of it and look after the other. The banks are thickly wooded; we are moving at 5 metres per second and will pass danger points faster than anyone can move along the bank.'

Laurel is impressed. 'It must be your military training,' she muses. 'Everyone should have it,' says Bill. 'Once a young man has been in sufficient danger to wet himself, he matures fast, and his mind learns to grapple with the essentials.' He pauses. 'Is that a green buoy there? Pass the binox. I wish some of our leaders had looked down the muzzle of a loaded gun early in their çareers, instead of swanning about Oxford screwing each other. Those of us who are frightened of wars, as I am, don't start them.'

We are just coming up to Kp 1414 – it is exactly 1000 kilometres since we entered the Danube.

It's 0730, at the Arpatin Bends. The Captains wanted to get through this bit in daylight and we can see why; it's not only a sharp series of bends but the river narrows, and for one huge tow of eight barges to meet another while negotiating these awkward curves would be dangerous. Ahead we can see a barge tow going the same way as we are; we are catching him up. This is good news, because (a) he'll show us where the channel is and (b) he's company. He must have slowed down considerably to get through the bends. We'll probably ease speed to keep pace with him. What do all those signs say? Danger! Sound horn! Call on VHF! Reduce speed! Keep 80 metres off! And, of course, No overtaking!

Bill says: 'Never seen so many signs clustered together. Is he Romanian, our barge ahead?'

It's the pusher tug *Giurgiu*, with four or five *schleppers* ahead of her, and as courtesy ensign she's flying the old Jugoslavian flag with the star in the middle. There seems to be some doubt as to what we should be flying. We're flying the Serbian flag, horizontal red blue and white stripes, but at the Customs post they were flying the Jugoslav flag without the star.

Bill says, 'I think we'll follow him. It's a bit cowardly but it's less of a strain than buoy spotting; one can sit and drive easily and not get so tired.'

We slow to one engine only, about 5 km/hr, following the tow. It makes for relaxed navigation, for the tug ahead with her eight barges 'sweeps' a large area of river, and it reduces our anxiety level a bit. Laurel can even get some breakfast, and then steer a little so Bill can rest.

While he is dozing, we reach Kp 1380, where River Drava joins, and signs indicate the turning for Srebrenica and Osijek. It is 0830. Laurel says, 'Captain on the bridge.'

She only uses this naval expression in moments of panic. 'There's a patrol boat on the Croatian side covered in camouflage netting and a bunch of soldiers has dashed out of a hut and down to the shore. Don't know if they're Serbs or Croats.' Bill has already got the binoculars and says, 'The flag is red, blue white with a badge, doesn't help much.'

'Are they coming after us with that little boat?' asks Laurel, trying to concentrate on steering. Bill says, 'Yes, they're coming.'

Medias *and her tow, blue-flagging*

They are coming.

Men in battle fatigues. With machine guns. This is it.

Their dory has a big outboard motor and is soon close to us and ordering us to stop. It secures alongside us. Bill puts the engine in neutral, then astern, and lets the ship drift in the current.

We do not know what to expect, and our hearts are somewhere up by our tonsils. Four huge men, looking somehow larger because of their machine guns and heavy boots, climb on board.

They are mature men, militia we suppose. Their commander is middle aged, with grizzled short hair. He speaks excellent English.

'Where have you come from?'

'This morning? From Bezdan.'

'Have you the frontier papers?'

'Yes, here they are.'

He glances at them.

'Where are you going?'

'To the Black Sea.'

'Why?'

'Good question,' says Bill. 'I am asking myself the same thing.'

The soldier laughs, and punches Bill lightly on the shoulder. 'You know that the treacherous Croats invaded Krajina this morning?'

Ah! So they are Serbs.

'Yes, we heard it on the BBC, but we were already in Jugoslavia, and felt the best thing to do was to get down river as soon as possible.'

'You are right, I think. You understand we are watching everything, we must search your ship.'

'Go ahead. Everyone else has. Why not you?'

He laughs again. 'You have a sense of humour.'

Bill does not feel very humorous, but at least they are polite, and not pointing their guns at us. They have the air of knowing which end of the gun the bullet comes out of. Bill is far more frightened of incompetent soldiery, of which there is too much in the world. Disciplined men do not shoot without cause. He leaves Laurel in the wheelhouse after making corrections to the way the ship was pointing and takes the soldiers below. One remains in the dory alongside.

Of course they are watching everything. They are defending their homes.

They soon realise that we are not a Trojan sea-horse full of Croatian soldiers, nor do we carry a cargo of arms to make rendezvous with anyone by the river bank. Within a few minutes they are back in the wheelhouse.

The leader salutes and offers his hand. 'I am sorry that all this is necessary. Have you a card with your ship's name?' We give him one of our postcards, with a drawing of Hosanna on it. Spoils of war.

They leave, wishing us 'Bon Voyage.'

We would have liked to talk to them, to hear their point of view, gauge better what sort of men they are, especially as the leader speaks good English, and his manners are impeccable. There are always two sides to every story, and it is difficult to cast him in the role of a war criminal. But they are on serious business, and so are we now; we all need to get on.

We listen to the BBC news at 0900. The Croatians are shelling Osijek, 22 kilometres away by river – 12 miles. Less than that, as the shell flies. If the artillery is man-sized, and we do not know it isn't, then the river may be already within range of the guns. If they were naval guns it would have been. There is no sound of gunfire, nor sight of anything, except of course the patrol boat.

When in danger, be somewhere else.

We soon catch up the Romanian tow again. The episode has had an effect on us. Bill says that he is no longer in such a cautious mood about diesel pirates and conditions during the night. He feels that if we hang about behind the slow tow, we will certainly not get to Kp 1202 tonight before dark, and he wants to stop before then. The soldier had favoured the idea that we should go through as fast as possible, and Bill was reassured by the professional attitude of the militiamen. He feels that the further downstream we go, and the further from the fighting we get, the less touchy will be the soldiers, and that at Kp 1300 we will be clear of the disputed territory and from then on it will be Serbia on both banks.

On to Kp 1300, he suggests, as soon as we can. Laurel agrees. Bill starts the other two engines and we radio to say we will be passing the tow, but we do so with difficulty as the *schleppers* are swirling about in the stream. From then on it is full speed, 7 knots. At least the stream is with us. Laurel is permanently on buoy-spotting duty with Bill steering. We are too busy to feel scared any more. We pass a Romanian tow going upstream and then at 1140 we round a broad, wide bend and are in Vukovar.

The city lies on the right bank at Kp 1333 and the channel is on the same side. Now the war comes close. On the outskirts is a burnt-out

Cranes at Vukovar

factory with shellholes in its walls. Then a gutted apartment building seven storeys high with blind black windows, the glass shattered, nobody living there. On the commercial quay the cranes stand, twisted, hurt, like wounded herons. Further on an elegant waterside promenade is littered with débris, its lamp standards bent or broken.

Vukovar is a devastated town, not a building is left intact; if the house walls are standing the windows are blackened by fire, the roof has collapsed, and the splintered rafters poke the sky like spillikins thrown by an angry child. The churches are in ruins. The empty water tower is pocked by shells. It brings it home to see a modern building so ruined; this is very recent war.

One block of flats shows signs of life. Half the windows are boarded up with hardboard or rugs, and some of the balconies hang awry, but the building blooms with washing, like a garden in spring. A whiff of hope in a devastated town, otherwise complete and utter desolation. It was as if someone had ordered the obliteration of the city in a frenzy of ferocity and had left a quiet seething fury behind, for such ruin will breed again its own bloodshed and destruction in years to come. As will the pit near the hospital where more than 200 souls were slaughtered in 1991. We feel the depression seeping into our bones, and hurry on. It has taken 20 minutes to pass through the city, 20 agonising minutes, while the two of us, both brought up in front-line, heavily-bombed towns, undergo a shocking reminder of the persistence of hate.

Bill navigates cautiously; all the channel marker posts are gone, and the buoys may or may not be marking the channel, there are a number scattered along the shoreline where they have come adrift, and nobody has had the heart to do anything about it. And who knows what débris may lie under the water?

At 1350 we pass Kp 1300 and are relieved to think that we are now into Serbia proper on both banks. A thunderstorm sends us running to close all hatches and we drive along isolated from the world, watching the lightning strike as God loses patience with the whole of creation. When peace returns, we open the windows, and on the banks everyone is in post-thunderstorm August mood, campsites on both sides – not military ones either. There is a complete change of mood – bathing and camping and barbecuing; everything is disconcertingly normal again.

We have been driving now for 11 hours, and we're getting tired. Bill does most of it. Laurel considers him a good driver; he has plenty of stamina, whether it's a car or a boat. He does about three hours, and then Laurel does a half or threequarters, maybe even an hour, while he sleeps in the chair. That way we cover the kilometres.

At 1640 we pass through Novi Sad. It's a big town, dominated by the great castle of Petrovaradin. There is a strand along one side of the river, a beautiful beach with trees and restaurants and cafés; people are bathing and eating ice cream.

Here in war-torn-Jugoslavia, it is a hot day.

Here is the lowest bridge by far on the lower Danube, rated at a mere 6.07 metres clearance above the highwater mark. We have read the *pegels* and seen that the river is half a metre above the minimum (ENS). Relu assured us that our mizzen mast would get under it, and we are glad to find it does. Watching masts go under bridges is nerve-wracking; in the last 10 yards it seems there is no chance, but it's too late to stop. Then suddenly one is under and clear.

No one in Novi Sad is worried about Croats and Operation Storm. Boats are out on the river, their occupants angling, or water-skiing, or just pottering. Dozens of them. There were none of these signs of affluence further up.

We are now expert on sanctions. We have just listened to a BBC reporter, told to do a story on them. He had torn himself away from the Hilton bar long enough to visit a Belgrade suburb, and file a moving piece about roadside vendors selling petrol by the bottle: look how fiercely sanctions were biting! Which was, of course, the official line.

There is enough diesel and petrol being used in boats this Saturday afternoon to fill 100,000 bottles; there is no sign of any shortage. Everybody knows that when fuel becomes short, private boating comes at the bottom of the list of priorities, after lawnmowers. If people are speeding up and down the river in their powerboats as they are today, the second day of Operation Storm, then there is no serious shortage of fuel. The BBC man might have seen more if he'd visited the Danube perhaps. It is interesting that in all our listening – and we listened to nearly every news broadcast – not one reporter ever saw the Danube as remotely significant. In fact we doubt whether any reporter even saw the Danube at all, and it is the main trade lifeline of the country. (It was reported in 1996, after sanctions had finished, that Serbia was investing over £100,000,000 to build 120 big barges, 10 pusher tugs, and 6 ice-breakers for the Danube.)

It's 1930 and getting dark and it's more than an hour to Kp 1202. Bill has been at the helm for most of the day since 0510, apart from short spells to eat or rest his eyes, and is tired out. Laurel has spent most of the 14½ hours standing, spotting buoys and marks through binoculars, and is in no condition to take over. In the dark it would be dangerous. We look over at a family of Serbs camping for the weekend by the riverside. There are little tents and people fishing. It is Saturday. This is real camping, this is not the Campingplatz such as we saw in Germany and Austria, with big sanitary blocks and a kitchen and a restaurant, where the tents have three bedrooms and a drawing room. This is old fashioned camping among the trees in little orange or green tents. The children are playing tig, father is lighting a fire to grill the fish he has caught. It is pastorally calm, with no suggestion of a country in the middle of a bloody war. There are half a dozen empty barges anchored there. Bill spins the wheel. 'We'll anchor here, too. I can't go on,' he says. Laurel stops holding her breath. We anchor behind the big barges, between them and the campers, about 100 metres from the bank. With the engines switched off, there is silence except for the shouts of excited children. It is nearly dark.

Bill says, 'I shouldn't think anybody is likely to cause trouble where there are families and small children. Children make good escorts.' But the massacre pits have not been dug up yet.

We are at Kp 1214, just past the confluence of River Tisa, itself navigable up and into Hungary. In fact logic says that the land between the Danube and the Tisa, called the Banat, should really be Hungarian, but they lost out in the great land lottery somewhere along the line.

We have a quiet night, disturbed momentarily about midnight when the Romanian tow struggles past on its way to Kp 1202.

• 26 •
THE SANCTIONS BUSTERS
Serbia

Bill is up before 0500. He wants to transit the rest of Jugoslavia in one day, and get the serious variables and unknowns behind him. After our long run yesterday, he must check and grease bearings and stern-tubes, check gearbox oil levels as well as oil and water in all the engines. It takes him about 20 minutes and we are under way at 0525.

The sun is rising, rosy pink above a bank of cloud, the mist on the water making it, as usual, difficult to pick out the buoys. We can see the shapes, distorted by mirage, but not the colours. The sun is reflected in the water, a rippled pillar of fluorescent orange. Overhead is a flight of egrets, and a lone stork paddles in the shallow water at the river's edge, lifting its red legs delicately to step over stones.

At Surduk (Kp 1207), and frequently thereafter for the next 30 kilometres, we come upon diesel pirates. This is the halfway point in the dash through Jugoslavia, and where the big tows anchor for the night. The Ukrainians, who are sympathetic, the Romanians and the Bulgarians, too desperately poor to resist the temptingly high prices offered, all sell their diesel here.

It looks like big business.

Drawn up on the shore are dozens of black skiffs, dory-like boats, about 5 to 8 metres in length, and each having a powerful outboard motor similar to the one the militia used to board us yesterday. Each boat holds between four and six 200 litre drums, and often some 25 litre jerricans too, and on the shore at every depôt the drums and jerricans are lined up in rows. We see a couple of dozen such sites, and it is apparent that each depôt is busy. We can see why we have not been bothered; we carry only 1500 litres and that is not enough to make it worth their while. Perhaps in times past it might have been different, and perhaps the 5 kilos of fish for 25 litres of diesel was the going rate for individual fishermen. Even if they were interested, two of us, even with two cats (keeping their heads down thank heaven), would have a hard time eating 5 kilos of fish.

We speculate how they have been able to get new Japanese outboard motors; it is evident that, quite apart from fuels, some countries' major manufacturers are happy to breach sanctions.

At 0830 we slow down, and occasionally stop engines to avoid fishing nets across the river at the approaches to Belgrade. We may be in the wrong channel, for the river is wide hereabouts and dotted with islands. The few channel markers are confusing, with separate channels for through traffic and those wishing to approach the city's docks. The depth varies alarmingly from 20 metres to barely 3.

Obviously sanctions are having some effect on certain types of traffic in Serbia. We pass trots of dumb barges laid up, with their tugs moored silently by the quaysides, so it is safe to assume that bulk cargoes are not making it on the river. Not legal ones anyway.

We are finding the lack of a good chart very irritating crossing this part of Jugoslavia. The sketch maps in Heikell's book, while admittedly not intended to be ideal for navigation, are badly enough drawn to be confusing. The river starts to get complicated, with channels going round islands, sometimes on the unexpected side, and the channel markers often absent. The standard of alertness required, and the tension caused by the political and military uncertainties make our anxiety levels dangerously high. Our nerves are as taut as bowstrings.

From the river, the city has no charm whatsoever, and we hurry past, dodging several blue-flagging barge tows, under the remaining low bridge at Pançevo (Kp 1166) which has a full 9.15 metres in the *Indicateur Kilométrique du Danube*, and in fact shows 10 metres on the gauge. The approach to the bridge is fraught, up sun and in mist, and the yellow diamond which marks the span we should go through is invisible until we are only 50 metres away and committed.

The odd early morning light has a mirage effect, which adds to our problems. The barge tows ahead are three times taller than they should be, and spotting leading marks isn't made any easier by the fact that the Serbs have other things to think about than cutting back the green growth round the kilometre posts and leading marks, often hidden by branches till you are level with them. You can still use a kilometre post if it's alongside, but a leading mark that you don't see until it's abeam is as much use as a marshmallow marlinspike.

We are taking turns to crash out in the reclining chair on the verandah, treating this as we would a night watch at sea, since we have already done six hours, a normal day's driving. We are already tired, and the tension leads to mild paranoia.

Laurel is at the wheel. A black skiff full of men, flying a huge Serbian flag, is hovering in our path.

She calls, 'Captain on the bridge'.

Here it comes, she thinks. Rape, pillage, and extortion. Here are the real pirates, the ones who are rumoured to take what they want at gunpoint, despite the Embassy saying that nothing had been recorded for a year.

Dry mouth, heart hammering, can't swallow.

And then they wander over to the shore and begin unloading bags of watermelons.

You feel a bit silly, don't you. And guilty, because you've woken the Captain, who needs his break probably more than you do.

The current decreases: about 3 km/hr at the entrance to Belgrade, where we noticed that the water level had fallen below normal, and now the current drops almost to zero at Smederevo itself.

The lowest remaining bridge will have at least 13 metres and possibly more, though it will be necessary to choose the very centre of the big arch at Smederevo, whose 10 metres nominal clearance is measured over a channel 120 metres wide.

Smederevo Castle is one of the most magnificent we have seen. We think the water level must have changed because any horse could jump the bottom wall. The pink brick ruins are immense and widespread, and there is a tower that leans at a dizzying angle.

We are at Ram. Not far now, to the Romanian border. The river is as wide as a lake. Suddenly there is a fleet of about 40 yachts, sails taut and pulling, a sight we haven't seen since Calais; in our delicate state it almost brings tears to our eyes. We happily give way to them, going under their sterns to keep clear of the race.

On the left bank at Kp 1075, we pass the confluence of River Nera, the border on that side between Serbia and Romania. Serbia will continue on the right bank for another 231 kilometres, after the Iron Gate. We should be safe from the effects of the Slavonic civil war now. Serbia will not want to offend her neighbour to the north, so the risk of incidents has lessened. The area is patrolled by both sides to see that nothing unapproved takes place.

A little further on at Kp 1059 lies the river port of Veliko Gradiste, the outcheck for Jugoslavia. It is set a little off the fairway where the river is wide, and being outside the buoyed channel we approach it carefully, especially as a dredger is working well out from the shore. The dredger signs are unclear, so Bill goes downstream of it and turns back inside it to approach the battleship grey empty pontoon. We make fast and wait.

Two men approach and ask if we are Australian. Our blue ensign often causes misconception. They tell us to take our papers to the office over there, indicating a building behind the café. Bill walks over. The ship is quite safe where it is, and after Laurel's experiences in Budapest he feels it is his turn to be brutalised. He is met by two young militiamen, one of whom speaks good English. After polite greetings are exchanged, and the usual bundle of papers and passports handed over, he is motioned to a seat. There is, as always, a soccer match on television, but the sound has been turned off as they enter the room. Though the English-speaking Sergeant concentrates on the job in hand, Bill notes the assistant's eyes swivelling TV-wards at intervals.

It is a pleasant room in the corner of the building. Along one wall is an iron-framed bed with grey blankets neatly folded, a big desk on which the chief features are a telephone and a carousel with about two dozen rubber stamps on it. The television is high on one wall. Facing it is a portrait of Tito, looking disapproving. On top of a filing cabinet is a VHF radio-telephone, switched off.

The young Sergeant looks up with a gentle smile.

'Why do you come here when the BBC tells the world we are animals?'

Bill feels this is not the place to express agreement with the pundits of Bush House. After what he hopes is a brief pause while the Sergeant looks him straight in the eye, he says: 'Every country has its animals, ours as well as yours,' and stares back.

Not bad, for one not normally addicted to tact and diplomacy.

'Yes,' sighs the young man. 'You are right. The man who destroyed Vukovar is an animal.'

Bill is not sure whether he is referring to a fellow Serb or a Croat, so he feels it better to limit his reply to an expression of sorrow at the state of the town as we passed through. The Sergeant stamps the papers and hands them back.

'Did you know they shelled Vukovar again yesterday just after noon? It was on the news last night.'

We passed through Vukovar yesterday at 1150. At noon we would have been about a mile past it.

We must have missed the shellfire by less than half an hour. Bill is speechless, a rare enough event, but probably appropriate. What can you say?

The Sergeant stands up. 'Enough of shootings and killings. Can I look at your boat? It looks a fine ship.'

We show him and the Harbour-master round the boat. The young man wants to go to nautical college, but in this crisis...? He finishes with a hanging question mark punctuating an unanswerable question.

We like him. He is a pleasant, good mannered official, one of the best we shall meet. How can countries produce him as well as the savages who kill in the name of ethnic cleansing? He waves us farewell as we push off from the little town, which reminds us of a dilapidated seaside resort. It is tourism on a small scale: paddling children along the strand, simple cafés, and shops with buckets and spades hung outside. We were tempted to go and find a plate of *çevepçiçi*: those little skewers of grilled meatballs that we ate in the old Jugoslavia, but once you are checked out you must go.

It is 15 kilometres to Moldova Veche, on the opposite bank, and marked as a port of entry to Romania.

The scenery changes as we near the Iron Gate, where the Danube has cut a way through the Carpathian Mountains. The Jugoslav side is hilly, there are some woods, but it is mostly pastureland, sere and brown in this hot dry August. The Romanian side is wonderfully romantic; high hills with crags heaving up from dark wolfhaunted forest – Dracula country. The romance is tempered by frequent goon-boxes set in clearings: lookout posts on high scaffolding, close to the river. There is no one in them, presumably since the fall of Ceauçescu.

We berth on the Customs pontoon after changing our courtesy ensign from the red, blue and white of Serbia, to the green, blue and yellow of Romania. It is 1800. At first it is difficult to find anyone awake, and when at last we do, we are told that we cannot enter here because the required visas are unavailable. We must go on to Orsova, only two hours on, they say. A quick check reveals that Orsova is nearly 100 kilometres further on. Do they really think we can do 50 km/hr in this old tub? The Customs people seem mystified by the distance. So far, is it, to Orsova? Fancy. But there of a certainty you will be issued with visas. Why not start now?

We manage to persuade them that after a fifteen hour day two days running 'sint foarte obosit' (we are extremely tired) 'Mi-e somn' (we want to sleep) if they don't mind us staying the night.

They turn aside and have a long and serious discussion among themselves about this unusual request.

'Not here,' is the answer, but they allot us a berth alongside a *schlepper* which is being loaded with firewood. All is quiet, this Sunday night. We are not allowed ashore and a heavily armed guard is stationed all night on the *schlepper* to see that two dangerous unarmed English pensioners do not invade Romania during the night.

The cats, as usual, do exactly what they like, released after two days stoppage of leave, and needing no visas. A tree trunk on the *schlepper* keeps them happily sharpening their claws for the night's work.

In the morning, 7 August, we observed that we were a sufficient menace to the state to qualify for *two* armed guards, one at each end of the *schlepper*. Their effectiveness was reinforced by the fact that the barge was too far out for us to get ashore anyway. At our urgent signals, one of the guards fetched an officer. A plank was produced to span the gap and Bill went to the office to get our papers, which had been impounded for the night. We slipped at 0840, the Romanian army stood down, and we headed for Orsova.

Listening to Relu, we had gleaned through his enthusiastic descriptions of the town an impression of a delightful riverside tourist resort, and we were looking forward to rest and relaxation, and reporting to our loved ones that we had successfully passed through Jugoslavia.

We were coming to a part of the river which has been much changed by the two dams in the Iron Gate scheme. These major works were undertaken jointly by Romania and Jugoslavia in the communist days and were heavily condemned by western Greens. They raised the water level by about 25 metres just above the upper dam at Kp 950, but such is the gradient here that 100 kilometres above it the water level is raised by only about 10 metres.

After Moldova Veche the river divides round a new island, once a low hill. The old river bed flows to the right, and we had been recommended by the tugmasters to take this route if there was a strong wind. Rod Heikell had gone this way in 1987, and had got himself lost among the trees of a submerged forest for a time, and had spent a night made fast to the top branches of one of them. His experience inclined us to the other route; there was not much wind at breakfast time, and it was shorter. It turned out to be shallower, the wind increased quickly and considerably from the east, and the early morning sun hindered us from identifying the markers, turning this too into a tricky channel. We reduced to half speed for 20 minutes in order more carefully to study the way ahead through our filtered binoculars. We are not surprised Heikell got lost in this tricky region; nor that he has drawn a channel the wrong side of a small islet called Babakai (Kp 1044.5), and only alertness saved us from taking it.

Where the channels reunite, the castle of Golubac stands against the cliff, steeped in history. There have been castles here since Roman times, and the present one is an impressive building. Heikell quotes the story of a knight, 'inevitably called George', who slew a dragon here. There was no regular municipal collection of *monstres*, as in France, and he was unable to sling the corpse in the river. The decomposing carcase became the breeding ground (in the legend) for a species of giant mosquito who thereafter plagued the area. We agree with him that this legend would be better transplanted further downstream where they have mosquitos that would be useful harnessed to a cart.

A feeling of mystery and awe was hard to shake off here, with the blank eyes of castle Golubac on us, the mist wreathing on the waters, among the stumps and rotting twigs of the submerged forest. The works are recent, but legends will certainly engender, perhaps of waterwolves and finny forest dwellers, and vampirhanas.

The lake shores came closer, crowded in on us, shouldering us into a steep and narrow valley, with a ledge carved out of the cliff a little above river level to serve as roads, one on the Serbian side, one on the Romanian side.

If we had thought that Surduk was big oil business, here was Mega-business. Over the 36 kilometres from 1056 to 1020 we counted 104 sites similar to the ones we had seen near Kp 1202, except that they were larger and busier. These were not related to taking the odd litres from tugs at anchor for the night; these were concerned with ferrying the stuff across the river from Romania to the Jugoslavian shore opposite in industrial quantities. The stacks of oil drums stood 4 or 5 high, and behind them huge articulated tanker-trucks waited in line as the oil was pumped into their tanks, a drum at a time. It was a continuous process: as one truck left, another took its place. Day and night the black skiffs, loaded with their 200 litre drums, buzzed back and forth, filling up by gravity from tanker-trucks parked on the new Romanian riverside road (which might well have been constructed for such a purpose), and discharging by pumping into tanker-trucks waiting eagerly on the opposite side. Some paused as we went by, others did not bother, assessing us as harmless. The Romanian Navy patrols the river, and at night their patrol boats are blacked out, but what can they do? Lookouts (at Golubac castle?) blow the whistle and everything stops for the time being, but not on the Jugoslavian side, for there the traffic is legal.

What about the Romanian side? We were to find out how corrupt officialdom is in Romania. There is a system of *baksheesh* beside which Levantine extortion appears infantile and ineffective. More to the point, Serbia is a land-locked country and Romania has traditionally been a trade route to that country, encouraged by Russia who has for a century been a champion of Serbia. UN Sanctions, coming at a time when Romania was shaking off the traumas of a terrible revolution, hit the Romanian economy hard. The temptation for their government, desperately in need of hard currency, to turn a blind eye to such a lucrative traffic must have been irresistible. And it must have been lucrative. We estimated that in a 36 kilometre stretch between 3000 and 6000 tonnes of liquid fuel must have crossed the Danube each day.

Gradually we left behind the scarred banks, cluttered with oil drums, black with spilt oil and churned with tanker tracks, and came to one of the most beautiful and impressive parts of the Danube's long passage to the sea.

Millennia ago, there was an inland sea west of the Carpathian Mountains, where now the great Danube Plain rolls over the fossils of sea creatures that log its past. Eventually the sea broke through the mountains, and poured over a sill about 44 metres above the level of the Black Sea. The channel it cut was shallow, and rocky, and the river cascaded down through spectacular crags, its waters shredded and roiled into rapids and whirlpools by the teeth of the rocks. For centuries, this stretch formed a barrier to navigation on the Lower Danube (from the Iron Gate to the sea) because the gorge was virtually impassable except for small craft. The Turks were not boatmen, and did little to encourage navigation on the Danube, though they ruled over much of it for centuries. It was the expansionist policies of the Austro-Hungarian Empire that led its Transport Minister, Gabor Baross, to order the blasting of a canal, the Sip Canal, in the river bed close to the right bank. It was opened in 1898, and it was but a modest improvement; barges had to be towed upstream against the fierce current by a steam locomotive on tracks on the bank.

Though this canal was constructed further down the river, we mention it now because although strictly speaking the Iron Gate (in the singular) was situated around Kp 943, custom has given the name of the Iron Gates (plural) to the long passage through the mountains, starting at Golubac, going through the Kazan Gorge, the Iron Gate, and down to about Kp 863.

The gorge loomed close on either side, steep grey crags dropping sheer into the river from immense heights, wild and rugged. There was a feeling of solitude, the noise of our engines echoing off the cliff was an indecency where silence should reign. It would have been difficult to find a place to stop, but a smaller craft than *Hosanna* could in places make fast to the rock faces. There were huge wild birds soaring across the narrow sky overhead. The slow beat of their serrated wings suggested eagles, but in the narrows we could not take time to check. Lower down between Kps 974 and 965, the cliffs became higher and the gorge even narrower – so narrow, and the bends so sharp that not only is it a 'no overtaking' zone, but it is forbidden even to pass vessels going in the opposite direction. Use of syren and VHF channel 16 is obligatory, and our syren's mournful note bounced off the cliffs as we approached the bends, and the birds

The Kazan Gorge

spun indignantly for a couple of circuits as if their tailfeathers had been ruffled by the decibels, before resuming the slow wheeling turns of the hunt.

The turns in the river, on the other hand, were sharp enough to cause *Hosanna*, at a mere 27 metres length, to have to pause and go warily. We were petrified at the thought of meeting a big upstream barge tow in the narrows, and did not wish to imagine the difficulties such a tow would encounter even without any other craft to consider. Knowing a little now about how they work, we decided they would probably take the barges through one or two at a time, as the Slovakian Captains did in the flood near Kelheim.

There were deeps below us, 35 metres to the bottom of the river which was at sea level. We had 1000 kilometres to go and 35 metres to drop.

We turned abruptly out of this limestone canyon to find Trajan's monument at Kp 964.7 on the right bank, a square stone tablet which was moved to its present position just above the water when the river level was raised. It commemorates the building of a road along the valley, the Romans being good at that, rather than water transport.

Before the end of the narrows we had a panic over a green buoy we thought we saw near the right hand shore, which would have meant going through a very narrow gap indeed. It eventually manifested as a little triangular green sail on a tiny boat. As we have said, there ought to be a law. You don't get this happening on a motorway: no one stands there imitating a traffic cone.

Orsova – pegel

As the river widened we met our first tow of the day, a nine-barge pusher, and were thankful we had emerged from the gorge. The country was beautiful, green and rolling hills on the Jugoslav side, the Romanian side a little more parched. The fields were of maize and sunflowers, and the haystacks were small and conical, like straw hats.

At 1550 we rounded into Orsova Bay. Old Orsova is now submerged on the bed of the bay, and New Orsova has been built on the shores of the lake that formed when the dam was built. We circled round the bay looking for a mooring, and were chased away from the Romanian Naval base. The chasers misdirected us to a disused pier, and we went further round the bay to what appeared to be a shipyard. The inner end of it was the Harbour-master's pontoon. There was not enough room, so Bill berthed sticking out a long way, but safe enough in the still water. It was about 1730.

De ce intirziaţi? Why are you late? Visas were not possible, we had arrived after 1600.

• 27 •
BUREAU-CRASS-Y
Orsova

We had taken so long slowly circling the great bay, looking for a mooring, that we were too late to check in. Yes, said Authority, it would have been possible to get visas this day, but the official had gone back to Turnu Severin, and his office was closed until tomorrow. There were urgent, but long-drawn out conferences between anxious uniformed men sitting on *Hosanna*'s verandah, smoking the cigarettes we had offered and drinking our ice-cooled drinks. Gradually the head-shaking stopped, and a more positive attitude appeared. Finally, as all the six men leant back and smiled, the one who spoke some English said we should move to the adjoining pontoon, and could stay there for the night, but we could not go ashore.

Bill looked longingly at the café-bar just opposite the berth and asked if we could not go there to eat. He regretted his request, as almost immediately the scrum re-formed, but this time, perhaps because a principle of BE NICE TO THE FOREIGNERS had been decided upon, the hooker quick-heeled the ball, and we were given permission to go to the café-bar. We would be allowed 30 minutes, and an escort would be provided.

We shifted berth, tidied ourselves up and were escorted to the café by one of the Harbour-master's assistants and an armed soldier. On arrival there was a certain amount of arm waving, and an obvious attempt to redecorate and furnish the basement on our behalf, but Bill preferred to sit on the terrace with the tin tables and rickety chairs, and enjoy the view with everyone else. They had thought we would prefer privacy. The atmosphere relaxed, our escort ordered us beer and wine to drink (both nicely cold on a hot, airless evening), clean paper was spread over the threadbare cloth and we had pickled salad and Romanian meat balls called *mitités*, grilled on skewers, the aroma of which had been wafting down to the boat and driving us mad with hunger. Our escort departed, saying he would see us later, and we were left with the armed guard sitting at the next table.

Bill does not like armed guards. Having no say in the presence of this one, he expressed his feelings by buying the guard an ice cream. The best way to cope with the feeling of menace that comes from an armed guard is to make him look ridiculous. Candyfloss would have been better, but was not available. However, an armed soldier eating an ice-cream cone should be enough. Bill was right. The scene had a surrealist air, the man's mouth smeared with strawberry mush, his tongue darting in and out licking his dummy, while in the other hand he held his sub-machine gun by the barrel.

From the beaten earth terrace of the café we could look across to the town of Orsova, nestling at the foot of hills dark against the setting sun on the other side of the bay, some distance away. As we watched we realised that *Medias*'s convoy had caught us up, and was anchoring in the bay.

From each barge a procession of unpainted, dented steel dories came slowly towards a spot close to *Hosanna* where they could be beached, the ripples from their progress punctuated by the circles of each stroke of an oar, spreading and interweaving patterns on the calm surface of the water. The boats were so heavily loaded that their crews had difficulty rowing them. We held our breath as they landed awkwardly with imminent risk of capsize, and dragged their loot up the steep bank to the Customs shed.

Their precious loads were the discards of Western affluence, raided from rubbish bins, municipal tips and second-hand shops, items we had seen about the decks and hatch covers of the *schleppers*. This was private enterprise, a shining bonus to add to their meagre pay. Every crew member had his hoard of old refrigerators, washing machines, trashy cocktail cabinets, metal grids, bathtubs, bicycles and pieces of carpet, all unobtainable in Romania and therefore saleable. Each item would be lugged up the steep steps from the landing, and looked over by the Customs officer on duty, money would be handed over, and the items carried off triumphantly to be loaded into trailers, and then away somewhere into the interior. Here a busy cottage industry mended what was broken and fixed and furbished the shabby.

This was clearly routine; every barge tow coming down from Germany and Austria would bring goodies. Everyone knew the form, and the goods passed continuously up the steps for hours. Our escort reappeared to take us back to the boat, and expressed his shame that his country should be reduced to living on other countries' rubbish. We could feel his embarrassment, and consoled him. We ourselves, like other seamen, are not above picking up some discarded object if it is something we want or need. The difference, one supposes, is that we have a choice, and the Romanians do not, but we did not add that. All economies have to start somewhere, we said. Romania had been ruined by bad men governing badly, and it was encouraging that people were beginning to pick themselves up, and think for themselves, rather than screaming for aid from the West, which must be the real humiliation.

We had enjoyed the early evening as the heat drained out of the day, and in the cool of dusk rounded off our meal with fruit and coffee. We were accompanied by our faithful armed spaniel who sat on the pontoon a few feet away. We did *not* feed him scraps from our table, but we did relent sufficiently to give him a cool drink now and then, and he would retire to a dark corner of the pontoon to drink it out of the gaze of passing NCOs.

As we sat in the evening cool a handsome young man in a purple

T-shirt waved cheerily to us as he passed. 'See you tomorrow!' he said. Only by his grin did we recognise Relu, who had now had the haircut and shave he could not afford in Austria. He looked very different from the wild and woolly man we first met in Komarno. Without his long black tresses and beard he looked very respectable. The change was staggering.

At the landward end of the pontoon was the building containing the Harbour authority, Police, Customs and Immigration, which might have appeared grand on the architect's plan, but was now dilapidated and peeling, its glass mosaics falling off in places, and the old steel window frames, though lumpily painted, were fighting a losing battle against rust. There was a state canteen in the building, which nobody used, preferring the tumble-down private enterprise café along the quay.

As we finished breakfast a man in plain clothes left the building and came towards us. He spoke a little English and invited Bill to come for the entry formalities for our persons. 'The ship will come after.' Bill had dressed himself tolerably smartly because most Romanian officials looked scruffy and he wanted the sartorial high ground. The man dismissed the sentry back to the building, and took Bill away in his car.

It was an elderly Renault, made under licence in Romania, and it was his official car. He was the Colonel in command of the area frontier police, no less, a kind and thoughtful man, and he had come down personally to see to our problems. Bill was sorry the Colonel was not allowed a smarter car, but perhaps he was lucky to have one at all. This had once been the General's, and was starting its downward passage. The Colonel's French was better than his English, so they switched.

They went first to the Iron Gate Dam on the way to Turnu Severin. They passed the derelict Orsova shipyards which had once built and repaired barges, and drove along the riverside. Bill was left to wait, and he looked at the wide river, with Jugoslavia on the other side. The enormous hydro-electric output generated at the dam is shared between the two countries. There are locks on both sides, but the Jugoslav lock was closed 'for repair', though we suspect the real reason was to save energy. It is a huge scheme, blending into the landscape now and not an eyesore, apart from the buildings themselves. It serves as a frontier bridge, normally busy, but less so owing to Sanctions. Workers went to and fro by bus, all of them being searched. Bill was summoned to an office in the administrative building.

A clerk typed out forms, and the Colonel drove into the city of Turnu Severin to the Bank of Commerce. Here the manager greeted and kowtowed to the Colonel, and Bill was able to cash two Eurocheques, one in dollars and the other in lei for local purchases. The Colonel asked if there was anything we needed. Bill asked for bread, they found a baker, and returned to the dam. The office resounded to the thump of rubber stamps for several minutes while everything in sight was covered in them, Bill being relieved that he did not have a bald head.

The Colonel was a pleasant, good mannered man. Bill asked him how they had all adapted to the new regime. It had been difficult at first, he said, all revolutions unsettled everything, and one never knew whether one's job was secure. He was materially worse off than before, but happier. Then he said how much the UN Sanctions were harming his country. 'We don't like war criminals,' he said, 'but the loss of trade is a cruel burden when we are least able to take it.'

Bill was dropped at the quayside. We now had to deal with the Harbour-master. If we had come across a charming and helpful frontier Police Chief, the Harbour-master was a man of different kidney; porcine, and coarse featured.

It was not that he was unpleasant in his manners. Bill was taken into his office, sat down, and the minions were dismissed. During the next two and a half hours his, and *Hosanna*'s papers were pored over countless times by this fat and dissolute looking man, who kept on murmuring 'difficult, difficult.' Bill could see no possible difficulty. If there were dues to pay, he would pay them. If there were not, then... He had plenty of time to study the relief map of this part of the river, facing him on the wall.

Laurel had been getting anxious as time passed. She knows Bill's inability to wait calmly, and his intolerance of bureaucratic fools. Had he finally over-stepped the mark, been arrested, and carted off to the nearby jail for torture?

She went to find Relu aboard *Medias*, but he was ashore. However, the Monitor came to her assistance. He indicated that it seemed to him that the Harbour-master was asking for a present. Not to give one was to start a long process of seeing who could outsit whom, and the Harbour-master had the advantage of his own WC next to his office. He suggested a bottle might do the trick.

In fact he meant a bottle of wine, and later he was horrified at her profligacy. So was Bill, but that is beside the point. She seized half a litre of Glenmorangie malt whisky, climbed two flights of steps to the Harbour-master's office, and peered nervously round the Harbour-master's door. 'I don't know what the problem is,' hissed Bill, 'he won't let Relu come and translate, but he won't let me go either.' Laurel produced the bottle from her basket, and offered it as a sacrifice.

In an instant the mood changed dramatically. The difficulties evaporated. From a cupboard came a tray with several little glasses. From the bottom right hand drawer of the desk came a bottle of wine and some wine glasses. The Harbour-master went to the door and bawled something out in a voice like a foghorn. Instantly two other men appeared with several bottles of ice-cold beer and beer glasses. Everybody sat down. Corks were drawn and bottlenecks gurgled.

'The Harbour-master of Orsova and his staff greet the English, welcome to the city of Orsova,' pronounced the Harbour-master.

Glug glug.

Not being used to formal speeches we nodded our thanks.

'The Harbour-master of Orsova drinks to the King of England,' (here one of the minions nudged him and whispered). 'The Queen,' he corrected himself.

Glug glug.

We drank to the Queen, but unfortunately were not able to recall the name of the present Head of State in Romania. However Bill knew the ground rules, and managed:

'The Captain and Mate of the Barge *Hosanna* drink to the prosperity of the Republic of Romania.'

Glug glug.

'To all seamen and sailors,' said one of the others.

Glug glug.

'To peace among men!' toasted Laurel.

Glug glug.

'To Princess Diana!' roared another man.

This looked likely to go on for some time. The Harbour-master had clearly had a start on us, but with the long abstemious interval he looked as if he was just limbering up for the real contest to come, and would shortly start on the heirs to the British throne. About the only former king of Romania Bill could remember was Vlad the Impaler, a person not exactly noted for his attention to the rights of man.

The etiquette was to empty your glass with each toast, Russian style, but not to throw the glasses at the wall. The Harbour-master and one of his assistants were toasting in spirits, Laurel and the other assistant in wine, while Bill had opted for beer, and was craftily using one of the little spirit glasses. He was cheerfully keeping his end up, having had to do this type of thing before. Slowly the speech of the Fat Harbour-master slurred and he had difficulty getting to his feet. The bottles were emptying. The assistant stood up, and we left, leaving the Fat Harbour-master silent, glass in hand, glazed eyes contemplating the wall.

There had been talk of our making a phone call; we needed to tell our children we had passed Jugoslavia safely. The assistant said he would call for us in an hour, meanwhile we went back on board. Lunch was late and rapid. We were not very impressed with Romanian officialdom. We felt it might be better to manage phoning and shopping on our own.

However, here was the assistant Harbour-master, Florian, come to fetch us in his car, a Brabant. We drove into the newly built town which looked quite attractive from a distance with tree-lined, wide curving streets. Closer examination showed that every building was finished in bare concrete, and that both the concrete and the fittings were already looking tatty. The telephone office was on the ground floor of a block of flats. It had the decor and feel of a rather dirty government waiting room of the 1940s. Anyone wanting to make an international call had to show their passport, fill in a form giving the number, and wait sitting on the windowsill because the few seats were already overfull; we might have graduated to a seat given time and a bit of ruthlessness, if the sitters had not been as leery-looking a band of cut-throats as we had seen since our acquaintance with the crew of *Medias*. We were saved by Florian. He told the woman behind the grill that he would take his guests to his flat to wait there for the call, which should be put through to his telephone. Then we would come back to pay. He seemed to have the stature to command this service.

His flat was on the fourth floor of a six storey block behind the telephone office. There were no lifts, and the public parts of the block were shabby. Families sat on the steps with their children in the hot afternoon. His flat was clean, but the small rooms were cluttered. He had a little boat, obviously, from the bits and pieces that lay about. He was the possessor also of quantities of copper wire, surplus to government requirements one supposes; it was in use everywhere instead of string, cellotape, or washing line. He offered us water melon from the fridge, cool and refreshing, especially after the session in the Port Office three hours before. He told us they were all having trouble coping with the new situation. The organised labour, such as the coal-miners, wanted to keep in power those old officials they knew they could manipulate, but everyone was fighting for a place in the sun and in the chaos nothing was getting done at all. There were other things he was ashamed of as well as the rampant second-hand goods market; 'Be patient with us,' he asked.

Our calls came through after about an hour, and we paid our bills and walked to the *piaţa* (pronounced piatsa), the market place. Many of the stalls were small trays from which a variety of goods were offered, three bottles of shampoo, two tins of polish, a dozen plastic clothes pegs, and a red cabbage, with strong plastic bags in colourful designs for sale to carry the loot home. Others were more like the farm stalls in any European market with small piles of vegetables, a few dozen eggs, and a couple of honeycombs. Laurel bought peppers, aubergines, and a bucketful of grapes for next to nothing. We thought of having a coffee or a drink in the market *cantina*, but Florian suggested somewhere nearer the waterfront, and we walked there and sat under a tree in a little park, where there was a light breeze. The kiosk belonged to his son, Dragos, a young man with a ponytail who spoke English. We had a cooling drink, and a chat and expressed our thanks to Florian, giving him half the grapes; there were far more than we could eat. Then Dragos and Mihaela, his girlfriend, drove us home. They, too, were given the two-and-sixpenny tour of *Hosanna*, and wrote in our visitor's book:

> 'Do you have nice voyage and Mary Christmas in this ship "Hosanna". Gut lucky!'

We were tired after so many visits and visitors, and decided to eat on board. Somewhat to Bill's surprise Laurel produced a really English meal of roast beef from the freezer, with roast potatoes, Yorkshire pudding, and cabbage. The nice thing about carrying your house with you is that you can occasionally shut out the country you are in, if you need a touch of home.

After dinner Relu called on us with a friend, bringing a bottle of Romanian Pinot Noir. By coincidence we were halfway down a bottle of Pinot Noir de Bourgogne, from France, so we were able to compare directly. The Romanian one stood up very well, a little sweeter, and a quarter the price. He'd bought it at the Station Buffet. We determined to do the same. Relu was longing to see his new wife downriver in Giurgiu, and he had no idea when. His bosses were a bit arbitrary, he said. 'They say come and I come, they say go and I go, they say stay and I stay,' never knowing from one day to the next, though he hoped he would be in Giurgiu before long. Despite a tiring day his company was relaxing. We did not realise the visit would be his last.

Coping with the officials had been partly pleasant, and partly quite unpleasant, but one common factor remained throughout: the going had not been easy, and produced personal tension at a very high level. Bill had been occupied with this all day, from 0830 to 1600, with only a short break for a snatched lunch. He was mentally exhausted.

We were left alone the next day except for a visit by Florian to ask when we were going. We told him we would leave tomorrow, and go to Turnu Severin, where we would like to take on fuel. He said he would see what could be done. We relaxed, reading a bit, gathering strength. Bill said, with some foresight, that we were going to find officialdom the biggest menace from now on.

There was a thunderstorm that night, a spectacular one with lightning shafting down into the water all round the bay.

We got up to a cooler day and had hoped to leave early. Laurel took the bag of papers to the Fat Harbour-master, and paid a modest mooring fee, after which further difficulties were discovered. He was not satisfied with our ship's certificate of registry. We had an old one, now overstamped 'cancelled' in red, which had been a most impressive document, little smaller than a bath towel, in a board folder. The replacement, which had our new engine arrangement on, was a scruffy-looking typed A4 sheet of paper. We had kept the old one to enfold the new as we thought it looked more worthy for places where great store is set by documents. It was a big mistake. Clearly the Fat Harbour-master was not impressed (neither are we; the signs of our becoming slowly a third world country are gathering) but his objection was that the stamp on the old certificate, saying CANCELLED was itself neither stamped, dated nor signed, so how did he know it was AUTHORISED? The logic, propounded by Florian, that a new one would automatically cancel an older one was not acceptable; the new one was a different type of certificate.

Bill, who arrived to see what the delay was this time, had no intention of providing more whisky to mollify this rapacious old man, and told him to call the British Consul. For over an hour the dispute went on, and finally Florian's argument prevailed: we clearly had a valid certificate, correctly in date, and the old one was irrelevant. The Fat Harbour-master walked rudely out of the room, our papers were released by Florian, and we left about 0950. Florian, who had been correct and well-mannered throughout our acquaintance with him, rang the lock at the Iron Gate to say we were on the way.

Our relaxed holiday in the Lake Resort of Orsova was over.

• 28 •
MISSING BELIEVED PILLAGED

We headed for the Iron Gate dam. The thunderstorms had put the *pegel* up by plus 4 centimetres. It was a grey, misty morning, cool and refreshing after the close hot weather. The tops of the tall hills in the gorge were wreathed with cloud, tatters of thunderstorm still caught there. Our deck-buckets were full of rainwater. We had been told yesterday that the drinking water at Orsova was wonderful, it comes from mountain springs, and we had wanted to fill our tanks. But in Romania there is always something; in this case the water system was under repair, and unavailable for at least 3 hours, and after that 3 hours it was another 3 hours, and then it was evening, and the following morning was too late, we had to check out. It had been a bit like that at the Post Office: our phone calls to England had raised only ansafones, and we wanted to send faxes. The Post Office had a fax machine. 'Wonderful,' we thought. Alas, they had no fax paper, and were not likely to have any for some time. We put lavatory paper in our pockets in countries like this, but it hadn't occurred to us that we ought to take a few sheets of fax paper as well.

We had no problems on the 11 kilometres down to the biggest inland waters lock we had ever seen. 'From now, we speak only Russian,' had said Relu, who had given us an invaluable aid, the *Ghidul de Conversatie in cinci limbri:* Guide to Conversation in 5 languages; French, English, German, Romanian and Russian. He had touching faith in our linguistic ability.

The Iron Gate lock (Portile de Fier, in Romanian) had 16 turbines generating electricity, 8 for Jugoslavia and 8 for Romania. There were double locks at either end of the barrage, one for the Jugoslav side and one for the Romanian side. The lock has 2 chambers, one after the other, and at best takes a long time to pass. One has to call in advance on channel 16, and we had to wait a few minutes while a Ukrainian ship came upstream out of the lock.

We started the flasher to indicate that we wanted to pass him starboard to starboard, as the entrance to the lock was on our left. He was a long time picking up our flash, but finally caught on. We were reminded of what Relu had told us about his old tug *Medias*, which has no mod cons at all. She has an enormous wheel taller than a man, which has to be spun fiercely to get a lot of wheel on. If another boat comes in the opposite direction flashing, and Relu is alone, he has to flash by turning a switch on and off, it's not automatic. His description of himself giving a great swoop of the wheel and dashing across to the side of the bridge to operate the switch, up and down for every flash, makes a hilarious picture.

We were invited into the lock at 1050. 'This is English boat *Hosanna*,' we said.

'British boat, two green, two green lamp, ist frei going in the sluys,' replied the lock-keeper, mercifully not speaking Russian, but mixing English and German.

'English boat, thank you, Merci.'

It may sound strange saying Merci, but the Romanians use that as thank you, and it was easier to say than *Multumesc*. We had also learnt the Romanian word *Poftim* which means, 'pardon, excuse me, didn't quite catch that.' We used it often, delighting in the sound. At 1113 the downstream gate began to open, and at 1123 we passed from the upper chamber to the lower. At 1155 we were clear of the lock, having passed through this enormous edifice all on our own. We did not at the time realise how lucky we were. *Rainbow*, following a few days behind us, had to pay $100 in cash before the lock-keeper would let them pass. He settled for Deutchmarks, which was all they had. On the other hand *Rainbow* didn't get charged any transit tax by the Serbians at Bezdan, so in the end it worked out about the same for both of us, only we had a receipt. Looking back on it later, we thought that maybe Florian the deputy Harbour-master had arranged our easy transit. If so, we had even more to thank him for.

There was a phrase the lock-keeper used on VHF: 'Attention to the sail,' which flummoxed us for a moment, our masts being down and our sails all bagged; what he meant was watch our ropes as the water surged out, *sehl* being a German word for rope. The concrete at the top of the lock was covered with graffiti, mostly in the Cyrillic alphabet. Laurel did something she does not often do, and painted *Hosanna*'s name and the date on the wall. We looked in vain for another English name, but there was one English sign: Happy Birthday Sasha.

It was only a few kilometres further on to Turnu Severin, where we berthed at 1255 at the Harbour-master's pontoon, outside a tug. All Romanian officials have learnt at least one English phrase, it's 'Just a moment please.' The only trouble is that a Romanian 'moment' is two hours long. The fact that we had already checked in at Orsova cut no ice at all, we had to do it all over again, the Customs, the Immigration, the Harbour-master, the lady who looked after the pontoon and who charged us ten dollars. It was very exhausting, everything in triplicate and needing the ship's stamp and our signature. The bureaucracy took two hours, and all Bill's patience. If Bureaucracy was to take, say, 9 hours every 30 kilometres we would be a long time getting out to sea. Bill was depressed and showing symptoms of anxiety. Laurel stepped rather more into the breach.

It started to rain. Laurel went ashore in a taxi to try to send some fax messages at about 1530. It wasn't easy at first as our two armed sentries would not let her land. It required some firmness of the 'Go and fetch your Officer' type to get things sorted out, which did nothing to ease Bill's state of mind. As soon as she had left, Bill was required to stand off for a passenger vessel. After returning to the pontoon he sank into the chair for a rest.

Two little girls about six or seven years old seemed to be asking if they could play with our cats. Bill nodded, and returned to his book. The cat Tansy would not play, she is not particularly gregarious with small children, but Bograt is amenable to being pulled about, and rather liked racing round the boat with these children. After a short pause Bill leapt into life on hearing a muffled wail, and recognising Bograt's banshee cry of despair (which we hear quite often; even when muffled it is audible at half a kilometre) he got up in time to see the two girls clambering down to the pontoon with a wriggling canvas bag containing something alive and struggling. He gave chase. The girls dropped the bag and fled. Bograt wriggled out of the bag, ran back on board, shaking herself indignantly, and sat down to imperative washing.

Laurel is very fond of her cats, and Bill is very fond of Laurel. He was distraught, not only by the kitnapping. Laurel was now missing believed pillaged, as it was well after 1700. He went in search. He knew she had intended to visit the big hotel wherein worked the UN Sanctions team. We had hopes they might send the faxes for us, especially our notes on the diesel pirate situation, but they had no fax machine. Nor did the hotel. Bill went to the main Post Office, but they, too, had no fax. His anxiety level was now dangerous, but he had no idea where next to look, so he returned on board to let his feelings fester. At 1800 he saw Laurel climbing out of a taxi, and behaved like any parent finally united with a lost child: he shouted at her. Laurel had by extreme persistence at the Hotel Trajan finally succeeded in her objective. It had taken three hours to send two faxes, and far too much money, but the taxi had cost only 30 pence, so she was in a good enough humour to ignore the shouting and calm him down. The atmosphere of the place was getting into us.

Neither of us felt like cooking. We went ashore to the restaurant at the big hotel, The Parc. It was huge, with terraces everywhere, but the restaurants which ideally should have occupied these terraces were closed. This left the restaurant indoors. There were over 100 tables, of which four or five were occupied. The carpet was shabby and none too clean, and the tapestry seated chairs were stained where hands had gripped the woodwork. The tablecloth was clean, but the table napkins were paper ones, and they had been cut in quarters for economy. Like us, the Hotel chef didn't feel like cooking; the meal was appalling. The hors d'oeuvres was turist salami (made from not very fresh turists?). The guidebook said: 'You will enjoy Crap fresh caught from the Danube.' Crap is Romanian for carp, but crap was probably the better word for it; our fish was freezer-burnt before being oven-burnt, and about as appetising as a suede glove. The service was sloppy, but the waitress spoke a little French. The wine was good, though, and we drank a lot of it.

A thoroughly bad day, not helped by the news of mass graves discovered after the fighting at Srebrenica. Bill needed a pill to get to sleep.

The next day we were back in action with the officials. To get our diesel fuel, we had to be checked by the Customs (Vama), there were more papers for the Harbour-master, and further papers to be shuttled between Vama and NAVROM who owned the fuelling point. When all this was done the Vama decided our proof of having brought funds into the country legally was not good enough, so Bill had to go to the bank at the other end of town and get a different form stamped and counter-stamped in a different way.

It was almost lunchtime before we shifted berth to the fuelling point, where two helpful men awaited, and found their nozzle would not fit our inlet; they were used to fuelling huge tugs. After about an hour of improvisation, all four of us decided, over a beer, that there was no way a *Hosanna*-sized nozzle could be put on the end of a pipe that had passed through the official meter. But the Customs forms had all been authenticated, signed, stamped, counter-signed, counter-stamped and counter-authenticated, and our Romanians knew that to undo that lot was akin to counter revolution. We *had* now to be given diesel. They asked if we had gauges. Bill, by now virtually foaming at the mouth, had the presence of mind to say yes. It was agreed to pump in fuel until we said we had received two tonnes. We know roughly how much our tanks hold, but in the interests of better accuracy Bill did some quick calculations on the litres per inch depth in the rectangular tanks. Then, while Laurel helped the two men hold the improvised nozzle in our filling tube, he watched the sight-glasses down below.

The diesel flowed in, hiccuping occasionally. Bill appeared. 'That's about two tonnes,' he said. The man in charge of the pumps said he did not want us to go short, we'd better have some more to make sure. Bill watched bemused while he put in what was probably another 400 litres. Unfortunately the stream was too powerful at one point, and an air bubble formed, blowing some diesel into the bottom of the boat which we had to mop up with kitchen paper. There was a smell of diesel everywhere as we gave the two men on the fuelling barge a bottle of wine each, re-berthed at the main pontoon and went to pay and get all the papers restamped, resigned, reauthenticated, counter-signed, etc.

After a time *Rainbow* berthed alongside us and the officials crossed our decks to deal with her. The procedure very nearly reduced Jean to tears, and *Rainbow* moved out to anchor among the barges for a quiet night.

The following morning we underwent the visit from the UN Sanctions team, a mixture of Americans and Turkish. No unpleasantness, but as a check it was not particularly effective. Perhaps they had decided we were not up to mischief. They were amused by Bill's account of yesterday's catnapping. 'Oh dear,' they said, 'you've deprived somebody of their dinner.' We had discovered that in Hungary a *Bograts* is a kind of cauldron. Bograt is somewhat cauldron-shaped, but we wouldn't want her to end up in one.

Laurel and Jean went shopping in the Alimentar. Laurel returned, grinning. 'I could have bought tins of crap at the Alimentar. I wish I had, it would make a nice present for one or two people I know.'

We left Turnu Severin at 0730 next morning, 12 August, and went downstream at full speed on our way to the last lock and Kalafat, where we would be checked again by the Sanctions Mission to make sure that we had not been extremely naughty on the way through Jugoslavia. We hoped to get to Kalafat today; though it was another five hours after we'd got through the lock.

It was flat land now, the great gorges and The Iron Gate behind us. On our right Jugoslavia looked extraordinarily peaceful, with little maize fields and a tractor or two here and there. But on both sides of the river were goon boxes, and they were manned, and everybody was looking at everybody else with deep, deep, suspicion. Bill was feeling edgy. He observed that the Black Sea had a weather pattern which would start to become unstable in September. He seemed unusually worried about it. Well, September was only 19 days away.

At 1235 we arrived at the lock complex known officially as Iron Gate II. Rod Heikell, in his book, refers to it as Prahovo (Kp 863), but that is the Jugoslavian side, which was not working at the time we passed. The remaining, Romanian, lock is in the Braţ Gogosul (Braţ is pronounced Bratch, and means arm). In spite of calling ahead we got a double red light.

For behold, some distance from the lock a Romanian tug was fussing back and forth shepherding her barges like a hen with chicks. We should know these barges, we thought; where's the bathtub? There's the chicken coops, and the woodpiles, and the useful bits of rope, but where's the bathtub? But they had unloaded the bathtub to sell at Orsova... It was, of course, *Medias* and her tow.

It was windy, and *Rainbow*, caught in the clapotage near the lock, irritated and uncomfortable, had earlier called us on VHF pleading 'Hurry up, they're keeping us waiting for you.' But *Rainbow* doesn't know what it takes to get *Medias* and her 8 barges through a lock. *Rainbow* called us again: 'Hosanna: this is Rainbow, you can relax, there's no sign of the damn thing opening, over.'

Well, no.

It was late afternoon yesterday when we saw Relu passing with his 8 barges, so it had taken him all morning to get the first batch through the lock.

Now as the gates open for *Medias*, but the lights remain red for *Rainbow* and *Hosanna*, she carefully separates the remaining 4 barges and arranges them in a tow of 2 behind 2. She tows these at very short scope, with a huge heap of tyres on her sloping stern, and glides very slowly into the lock. As she stops at the end of the lock chamber, the barges ride up over the tyres protecting her stern until at last all come to a halt and are made fast. There is just room for us as well. The green light tells us to follow in, and the lock gates close at 1500, two and a half hours after our arrival.

'Oh gracious me, a soldier with a rifle,' said Laurel.

It took two and threequarter hours in the end to get through the lock, our 273rd, the last one on the Danube, and about the longest we'd ever seen. It was built in 1979 but from the crumbling of the concrete and the decrepitude of the construction, plus the fact that a gang of men was needed to close the gates behind us, it is not in good repair. There were now 963 kilometres to go to the Black Sea.

The soldier with a rifle stopped Laurel from photographing *Medias* in the lock. 'But it's my friend!' she exclaimed. 'No good,' he said.

We were through and clear at 1520, but not *Medias*. She had to anchor the barges she had just towed through with those she had brought through already that morning, and reform her 8-barge tow before following us down river. We contemplated for a moment the work they did, these Romanian Tug Captains, with their ancient tugs and huge tows, what long hours they worked, and how poorly paid they were. We did not envy them.

We did not realise then that we should not see Relu again. We owed him much; his friendship, his knowledge, and practical advice had greatly helped us. There could have been no greater contrast with the Fat Harbour-master at Orsova collecting half a bottle of whisky for sweet Fanny Adams.

There was no chance now of getting to Kalafat, so we looked for an anchorage. We were very close to the border on our right between Jugoslavia and Bulgaria. The trees had been cut down to form a big swathe of bare territory. On the left was Romania, with more goon boxes and gun emplacements.

We passed the right bank frontier at Kp 845. At 841 we anchored close by the left bank; *Hosanna* rode quietly in a strong stream.

With no more locks the currents were now governed entirely by the gradient of the river bed and the water flow. The water level had been falling fast, but we had been told at Orsova that the up-river regulators were asking the lower ones to keep the water level down so as to continue draining the upper reaches, which were still full. This meant that the currents were beginning to strengthen in this reach below the last lock, and we could expect the water levels to go down further.

Rainbow came by, ran aground, got off again, and accepted our invitation to raft up, and join us in an informal supper party of boiled bacon and beans. There is not much choice of delectable foods once one gets to Romania, if caviar is out of season, and it was.

We watched Bulgarian goats browsing on the strand, and celebrated the comfortable feeling of having achieved the transit of Jugoslavia unscathed.

• 29 •

ORDEAL BY SANCTIONS
Kalafat

The current was stronger next morning, Sunday, running at about 10 km/hr. We got under way at 0810, and at about 0920 came up with *Medias* and her tow, who had passed us during the evening, working as usual till long after nightfall. They were anchored at Kp 825. We wondered why she hadn't started again at dawn this morning. Just beyond her was the big tug *Durnstein* (Austrian), a rare sight down here, also at anchor with 3 barges. There was incomprehensible Russian chatter on channel 16. At Kp 822 there were dozens of barges spread all over the marked channel and we dropped to slow ahead to take stock of the situation. A big Russian tug without any barges was working hard upstream close to the left bank, well outside the marked channel. She was making slow progress in spite of two huge plumes of white water astern of her. Five minutes later, in the middle of the buoyed channel, we hit bottom upstream of the barges, and knew why *Medias* had anchored higher up. We would not see her again.

Bill tried to refloat *Hosanna* while watching the Russian tug. There was evidently deeper water over there, and the tug was deepening it by brute force, his big five-bladed propellers spreading the loose sand about. Another Russian tug took two of the abandoned barges and followed him upstream. *Hosanna* came off the ground, and we were able to creep past the remaining barges and find deeper water (1.60 metres, and we draw 1.50) before a third Russian tug could start to take through two more barges. We heard our friend Relu on the radio, for the last time: it seemed that up- and downstream tows were alternating, passing the shallows with two barges at a time, big *Durnstein* being the first downstream. We kept speed down to 1 knot because to have used any more power would have dragged our stern deeper (a phenomenon known as 'squat') and run us aground again. It was sexual navigation (continuously caressing the bottom) for the next 5 kilometres. The *pegel* at Cetate showed the river had fallen a metre in one night. It was now well below normal navigating level.

Then we were in 5 metres again and picked up speed. The current increased and we made fast to a pontoon at Kalafat on the left bank in time for lunch. A marine festival was in progress, with music and flags, and in order to moor we had to avoid the greasy pole, which had been placed without much thought to anyone mooring at the pontoon.

There followed a surreal afternoon in which the Sanctions Team and the Romanian authorities boarded us while water frolics took place all around us. There were tugs-of-war, and a duck race, where mallards with their wings clipped are thrown into the water for the local youths to dive after, swim, chase and catch. And all this time the Sanctions Control people were on board, Dutch and American among them this time, asking questions, making sure that everything was in order. And so were the Customs and so were the Immigration Police, and so were the Port Police and the Harbour-master. All of them were slightly distracted by the water frolics, the Dutch and American rather disapproving. We could hear one of them muttering: 'Don't drown the ducks... you drowning the ducks... don't go drown the ducks.' It was no good trying to hide and thinking of the RSPCA; one was in a different culture here. Not that different, however. We had no time to mention that the last duck race we saw, just as cruel as this, was in southern France.

King Neptune arrived by boat, with trident and attendant mermaids, to much applause. Nothing to complain of there.

Then a piglet was put in a sack and suspended under the greasy pole, which was about twenty feet long and springy, and as the young men tried to clamber along it and fell off, the pole would spring and the poor pig would be tossed up and down squealing frantically. Another of the Sanctions Team could be heard muttering: 'Sick, man, sick.' We had not realised to what degree our festivities in the West have been sanitised in the strainer of political correctness, and made to be environmentally friendly to a point where young men like those in the Sanctions Team have forgotten some of the rough and hearty pastimes of their forebears. Except, perhaps, football.

We were in any case diverted by the necessity of making our final clearance with the WEU Sanctions Inspection Team. It was as big a frolic as was taking place all around us, but less fun. Laurel explained to the Sanctions Team that Bill was on a very short fuse because we'd been aground for half an hour that morning, which they seemed to find amusing. They were less amused to hear that we had taken on diesel, legitimately, at Turnu Severin. We produced the receipts.

The Sanctions enforcers at Kalafat had had no idea that it was possible legitimately to take on diesel between Mohács and Kalafat. Nor had they any knowledge of the trans-Danube fleet of diesel pirates. Had they never thought of checking? Well, they had to get diplomatic clearance before they could venture into that area, and when they did so, they saw, surprise, surprise, absolutely nothing. Had no one ever thought of passing through in an innocent-looking boat like ourselves? Well, no.

It is time to round off our view of the whole subject of Sanctions which had caused us, personally, great delays, and considerable anguish. We have already told how modest amounts of diesel oil were sold from the commercial vessels into Jugoslavia at around Kp 1202. Other materials of a non-bulk nature went too, because it was impossible for the Inspection Teams to be completely effective, and the gains for the crews of the ships were substantial. Consider that a senior tugmaster in Romania earns $50 a week. With the 'frontier price' of illicit diesel at about 40 cents per litre, the crew of a ship could make more out of 'bunker-spillage' in one night than they would earn in a month, with no chance of being caught. No chance because the amount required for the 400 kilometre passage had to be an approximate estimate; one could suspect, but it would be very difficult to accuse anyone in respect of the odd 500 litres discrepancy because of the vagaries of the load towed, varying friction according to the depth of the channels, and variable current. Who in any civil service would know enough about the techniques of towing to call these experienced tugmasters liars? No-one outside their own tight little confraternity.

But the amount Serbia got this way was as nothing compared with the wholesale trade across the Danube between Kp 1020 and 1056. This was enormous, and embraced goods other than oil fuels. It was highly organised, and one needs to consider the dollar fortunes made in a very few years by certain Hungarians and Romanians, currently attributed to property speculation.

When laws are passed we tend to have faith in our leaders and support those who enforce the law. We did so this time automatically. We wrote to *The Times* and sent them photographs of the diesel boats and the waiting tankers. They did not want the story, though they are normally only too keen to expose the incompetence or corruption of governments.

Bill has taken part in blockades. He has seen what *can* be done. It is inconceivable that any administrators could be as incompetent as this. The conclusion we must come to is that the Western governments, who took upon themselves the enforcement of Sanctions, did not want them to be effective. Certainly the Germans continued to supply Croatia.

The reason could not be found at Kalafat, because the people on the ground were not in the policy-making echelons. Like the team at Mohács, they did their duty knowing they were wasting their time.

Rainbow arrived, and berthed alongside us, Jean went ashore for cigarettes, and we sank into restful peace (as we thought) for the rest of the afternoon, only to be visited by the Customs who hadn't had their slice yet and wanted to make out an inventory of everything we had on board. Fortunately we managed to dissuade them, saying it would take them three days, they'd never catch up with the paperwork. They contented themselves with the larger items, as on a Greek transit log, recording things like sewing machine, television, outboard motor? (we hadn't got one; that surprised them) bicycle, two boats, one of which was a lifeboat, and so on.

They discovered that Jean had gone ashore before being checked in: Wicked! Unheard of! She would have problems! We tried to explain the European attitude to documents, that we did not even have to check in between France and England, we said, let alone every village we stopped at. They agreed that time and expense would be saved by less paperwork, but change, they shrugged, was slow. And we thought, but did not say, that less paperwork meant fewer jobs. We did find out that if you stayed less than six hours no paperwork was necessary, presumably because six hours was insufficient to accomplish both a check-in and a check-out.

After all that was over everything calmed down, the festival subsided into post prandial snoozing, and we had a quiet afternoon.

Until Laurel tackled the chicken she had bought in the market in Turnu Severin. A shriek from the galley brought Bill down to see what was wrong. He found Laurel helpless with laughter. She had put her fingers inside to remove the giblets, and they had been grabbed by a little dry scaly hand. Out came two feet, and a head. It should not have been a surprise, as we knew hen's feet soup was a popular dish in these parts, but we had forgotten. In China one would have been surprised *not* to find the feet: they are a delicacy there.

The day ended with a chat and a drink with *Rainbow* and a mutual commiseration about the bureaucracy of Eastern European countries. Their morale was as low as ours. We promised them they would love Turkey; it would be something for them to look forward to.

The day was not quite over. At 2200 there were wails from the top of the cliff on shore; Tansy couldn't find her way back down to the boat. The pontoon we'd ended up on was broken and damaged, and the quay under the cliff at that point was also completely ruined. The clamber ashore was more than Laurel could manage unless thoroughly motivated. A cat in distress was enough, though. If it was hard for a cat, it was almost impossible for Laurel. Willpower took over, as it so often does, and with some difficulty in the dark she led the lost cat back over an obstacle course of steep cliff, broken concrete, derelict cranes and twisted girders.

In the morning, it fell to Laurel to go to the Harbour-master's office and get the papers seen to and pay our one dollar harbour dues. It took only an hour and a half – less than a Romanian 'moment'. The walk, or rather scramble, along the ruined quay was one of the worst she'd ever had in her life; if it hadn't been for a friendly sailor helping her over a chasm and a scree she would probably not have made it. Rather than attempt it again she came back along the cliff top, which involved going through something secret and private and military. She was challenged by a sentry, but continued with imperturbable determination, pointing to *Hosanna* below; not even the sentry's gun could persuade her to brave the ruined quay again.

At 0900 we were given permission to leave. Laurel had taken the precaution of asking by mime whether there were any shallow patches; it seemed there was one at Kp 760. Off we went, looking longingly at the Bulgarian side, which compared to Romania looked clean, and cared for. Laurel had coal dust in her shoes, and we were beginning to wish we had visas for Bulgaria.

• 30 •
HARD AGROUND
Kosloduj and Dolni Vadin

Warned of shallows at Kp 760, we reduced to one engine and threaded our way through a winding, narrow, channel, marked in the *Indicateur Kilométrique* as a sill. Between Kps 754 and 751 we spent over an hour feeling our way through a patch of islands with drying sandbanks, looking for a channel that appeared not to exist. We nosed through with several gentle groundings.

It was a day of mist and mirage, the islands were mirrored vertically, buoys stretched halfway up the shimmering trees on the shore behind them, and we never knew whether it was birds sitting on the water or withies to mark the shallows.

It was tense navigation in strong currents. Bill remained calm while concentrating and vented his feelings in deeper waters, but the Danube rolled on, and heeded no complaints. We were both tired out, and anchored in a deeper patch, off the channel, at Kp 705 in time for tea. We rested, and later barbecued some Romanian pork chops, tasty and wickedly marbled with fat which made them grill to perfection, after which we turned in early.

We had a peaceful night disturbed only by a Ukrainian convoy noisily weighing anchor at 0500, like someone dropping bolts one by one onto a tin roof for half an hour. We had a lie-in, and after a good breakfast – a deliberate attempt by Laurel to generate calm – Bill changed the engine oil and filters on all three engines. This was normally the last thing calculated to produce a calm frame of mind but, as he said, if that was all there was to worry about he would be happy. It was a cool morning, during which *Rainbow* went past, cheerfully knocking on our hull and shouting, 'Vama. Vere are de papers?' It sounded as if anchoring was restoring their sense of humour, too.

We weighed anchor and left at 1300 and passed one of Bulgaria's nuclear power stations, the same type as Chernobyl. The Greens are unhappy, they want it dismantled; who can blame them?

As we approached a long straight stretch with a sharp bend at the end, we sensed something wrong. The channel shifted to the other side of the river halfway down, the changeover being marked by a floating plastic drum that some kind tugmaster had left. After the bend the channel passed the wrong side of several small islands. There were no more kilometre posts or markers. We felt our way, touching bottom from time to time. This stretch commonly closes for lack of water. We had come to know the signs of shallows; the change in colour, the overfalls, the little ripples and whirlpools, the branches, the stumps and withies. We had learnt a great deal at some cost. On the right was a village, its name written in Cyrillic on the pontoon. It came home to us that these were the only written words to be seen on the river. No advertising hoardings, nothing saying HOTEL or BAR or DISCO, no signposts or traffic signs.

Bill said it might be nice to find a little village and stop there as we do in Greece, but we both knew what would happen. The village would have only one policeman, and imperative phone calls would go to the next big town and we should be held at gunpoint while they rounded up officials from 20 kilometres away to come and spend hours poring over our papers.

On the left was just such a Romanian village, whose name seemed entirely composed of Ls. We recognised a typical Harbour-master's pontoon: a flat black barge with the inevitable yellow paint on the top of the cabin. We don't know who in the Romanian government bought millions of gallons of yellow paint, but the State has tons of it. If an object is painted at all it's yellow.

We did not stop; we were tired of officials, and sought an anchorage further on. There was one marked at Kp 666 and another one at 660. Neither of us fancied 666, the Mark of the Beast. Sailors are swayed by superstition, though they are apt to call it prudence. There were plenty of more comfortable beasts about; sheep, goats, cows, horses and pigs, all came down to drink from the Danube.

On the Bulgarian shore women were washing huge hanks of wool, swirling it in figures of eight through the toast-brown water and setting it to dry. The finished product, woven rugs in natural colours of oatmeal, fawn and a cool brown, were washed and drying on the strand. The wooden carts standing on the shore were similar to the Sicilian ones with big wooden wheels, but without the gaily painted scenes. The shape of the beached boats had changed, they were narrower, and pointed at the ends, more like a canoe than the squarish steel skiffs of Jugoslavia.

The anchorage at 666 had disappeared. The channel is now on the opposite side of the river. Once more tired out by the strain of navigating in swift shallow water, we anchored for the night off the village of Dolni Vadin at Kp 652. There was a *pegel*; the river was about 60 cm below normal.

While we had supper in the verandah we watched families on the Romanian side bringing carts down to the water and washing their blankets, up to their knees in the Danube; it was a gypsy camp. The Romanians had told us that it was gypsies who give them a bad name for thieving. 'They break our faces,' one sailor said to us, a good expression meaning 'they spoil our image'. Every country we had been through had warned us against Romanian thieving. So far, we had

Beehive caravans, Romania

found them honest if subornable. Compared to Budapest, Romanian taxi drivers were archangels.

A flight of cormorants went over, storks stepped in the shallows, a breeze rustled the woods. Gradually the strain began to drain away with the peace of evening. Sighing with contentment, we revelled in the thought that we didn't have to produce documents for the cormorants.

Bill rose early and checked the injectors on the port engine, which he thought might be causing a smoky exhaust. He found nothing wrong; he forgot until much later that the problem was probably due to dirty air filters. While doing it he dropped two spanners into the bilge under the engine, a hole so constructed (aren't they always?) that the tools were irretrievable without foot-long double-jointed fingers.

When he had recovered from sweat and swearing we weighed and immediately ran into difficulties searching for the channel. The markers, where they existed, were completely unreliable. We spent an hour going slow ahead on one engine, borne along by the current. Exhausted by lunchtime, we anchored.

During dessert a Ukrainian convoy passed us, so we weighed and followed, but couldn't keep up. Gradually we dropped a mile or two behind. There was a one-way stretch at Kp 569, and seeing an enormous upstream-bound tow at the other end we anchored to one side to give him priority. He did the same at his end. We were unwilling to argue about it: 'After you, Ivan Ivanovitch.' 'Nyet, after you, Vassili,' so we gave up for the night and shifted our anchor berth further away from the channel. Another tow arrived at our end and anchored, and the tugs towed each other's barges through one by one, weaving back and forth as if fitting the Danube with new shoelaces. It was obviously a bad passage. Both tows anchored for the night and there was much radio chatter with many *Da*, *da*'s, and *Spasiba*'s. *Spasiba* is Russian for *Merci*.

The Ukrainians sounded cheerful, especially one with a deep bass voice. We expected him to start singing at any moment: 'Otchi chyorna', or perhaps the song of the Volga Boatmen. Later on that evening he did sing, a slow mournful song; the nicest sound we've ever heard on channel 16.

Laurel had changed the sheets. Jugoslavian trauma and fast passage making had given clean sheets a low priority but now, oh! Clean sheets, what bliss: the freshly laundered smell, and the knowledge that we ourselves had had a good scrub and were not unworthy to lie in them. How wonderful simple pleasures are when you have been deprived of them.

Next morning we noticed a survey launch running lines of soundings across the channel at about Kp 568, so we took even more care than usual. There were several sandspits appearing to go right across the river. Then we saw a line of dhan-buoys which seemed to indicate that the channel crossed almost at right angles from left to right, and Bill turned to follow them. There was a fierce current across the channel, and we had to aim off about 45° to stay in it, with no leeway either side, so narrow it was. As the temporary buoys did not differentiate between left and right hand marks, Bill fell into a trap and went the wrong side of the last one. We grounded by the stern. The current was across the ship, about 8 km/hr (4 knots), and it pinned us broadside on to the shoal. We tried the engines forwards, and backwards, but the force of the current would not let us move, and we were merely digging ourselves into a hole. When already in a hole, stop digging.

Our friends in *Rainbow* appeared. Sidelining our shame, we accepted their offer of help. *Rainbow* was a small yacht of about 8 metres length, with a small engine. She drew only a metre, so was in no danger of grounding, but she had little power. She found she could stem the current and make some way against it, so Bill asked if they could lay out our 100 kilo anchor for us. We slung it off their stern and they started off upstream but the resistance of the anchor made it difficult for them to steer and in a matter of seconds they were being swept the wrong side of us and, despite gallant efforts, had to let go the anchor in the wrong place, downstream.

Bill tried to winch the anchor home by brute force with the hydraulic windlass, but the holding ground was superb, it did not budge. There was nothing further *Rainbow* could do, so we bade them farewell and waited for assistance. Someone would have to do something; we were blocking the fairway on a bend.

Soon after 0900 the Romanian survey launch arrived and attempted to tow our bows up into the stream. They knotted two ropes together to do this and the knot, one unknown to Bill, gave way. They tried with another rope, and Bill simultaneously ran all engines and Laurel worked the anchor windlass as well, but we were stuck fast. Worse, the lever on the anchor windlass went dead, and with a sinking heart Laurel realised that the drive belts in the engine room had parted: she knew the symptoms well. As she imparted the bad news, a second harbour launch arrived flying the Bulgarian flag. The cooperation between the two launches suggested that they had worked together many times before. The two attempted to tow in tandem, but without success. They had, however, moved us nearer our anchor, and when we signalled to them that the winch was *kaput* men came on board to weigh by hand, heavy work. We cheered as we juddered off at about 1015, after a further, successful, attempt to tow in tandem.

The launches made fast one each side of us and got us through the narrows as a multi-national sandwich. Then we unknotted the cats' cradle of tow ropes, thanked our benefactors profusely and asked if we owed anything. Smiles all round. No. What, no paperwork? No dollars? No, no. How about some French wine? Delighted.

The crews of these launches were admirably competent. Bill recognised this in spite of the false start, and once they were working together he more or less left it to them. He could not understand what they were saying to each other, and accepted that he was in some ways more of a liability than a help, not a feeling he is used to.

The Bulgarian, who had arrived from downstream, led us round some difficult shoals while the Romanian launch moved the markers. There were two big tows waiting to go through, and they did so one barge at a time. Finally, when we had reached deeper water, the Bulgarian bade us 'bon voyage' and we continued for a while until about 1100 when, with visibility down to about 1 kilometre, Bill announced that he had had enough. We declared a Sunday and anchored at Kp 558, having done only 10 kilometres. The river level was 50 cm below the minimum navigable level.

Bill, depressed, sat for a time with his head in his hands not speaking or answering. At last he went down to the engine room to fit new belts to the hydraulic pump, but everything was still too hot to touch. Instead he fitted navigation lamps to the new foremast which he had been preparing to step. Laurel scraped some rusty patches on the foredeck which needed attention before painting. Then she cooked one of his favourite suppers, duck pilaff, and with fresh plums as dessert, and a glass or two of calvados to follow, he went to bed a little happier.

Bill is prepared for the occasional grounding in inland waters, but takes pride in getting himself out of trouble. Too much pride perhaps, so that he feels it deeply when he has to accept help. It is a rare enough event.

• 31 •

THE SUNSET HORSES
Giurgiu, Braţul Borçea

In the cool of the morning Bill fitted new belts. While there, he discovered a leaking sterngland and dealt with that. Laurel did some work chipping and priming the foredeck; if you have a steel boat there is always painting to be done.

With new belts, the anchor came in sweetly when we weighed at 1050. It was misty, with visibility down to a kilometre, and spotting markers required concentration, so we dropped a lunch-hook at Kp 539. We were still eating when a Bulgarian tow passed us, so we weighed hastily, following and swallowing. It took off much of the tension to have someone to follow. This time his speed matched ours, so we could follow him at dead slow over a complex stretch at about Kp 524. The channel narrowed to under 50 metres wide, was only 1.70 metres deep, and was alarmingly close to the bank: we could have touched the trees with a boathook.

Our leader was active on channel 16 all this time, telling everyone where he was and what he was doing in Russian, though we noticed that the words he used for downstream and upstream were not the Russian or German words we expected, but the French canal words *aval* and *amont*. After this we had an easy ride to the towns of Rousse (Bulgaria, Kp 495) and Giurgiu on the Romanian side. We headed for Giurgiu, Relu's home town. Was he here yet? He had warmly invited us to his home.

We had discovered that entry visas for Bulgaria cost $66 per person. We might have been prepared to pay that and do a little travelling on the Bulgarian side, which Rod Heikell had found the more congenial, had we not also discovered that the Bulgarian authorities consider that by leaving any port you have left their country, and demand a further $66 per person at the next port of call down the river. We just did not have enough bunches of $132 to go down river that way. The Romanians followed the normal international practice of allowing you to pass from one port to another on the original visa, as long as they put another stamp on it.

After the usual tiresome formalities, which Laurel saw to, we shifted berth and lay alongside a tug called *Filiasi*, so dodging a threatened $100 charge for the pontoon.

Thus started a most difficult evening. *Filiasi* was a tug of the same company as Relu's *Medias*, but was a very different proposition. It was much newer. The Captain and engineer were pleasant people, but we didn't take to some of the crew, who were over-friendly to the point of intrusion, and we fended them off with difficulty.

The Harbour-master brought a French speaking friend with him, and we unwisely gave them the two-and-sixpenny tour of the boat. The friend was anxious to know if Bill was a ham radio man. He isn't. The man's face fell; he desperately needed spares. In our cuddy workshop he was over the moon at seeing Bill's neat drawers full of assorted screws and nuts and bolts, and with barely a pause to ask permission, began to fill his pockets with our precious brass and stainless steel screws, saying they were unobtainable in Romania. 'Just so,' said Bill, cutting down the flow, allowing him a few of each and firmly taking back the stainless steel wood screws, since we haven't finished building this boat yet. As he went round our decks, his eyes were everywhere, and he shamelessly asked to be given any item he fancied. We were firm. On a journey such as ours, little is surplus.

Venera-Maria, the 16-year-old daughter of the pontoon lady, offered to take Laurel shopping in the town which is about 4 kilometres from the docks. Though it was already 1800 the market would still be open. The offer was made in a mixture of languages and signs, and Laurel accepted gratefully. Venera-Maria's mother was a Captain in her own right; her pontoon job was temporary, between ships. Father was also a Captain, away with his ship. Afterwards Laurel could not explain why she assumed that they were walking to her mother's car. Not in Romania. And why, when her companions apologised sweetly for not having a car, did she assume there must be a bus? After a kilometre it dawned on her that Venera-Maria and her young friend Florian planned to walk the 4 kilometres to Giurgiu. Laurel has a maximum continuous walk, unencumbered, of perhaps a kilometre if all conditions are exactly optimum, and here they were not. The youngsters were charming. 'Take your time,' said Venera-Maria. 'There is no hurry.' Apologising as best she could, Laurel explained her predicament, and they got a passing taxi. The two youngsters were sympathetic and helpful, Venera-Maria's English was good.

Did they visit Rousse in Bulgaria, just across the river by ferry? Laurel asked. No, no, they said, a little shocked at the idea. Rousse was Hollywood, the Côte d'Azur, Bond Street, an unattainable Paradise. You could get anything, but it was expensive beyond the means of most Romanians. Imagine, an ice cream that cost nearly 1600 lei! (All of 50 pence. And that was twice a Romanian taxi fare. One could see the problem.) Laurel bought vegetables, pork and beef, and bread. The butcher was surly and had no time for foreigners. Venera-Maria chipped in to see that Laurel got what she wanted, though from her hesitancy it seemed that she did not buy meat often. Florian had insisted on paying the taxi fare, which wrung Laurel's heart; she made sure that his generosity was not repeated on the return journey. We gave the two youngsters the two-and-sixpenny tour with love and gratitude, even though by now it was getting late. We then had a rest and a drink before tackling supper, and were enjoying the peace when one of the tugmen strode on board, climbed on to our poop and beckoned Laurel imperiously. Her bones could be heard groaning as she unwillingly got to her feet, cursing.

He wanted our geraniums. Impossible to get in Romania.

The tug crew would not leave us alone. They had been teasing the cats in Laurel's absence, and Tansy, after several audible warnings, had bitten one of them. Laurel offered to take cuttings of the geraniums, and did so. ('He's the one Tansy bit,' whispered Bill). We were conversing in five words of German (his), no English, and Laurel spoke no Romanian and a different five words of German. He took the cuttings and disappeared. Ten minutes later he was back, wanting one of the best plants. A complete and beautiful one, he said, as a souvenir of Romania. Laurel couldn't quite see the logic of this. How could giving *him* a geranium be *her* souvenir of Romania? Or even *his*? She lost her cool. 'Off! Out! Go!' she said, making shooing gestures.

We confined both cats, fearing trouble.

The cats showed their displeasure, one on the saloon carpet and the other in the wheelhouse. Bill blew up like a volcano, which meant that Laurel couldn't, as only one of us is allowed to do that at a time. Supper was rather a tight-lipped affair. At bedtime Bill said helpfully, 'I'll bring the geraniums indoors. The best ones, anyway. The leggy ones can stay outside, in that wooden tray.'

There's more than one way to say sorry.

In the morning attempts to discover where Relu was had failed; he was still upriver somewhere. We could not wait for him. The leggy geraniums had gone, tray and all. Laurel was at the port office to collect the documents at 0720 and surprised a man putting on his trousers. He spent half an hour looking at the documents, studying them, and making a lot of phone calls. After another 40 minutes, when her irritation and tapping feet began to make themselves felt, he invited Laurel out on the steps, locked the door, and went off on a bicycle. She said later that if he had not locked the door she would have used a little Romanian enterprise, taken the papers, stamped or not, and fled for the boat. He was back in 20 minutes, probably checking that we had committed no crime overnight other than having our geraniums stolen. The whole process of getting our documents back took 90 minutes, and we were the only customers. How they would cope with more than one boat a day beggars belief.

It was a fine sunny morning. The river level had risen in the night by about 30 centimetres. It was altogether a better day, though things were still not easy. In one stretch of 10 kilometres we counted more buoys washed up on the shore than in place. We had difficulty finding an anchorage, so it was 1805 when we settled down at Kp 389. We were beginning to feel the tug of the sea. All we wanted was to clear out of this river and revel in some searoom, to get once again to a country where the officials were polite and friendly, and where they left you alone once you had done the necessary. This, we knew, would be the case in Turkey.

Next morning Bill worked on the masts, and Laurel painted the foredeck and sprinkled it with fine sand to make it non-slip. We left after lunch. Bulgaria finished on the right bank by the town of Silistra, and we were called in to report ship and crew details at the Romanian port of Calarasi (Kp 373), and from then on the sinuous channel became once more a nightmare. We have to keep referring to kilometre post numbers; there are few named landmarks in this part of the river. At about Kp 357 there was an 80° turn round the end of an island that was hard to spot, and after that the channel crossed from the left bank over to the right, with no markers. By now it will probably be doing the opposite. We hate to labour the point, but no chart or guide can be of much use in these circumstances, because even if well drawn, it would quickly be out of date in the shifting channels. Professionals help each other; one picks up the tune, if not the words. One can hear them advising: 'Watch out at Kp xyz, the channel now goes over to the left for half a kilometre.' We were cut off from this help by a lack of Russian, but one or two tugmasters gave us the occasional warning in English. Nice of them. We anchored for the night at Kp 348, after the really difficult bit, worn out.

Fishermen were out with their narrow skiffs, one or two men per boat. They anchored with a big stone, and lay to the current, with the line in their right hand, and a tube like an ear trumpet in the other. With this they hit the water rythmically, making a hollow plomp that the fish must find attractive. We had never seen fishing with audible bait before.

The river started to divide and re-form round islands several miles long, and one had to keep alert. Heikell shows only the arm that he used, and this was not the one in use in 1995.

Our leading tug opted for an arm called Braţul Borçea, which we heard pronounced over the radio as 'Brátch Bortcha'. We had no data whatsoever for this channel, and had to make up our mind very quickly. Bill, reasoning that the Ukrainians were almost certainly bound for the same place as ourselves for the next 150 kilometres, swung the wheel over and followed. It was a narrow, deep channel with a stronger current. After 10 kilometres we lost our guide in the fog, but were not much inconvenienced because, as the water widened and shoaled, we came across good markers.

The land was flat with the occasional small hamlet of a few houses. There were birchwoods and many big plantations of poplars in various stages, presumably destined for the pulp industry, but apart from that the land showed no signs of cultivation.

In a clearing on the shore a cluster of caravans appeared at first to be the homes of gypsies. Through the open door at the end of the van a bunk was visible. Then we noticed that the sides were composed of multicoloured rows of flaps, 15 or 20, like pigeon holes. They were beehives, and we contemplated the happy thought that the bees knew their hive by the colour of the door. Did they have to produce documents on their return from foraging? 'Worker Bee number zo-and-zo, My rezidenz iz ze azzure door, zecond row, zevenz van, cargo two zacs pollen from azzorted plantz.' This was the source, then, of those honeycombs we had bought in the market, sweet and golden, and deliciously crunchy.

While honey seemed the only crop, animals were here in plenty. There were herds of pigs, semi-wild, horses roamed free, and occasionally one would canter along the bank beside us, mane and tail blowing out; handsome creatures. Timeless pictures were etched on our minds; wooden carts, mangers of hay for the horses, wood piles, a beached fishing skiff with nets hung to dry on the shore. Nothing from the 20th century intruded, except the hum of our engines.

By going this way we missed the turning at Cernavoda, where one can leave the Danube and take a short cut down a new ship-canal which comes out into the Black Sea by the port of Constanţa. *Rainbow*, who was now behind us, went that way, fed up with the Danube and wanting to be out of it as soon as possible. They had to take a pilot, do the whole canal length non-stop, and pay a substantial fee for such a small boat.

When we passed the small town of Giurgeni, we were interrogated by VHF, in English, and informed that we should always report in to the control stations as we pass them. As we have no idea where the control stations are, this would be difficult.

Conditions improved. We could use the autopilot on straight stretches for about 15 minutes at a time. It had to be 'tweaked' occasionally, but it enabled Bill, who did almost all the driving, to do his own buoy-spotting with the binoculars, and so eased the all-round tension. We anchored at Kp 212.

Now that we were nearing the delta, the land seemed vast and desolate. A sandy cliff about a metre high rose from the beach, and over it was grazing land with a few silhouetted trees. The current was about 9 km/hr. There were thunderstorms about, towering cumulus grumbled over the horizon, and we barbecued a mixed grill for supper. During our meal a herd of 13 graceful horses came down the sandy cliff to look at us. They halted to drink, about 50 metres away, gilded by the setting sun. They watched us eating for a few minutes, then together they tossed their heads and raced along the bank and out of sight. A skein of geese flew by, honking.

This, we decided, was a good spot to ready the masts and step them where there would be little chance of interruption. Laurel painted the base of the mainmast while Bill fettled the rigging screws. Then she went below, and when we finished for the day the mainmast was ready to step. The horses came back to entertain us again at dinner, and stayed until sunset, which was a dramatic one.

In the morning, while Laurel baked bread and pastries, Bill moved the foremast so that he could step the mainmast. Unfortunately he let the foremast slip out of its tabernacle jaws down to one side. He was unable to manhandle the 400 kilos of galvanised steel tube, so he left it where it had fallen and carefully raised the mainmast with its main-boom. He got that done by 1015, which is a record.

We used tackles hung from both the mainmast and the mast-raising sheerlegs to hoist the foremast back into its tabernacle jaws and slide in the pin. This was a new mast that had never been stepped before, and needed some fiddling adjustments as well as getting all the rigging bent on. It got hot in late afternoon as the wind dropped, and both of us were tired, so we stopped and had beef and egg curry (the last of our fresh meat) for supper, joined as usual at sunset by the horses. This time they had told their friends and family; there were far more of them and several foals too. All went in to the river to bathe.

We followed a Bulgarian convoy down to Kp 175 after lunch. This point is marked as an anchorage, but it had its drawbacks, being near a noisy factory. We were told to move by a Romanian warship going home to the naval base up a side stream, but it was late and we ignored him. It was our last chance to stop before Braila, and we wanted to finish work on the mast so as to have the decks clear for manoeuvring near the pontoons.

The foremast went up next morning, Friday 25 August. The wind was rising as we finished, and we secured the shrouds that hold up the mast with some relief. There's an art in moving heavy gear around and lifting heavy weights, not by your own efforts but by machinery. It takes time, planning, and thinking, then doing it and checking for snags. Now the decks were clear of the clutter of spars, wires, ropes and halliards that had been there since the long wet winter. We stood back with satisfaction and contemplated our work. We felt a complete ship again.

• 32 •
TO RUSSIA FOR LUNCH
Braila and Ismail

At Braila it was Bill's turn to tackle the formalities. Deciding on heroic measures, he got out a naval uniform shirt, with Master Mariner shoulder straps. He wore navy-blue long trousers instead of his disreputable shorts, and put the white cover on his ancient Gieves yachting cap with the RNSA badge. He crossed the pontoon resplendent with four gold stripes on each shoulder.

The effect was gratifying. Both sentries presented arms. The Customs Officer leapt to his feet and saluted. Bill was offered a chair and a cup of coffee in the Harbour-master's office, and was back on board in 40 minutes. A record!

He changed before we went ashore for a walk. Braila is the old port of Romania and the home of most of her seamen, and is pronounced to rhyme with 'sailor'. The architecture mostly dates from an age of elegance with Italian influences. There is a charming town square with a park in the centre. It fails to be beautiful because it has become tatty and neglected. There were two small pavement cafés, where in a Mediterranean square there would have been 30. They were full. We sat down to have a cool drink, but there was no service. After a while a pleasant young man at the next table told us the waiters were too lazy to come to us: one had to go to the counter and order. After a time they might bring it to you. Bill went to the counter, and after a time the drinks arrived. The waiter did not wipe the previous spills off the table. He did not have a cloth; it was not his job. Nor did he empty the over-full ash tray. State employment at a low, secure salary seems to lead to a total lack of motivation, especially in service industries. The concept of a customer as someone to be pleased does not exist in Romania. If the waiter throws the food in your lap, he is still doing you a favour.

A wedding party emerged from the photo-shop next door to have a group photo taken. The dresses were home-made, bright coloured but skimpy on material, as in wartime Britain. The adult bridesmaid was dressed in magenta satin, the seams puckering a little here and there. Only the little bridesmaids had an extravagance of frills, and the bride, clad in icing sugar white with a profligate flurry of ribbons and bows, eased off her stiff satin shoes and wobbled, as she rubbed her left instep with her right toes. Several other women were teetering for the same reason.

Clock in the park, Braila

We did some food shopping and stayed for a meal at what was considered the best restaurant in town: the *Locksha* (Galleon).

The wedding party was in the next room. The bride was in tears; there appeared to be a disagreement between the wedding party and the management. We were not surprised: poverty and shortages have led to arrogance and a feeling of power among those who provide, and abject submission on the part of those who consume. In the adjoining room we were the only customers. There was a menu, but almost everything was off. We had pork chop and chips. The service was friendly, but casual, with the staff sitting smoking at another table when not busy. Laurel caused an upset by asking for the other half of her paper napkin. We thought for a moment that it might be added to the bill.

It was spitting with rain as we left. We walked across the square to the rococo turquoise blue tile clocktower and found a taxi to take us back. It cost us 700 lei (3250 lei ≡ £1). When we got back the pontoon guardian gave us six bream that he had caught, so we all had a drink together.

Pontoon guardians are either employees of NAVROM, or in some cases are on the staff of the Harbour-master. They supervise everything that happens on their pontoon and live on board it with their families. Some are men, but very often they are women. A few are good natured, but not many. Bill substituted the word Gorgon for Guardian, after one such. They make a charge for the use of the pontoon, which appears based on the best capitalist principles: charge what the market will bear. A bottle of wine presented early on in one's stay can earn more than its cost. The charges (always in dollars) varied from 1 to 23 for a night. Sometimes a receipt is given, sometimes not. There is no certainty of charge, no peace at night, nor any feeling of security. But the man at Braila seemed trustworthy.

We took on fresh water. Most countries now have potable water systems, even though they might contain locally bred bacteria that we are not used to. Tough; we get used to them. In fact most countries have better water-treatment systems than we have in Britain where many are Victorian and have not been modernised, whereas in the more backward parts of the world the Western countries have helped the locals install brand new systems that the donors themselves can no longer afford.

We compounded with the weather and rested. We dined on the verandah as usual, but were driven below by a mixture of cold and mosquitos.

The news next morning, 28 August, was grim. Shells had landed on Sarajevo market, with appalling casualties. We shopped gloomily, the market was sparse and the vegetables dubious. The cabbages looked awful, as the shopkeeper had not troubled to remove the discoloured outer leaves. The inner part of the cabbage was perfectly good, and it cost only a couple of pennies, but the idea of presenting something for sale in an attractive way has not occurred, because anything will sell to someone desperate enough. Bananas, being imported, were probably the most expensive fruit at 1000 lei a kilo, most other fruits were 800, and most vegetables were 600. Meat was between 3500 to 5000 a kilo, but the butcher was cleaning his shop and shooed us out; evidently he didn't feel like selling today. Laurel found a chicken elsewhere. Shopping becomes simple when there's not much choice. If it isn't there, you don't get it. We had become very undemanding. The Romanian white wine was good in its class, a simple *vin de table*, and we bought two bottles of vodka. The vodka was to give to fishermen; we were told that this was what one did in the Delta. We are not vodka drinkers, and were not sure we dared to try it at 30 pence a bottle.

We left at noon, and reached Kp 150, where the kilometre posts change to mile posts, all distances now being in nautical miles. We were at Mp 82, Galati, a sea and river port, with extensive docks, wharves with cranes, and honeycoloured blocks of flats behind them.

The port pontoon, Braila

Laurel read from the Admiralty pilot: 'During the summer there is a great deal of Marsh fever here, to which newcomers are especially liable.' Malaria is not so rife nowadays. Should we succumb, it was comforting to know from that same source that: 'A berth is available for British sailors in the hospital at Braila.'

Barges were anchored in midriver, and naval patrol boats up a creek. The shipyards are one of Ceauçescu's grandiose plans, which have polluted the skies with smoke, and buried riverside towns in badly made concrete, already sliding into the river in broken slabs barbed with reinforcing rods. Here the docks seemed in better order; the yards were building ships of about 10,000 tons. Two were completing for a Chinese company, the Mei Yuan and the Dong Yuan, registered in Kuang Ju. That the Chinese should find it economic to have ships built in Romania says something for their respective economies.

We were in seagoing waters now, with big coastal steamers and Black Sea ships from distant ports, one from Limassol, another from Beirut, and a Turkish coaster. We passed under bridges and power cables with our masts up and headroom to spare. Another freighter passed, from Gdansk in Poland; would he have come the long way round from the Baltic, or down the Volga? We had not seen ships like this since the Scheldt in Holland, nine months ago. There was something approaching an attractive waterfront, a café and a row of those blocky sculptures beloved by Communism; shapes reminiscent of spanners and other tools, as high as a house. The blocks of flats reminded us of the beehive vans, with their little coloured doors. They weren't much bigger.

Ceauçescu's classic motor yacht dripped and rusted at the quay, beautiful, but neglected since the fall of his regime. It was called the *Libertatea*, as if Ceauçescu knew anything about liberty. She flew an ensign, but the halliard was broken, so the flag streamed out untidily.

The opposite, right, bank was a world away from the busy docks, green and pastoral, with willows and grazing cattle. The docks and cranes on the left gave way to willows and dunes too, and we hoped for a peaceful anchorage like 212, that of the sunset horses, which we now recalled with affection. Mile posts were scarce, but a vicious looking fence at Mp 78 suggested frontiers, and a short time later there was a goonbox, and some men fishing, wearing collars and ties. A nice relaxed border, we thought, if the officials could spend lunchtime fishing.

And suddenly the Ukraine was on our left. Old Russia, ex-USSR. The dunes and willows and the line of wooden telegraph posts with two wires strung on them did not look different from Romania, but shortly there was a wooden railway station straight out of *Anna Karenina*, 19th century with pediments and pilasters in a delicate almond green. The Russians were not here in the 19th century to build it, but at least they have cherished the building and not flattened it under concrete monoliths as Ceauçescu has done. The difference from Romania was now apparent: the houses were neatly painted and well cared for, and there was no sign of the tracts of rubbish and ruined desolation that the Romanians seemed too disheartened, and perhaps too poor, to tidy up.

Every 100 metres or so was a goonbox with a bank of floodlights. Nobody was going to surprise the Ukraine from the Danube.

We found our anchorage at Mp 61, and barbecued steak for dinner, with ratatouille and Romanian Pinot Noir.

What made us divert to the Ukraine? When the Soviet Union broke up, her frontage to the Danube delta passed to the Ukraine except for a short length of under half a kilometre which went to Moldavia. Were we collecting courtesy ensigns? We have enough of those in our locker. We were fed up with the bureaucracies of the former Russian satellites; why go to a bit of old Mother Russia herself? In the name of sheer curiosity we do some daft things from time to time.

We turned left at Mp 43 into the Braţul Chilia (the ch is pronounced as in the Scottish loch), punching into a strong wind that blew spray over the foredeck, flushing Tansy out of her favourite outdoor spot under the dinghy, and kicking up waves that would have made a small yacht bounce.

There were no mile posts. 'Wish I knew exactly where we were,' said Bill. 'Why not use GPS now?' asked Laurel. Bill chuckled with delight. Of course, on an Admiralty Black Sea chart. What a difference after the inaccurate diagrams we'd had to use for so long. Unfortunately the chart was an old one, pre GPS, and it put *Hosanna* on a railway line ashore, about a mile and a half out.

We had had no weather report for weeks; requests to Harbourmasters for forecasts had produced only a sleepy Balkan shrug. Our Navtex ought to receive Odessa, but didn't. It had received Ostend all right at the start of our journey. We noted a conical black buoy, and deduced that Ukraine had stuck to the pre-IALA buoyage system, but

Ukrainian church and strand

the 'Bacon and egg' sign, as we called it (a vertical bar meaning WARNING beside a black circle meaning HOOT) was in use.

Two hours later, we arrived at the Ukrainian port of Ismail, fully prepared, in all but one respect. No visas.

Our phrasebook was open at the Russian section, and we flew the Ukrainian flag at the starboard yardarm. After a frantic hunt the yellow flag, unused for years, flew at the other. We had been told that yachts arriving at the Ukrainian port of Odessa the year before had not needed visas. We hoped for the same reception here.

As we berthed on a spacious empty quay, officials arrived and kept on arriving. This was clearly their big moment, for obviously not much was happening in this port, which had once been the centre of a big up-river Russian trade.

We were ordered to a different pontoon, one which had once been used for a hydrofoil service but the seven hydrofoils were now laid up. The wind was near gale force so we were relieved to accomplish this successfully. We had a soldier to guard us, a handsome tall blond man, who did not bear firearms, but had a most bloodthirsty looking dagger in his belt.

The person in charge appeared to be a lady, attractive, tall and shapely, 30 to 40 years old in a smart grey-green uniform with officer's shoulder straps. Passports were inspected. What a pity we did not have visas. 'Our information is that we can be issued with them here,' we said.

Nyet. Regretful, but *Nyet*. Once perhaps, but no longer.

Until this problem was solved we could not go ashore. We told her all we knew about the reception of the yachts in Odessa. She said she would make enquiries. Off she went with a small platoon of assistants, leaving us with barely enough uniformed men to organise a rugger match. They wore camouflaged fatigues, and fur-lined boots. A couple of dockworkers got near enough to murmur hopefully: 'Whisky?' but were shooed away.

Our cat Tansy jumped onto the pontoon and fraternised, rubbing herself against the ankles of various officials. Someone made a joke; it was translated for us: cats do not need visas in the Ukraine. The lady returned. Her chief had said 'No visa, no visit'. She had persuaded him to refer the matter higher up. 'I would like you to see our town. We are hospitable people,' she said.

Higher authority arrived. It was evidently high enough to cause some of the crowd to disperse to a respectful distance. He was sorry but the rules were strict. It was possible to enter at Odessa without a visa; perhaps they should have the same rule here, but nobody had thought of it. But perhaps we had need of stores? Of water? Alas, no.

Bill had been getting a little short of patience confronted with an unresolved situation which had dragged on for over two hours.

As we bade them farewell and left, we detected a slight wistfulness, as if they had wanted very much to be hospitable. We too would have liked to stay and talk. Perhaps we missed something. Perhaps, if we had asked for stores (had the senior officer been hinting?), we would have been taken shopping, and we might have been allowed to stop the night. There might have been a vodka party on the pontoon, men dancing Kazak dances, and singing mournful songs. Who knows.

We retraced our steps to the confluence and anchored for the night where the river was wide and deep. The wind rose further in the night. Bill had to turn out to veer more cable, and our halliards, newly in place and not properly tightened, beat against the mast and disturbed our sleep. Not a comfortable night.

• 33 •

THE WINDY LEVELS
Tulçea to Sulina

We were up early because it was blowing a gale from the west. It was pouring with rain, and visibility was bad as we went 6 miles downstream towards Tulçea, a big-ship port. It took only an hour, but was trying, and got worse. Barges were anchored in trots, and a thunderstorm brought cloud and torrential rain which reduced visibility till it was black as night. We lit our navigation lights, though other ships did not, and we navigated entirely on radar.

We berthed at the Harbour-master's pontoon, and were rebuked for not announcing ourselves by radio before arriving in the port. The formalities at the port were reasonable; it seems that once one gets into the world of real merchant shipping where the officials are more used to foreigners, things go with a little more certitude. But that was only half the formalities. We now had to move to Pontoon Number Five, outside *Danubia* and the Good Ship *Venus*. While unberthing we were caught in an eddy that Bill had not noticed, and slammed into the protruding anchor of the passenger ship *Moldavia*, bending our guardrail and wounding our Captain's self esteem. That recovered from, we had to negotiate with the Pontoon Mafia.

The Guardian on our pontoon was no problem, but the Chief of Pontoons had to be bearded in his den. He did not visit. He held court in Pontoon Number One. Bill found a scene vaguely reminiscent of a gangster hideout in old American films. Round a table in the centre of the room sat three or four men, all wearing trilby hats, all reading newspapers. Everyone wore a suit which had seen better days, and had a cigarette dangling from a lower lip. All but one were fat, some very fat. Bill was an interruption to some important item on the agenda. The fat man at the head of the table (the Godfather?) motioned him to be seated.

After several silent minutes during which only strained breathing could be heard, the Godfather put down his paper. Bill did not understand the question put to him, and they realised he was a foreigner. The small, thin man stepped forward, speaking English with a strong Chicago accent. One night on the Pontoon Number Five would mean a reduced rate, special for you signor (he consulted a well-worn notebook), 23 dollars. This was the most we had ever had to pay. These pontoons were primitive landing stages, there were no luxuries like a shower block, or shore power, or a convenient telephone. You thought yourself lucky if the deformed and rusty girders that gouged your hull were disarmed with rubber tyres. Obviously the local Mafia were short of funds. Bill got a receipt, probably dubious in a Romanian court of law, and left. He had an image of two of the men with their right hands inside their coats all the time he was there.

Laurel was unduly tired and did not go ashore. Bill went off in the cool rain to post letters, and phone our children with news of our progress. He was in need of a walk and went round the back of the town with its newly built but dirty streets. The whole place had been in course of reconstruction when Ceauçescu fell. It had been planned to make it the centre of a tourist industry based on the Delta. Boards had been erected advertising boat trips and sojourns in the Delta, but there were none. The waterfront had been rebuilt with vestiges of elegance, but the new trees were not thriving. In the old town, small narrow lanes had once run down to the river from the high ground at the back, but now were only there in traces. The people had re-opened the old ways, tracing paths across building sites strewn with rubbish.

At the bottom of the hill was the *piaţa* with a butcher's stall, and a fishmonger, and vegetable stalls. There was a supermarket on the frontage which had little to sell.

It was a sunny morning as we left and went downstream. The current was much weaker, probably about 4 km/hr, and the channels were deep and easy, but there was wind in the sky.

Shortly after starting, at Mp 34, the channel forked, and there was a signal station which controlled traffic over a one-way section. A 'no entry' sign here would mean a big ship coming up channel. The signalisation near the coast was efficient.

Just before Mp 31 another of Relu's warnings came into effect. He had told us about the wreck of the passenger vessel *Rostock*, and what a hazard it was to navigation, and Bill had asked the Harbour-master at Tulçea to chart its exact position. One had to call on channel 16 to warn the salvage crew working on the wreck, which had capsized and sunk across the channel.

One could hardly have missed it, so to speak. The ship lay across a bend like a crashed zeppelin, with the arm of a huge floating crane above it. They were breaking her up and removing her piece by piece. If the Danube had been running high she would have been difficult to see. A narrow way was kept open past her stern, and caution was needed to negotiate this channel, even for a modest sized craft like *Hosanna*.

We had wondered about going up a side arm of the Danube (there are many) to the village of Milia 23. This small village is peopled by Lipovenians, a small orthodox religious sect who occupy themselves with fishing the Delta, and with drinking enormous quantities of vodka. Every Romanian we met had wild tales to tell of their drinking habits and hospitality, but the weather seemed on the turn into autumn, and we felt the need to get on. From Tulçea it was 38 miles to Sulina, and the Black Sea.

There were signs on the banks of attempts to attract tourism. Every now and then a reed-thatched chalet and a small pontoon with a map of local bird habitats suggested boat trips. There was even a small hotel, shuttered and deserted. The birds, meanwhile, revelled in sovereign rule of their domaine, undisturbed by intrusive twitchers. We saw storks' nests on the telegraph poles, and geese, and herons. A swallow flew into the wheelhouse, a darting arrow of navy blue shot silk, and we were able to set it free before the cats woke up to its presence.

At Mp 18 we passed a fishing collective, where they were unloading blocks of ice. We thought they were washing a rug under the trees, and then they picked up an enormous leg of beef, newly hacked off, and carried it in to the ice house. Backyard butchery.

We dropped a lunch hook for one of those idyllic stops that remain in the memory for ever. Green water, willow, clumps of reed thatch drying by the riverside; peaceful, just us and the birds in the sunshine.

We would have liked a little more time in the Delta. This kind of land, flat and marshy, whispering with reeds under a windy sky, and full of the chuck and chirrup of waterbirds, is bred into our East Anglian bones. We know the old Anglo Saxon names of birds, such as boomer and harnser, which the Norfolkman still uses, better than we know those adopted by ornithologists. We had not dawdled in the Danube's upper reaches; the passage from end to end is a long job, and if one is not to be under way all the hours God gives it takes several months, and the Black Sea had sent us a taste of September weather in this morning's thunderstorm. Since then the weather had been fine, but unsettled.

We stopped for the night at Crisan on the right bank. There is a NAVROM pontoon, but we were hailed by the Harbour-master, a pleasant man who moved another boat to give us room and made us free of his pontoon.

Authority had once decided that the tiny village of Crisan would be a viable base for Delta tourism. Next to the electricity station, therefore, was a campsite, behind a fence overgrown with creeper, where a pig stood guard, snorting. It consisted of a number of wooden huts, a derelict skittle alley, and a toilet block. All were recently built, but deserted, the varnish already weathered. There were signboards about birds and fish, faded and illegible. The Harbour-master told us there was a restaurant at the campsite. We found it; a forlorn looking building in the inevitable reinforced concrete. An old freezer cabinet lay outside its door, rusting. Inside, the floor was bare concrete screed. A stack of tables stood to one side, a counter with faded advertisements for soft drinks on it, and a wall poster announcing cruises in the Delta, all faded into the blue that remains when the other colours leach out. A woman was ironing as she watched television. We sat at a table for a few minutes, while she finished and folded her ironing. Not by a movement or a glance did she register our existence. She then fetched a baby from a back room and began to feed it. This was going to be a long business. We decided that the baby was probably enjoying the best of the menu and beat a retreat.

By the pontoon was a kiosk with two tin tables and a man selling melons. Bill had a beer; it was the worst he had ever tasted and he surreptitiously poured most of it away. Laurel declined a drink and investigated the melons; the vendor had three to choose from. He was delighted to sell us one, and it turned out to be sweet and juicy when we had it for dessert later on. It cost sixpence. As we sat there in the sunset, the ferry arrived from upriver, and for a while the village sparked into animation. It was like the arrival of a Greek island ferry, and for much the same reason – there is no other transport in the Delta. Towns and villages are linked not by roads, but by water. So no cars met the ferry, and no buses. There was, however, a wealth of other transport, from horse drawn carts and buggies to wheelbarrows and handcarts, as luggage and parcels were offloaded. One solitary tourist appeared with a backpack, and stood irresolute, while the locals swirled busily around him like the current round an islet. When the ferry left and the quay was once more deserted, he was still looking round vaguely for the *Turist Biroul*. Unlike the Greek ferry, there were no determined landladies to select their prey, seize his luggage and place it on a handcart, and wheel him off triumphantly to 'Clean room! Near sea!'

1 September dawned cold and grey. We left Crisan on the last hop to Sulina, in the teeth of a force 5 wind from the east, right on our nose. It kicked up a choppy sea in the straight stretches, and at Mp 9 we overtook a small fishing skiff in which two young men were struggling to row into the wind and waves. We slowed down and offered them a tow. They were touchingly grateful; they were trying to row upwind the 8 miles to Sulina to take their catch to market. They were soaked with spray and making no headway at all. Juli and Gigi hid further under the binbags that served them as waterproofs, and sat back to rest as we hauled them along. Every now and then Laurel checked that the skiff was riding safely, but the lads were capable, and slackened or tightened the tow according to the conditions. Towards the end they called Laurel and offered her a choice of their catch, displaying a catfish as tall as she was. Laughing she declined, managing to explain that two persons and two cats could never eat so much fish. She picked out two fine zander.

Coming into Sulina, cows grazed on the bank, and multicoloured hens and a turkey scratted happily, till the rural scene gave way to a skyline of low buildings, nothing more than two storeys high. There were thatched cabins with gardens of maize and sunflowers, all along the river bank. Like Crisan there are no roads into or out of Sulina, and therefore no cars. It was a town about 3 kilometres long, and one street wide, though wide is not the right word for the riverside lane that barely permits two handcarts to pass each other. Since the Danube itself is the High Street, the bus comes in the shape of the passenger ferry, taxis are horse drawn, or else one goes on foot with one's luggage on a handcart. Cargoes come and go by boat. The boys asked to be dropped off just before the town, and we waved each other farewell.

At about 1100 we berthed at a concrete quay at Sulina, near the first yacht we'd seen since *Rainbow*, the Dutch *Sea Lion*. Early in the afternoon the sky went black as a bruise and another violent thunderstorm burst over our heads; for two hours torrential rain pounded down, dense as a waterfall. It stopped as suddenly as it had begun, and an eerie silence ensued. We put on waterboots and ventured ashore.

The riverside lane was flooded to a depth of 15 cm. Anyone wishing to cross took off their shoes and went barefoot. We were privileged to glimpse the only motorised vehicle in Sulina: the fire engine, busy pumping out a flooded store. A horse-drawn cart splashed past, the horse enjoying stomping in water up to his hocks. Some public spirited citizens were poking at the blocked drainholes with hoes or broom handles; where they had succeeded in freeing them a chair standing in a whirlpool 3 feet across warned passers-by of the hole beneath the fast draining water. Fishermen were baling out their skiffs.

The supermarket had about five packets each of what Romanians would call everything: sugar, macaroni, flour, and powdered milk. There was a short row of tins, mostly fish, and three pots of jam and some honey. Large empty gaps separated these items. On the floor, tin bowls had been placed to catch the rain that had come through the roof, with a baby's bath under the worst leak. The shelves had been cleared under the leaks; just as well as it was the pasta section that had suffered most. Laurel was after longlife milk, but that had not yet arrived in Romania, and the packet of powdered milk she got instead cost more than a bottle of vodka.

We spent another day at Sulina, in the hope of improving weather. We took the Navtex aerial apart, and clumsily soldered up a stray wire, thinking it would be a miracle if it worked. We stowed for sea, put away the breakables, bent on the sails, tidied up and lashed loose gear. If only we could get a weather forecast, we were ready for sea.

The next morning, Sunday 3 September, we were up at seven, delighted to find the weather report from Odessa on our Navtex. It was like a birthday present. There was a low over Russia, a cold front extended to Romania and Bulgaria, and a warm front to the Danube and Georgia. Nothing awful there, to delay departure.

Uncooperative officials, however, did delay us, insisting that a full team should gather simultaneously to clear us; there always seemed to be one of them out of step. As we waited the sound of chanting came from the church nearby, so we went in and gave our last few lei to the man selling candles, to light one for our coming journey. It was 0930 before we could leave, and just after 1000 when we passed between the pierheads, carried along by the silt-laden current of the river, past a working dredger, and as we felt a slight lift from the first sea-swell for many months, we left the Danube behind us, and were out into the Black Sea.

• 34 •
SAILING TO BYZANTIUM

The Black Sea was blue, as the Danube had been only twice in milky dawns. The day was sunny, not a thundercloud in sight. 'Go to the last buoy,' the Capitan had said, 'before turning south.' One journey ends, and another begins.

Most Communist countries had mines laid around their coasts. We followed the Harbour-master's advice and kept to the channel marked on the chart as free of mines; though it was a dog-leg we felt it better not to take chances. Officially, the minefields had been cleared, but Bill had seen two minesweepers laid up at Galati, and was unimpressed. The mines were old and many would have been carried off station; detonators become unstable with time. The channel was not marked, and with a cross current we were glad of our GPS to keep us on track. We were relieved an hour later to clear the danger area.

Now we could relax in a way that had been impossible in the river. There were no ships in sight, no buoys to worry about, deep water under the keel, and a large school of dolphins, welcoming us back to sea. The autopilot hooted quietly keeping us on a southerly course, and left us free to sit, or make coffee, or review our journey, and boost our morale with a little self congratulation. It was 4100 kilometres since Calais, 2216 nautical miles, and it had taken five months. It had been the most wearing journey we had ever done, the anxiety had taken a toll on Bill, and he was very near both mental and physical exhaustion.

The weather forecast came in on Navtex from Istanbul, predicting winds from N or NE force 3 to 5, which could not have been better. We were thrilled by the first contact, even by Navtex, with a country we knew well, and where we were confident of a welcome.

We had taken the precaution of clearing for Constanţa in case of bad weather *en route*, but with a favourable forecast Bill decided to head for the Bosphorus, due south of us and 222 miles distant. We set the sails to help us on our way.

By 1730 the wind freshened from the south, instead of north as forecast. Bill furled sail, and decided to edge over towards Constanţa in case of an increasing wind; we had been land-locked for 12 months and it is wise to be prudent on one's first voyage after that time. The evening forecast was for northerlies force 3 to 5 (don't meteorologists ever look out of the window? Or do they consider an error of 180° close enough for working purposes?) and the wind continued to strengthen against us. We discovered our after bilge to be a few inches deep in water. Bill went down and tasted it. 'Chateau Margaux 1947,' he announced cheerfully. It was fresh water; we must have overfilled one of the tanks. It was the decider. He took half an hour to suck it up dry with the big hoover, and in the meantime Laurel took charge of the boat and headed away for Constanţa while the wind further freshened from the south.

We approached Constanţa at 0100. Ah yes, we remembered, there is a downside to seagoing. Rolling and pitching in the black night, puzzled by the entrance to Port Tomis harbour where the pierhead lights appeared to be round the wrong way, relieved when at last they showed up clearly on radar. We called the harbour authority on VHF, and to our delight they said, 'It is very late, papers will wait till morning.'

As we made the sharp 150° turn into the harbour and rounded up under the lighthouse, whistles blew and soldiers ran out of a hut at the base of the lighthouse. One man beckoned and another levelled a rifle at us.

Welcome back to Romania.

It is not difficult to get *Hosanna* alongside a berth 50 yards astern of her at short notice when she is still going ahead. It just takes time. It takes time for a ship even to stop, never mind go backwards. The two soldiers seemed to be going berserk: one with his silly whistle, while the other waved his gun about like the squire after a good lunch. Bill sounded three short blasts on the siren. We don't suppose they knew what that meant, but it drowned out the whistle and relieved Bill's feelings, which get heated at moments like this. Possibly it woke half the town.

After several minutes we got alongside close to the two soldiers who proceeded to come aboard uninvited. One gave us a form to fill in, while the other asked Bill to make entries in his book. We did not know what the column entries were, but it was not difficult to guess. Bill signed it H Nelson. 'Where do we berth?' Bill asked, mostly by sign language. They shrugged, their duty being done, and went back to their hut under the lighthouse. We moved as far away from them as we could, and turned in. It was almost 0200, and the 'northerly' wind was blowing hard from the south.

Three officials turned up by car at 0750. Bill was still in bed. They were reasonable and efficient. Afterwards they invited us to connect up to shore power, which was a pleasant surprise. The 'marina' had about 10 occupied berths: some commercial craft and 3 Romanian yachts, a possession beyond the dreams of most nationals. Evidently the leisure use of boats is still a rare concept. We were in contact with fat cats for the first time. How many foreign yachts did they get, we asked the harbour authority. They were evasive, but admitted that *Sea Lion* came in sometimes, 'and now you.'

We explored the town, which was the most attractive we had come across in Romania. Here was something like a resort, built on cliffs on

Mosque and museum, Constanţa

a promontory, the buildings dominated by the dome of an old mosque among stately trees, and an oriental-looking Historical Museum. At a distance it was picturesque, but the flights of steps that took us up to the town centre, past what were probably remains of ramparts, were decayed and perilous.

We had letters to post and telephone calls to make, and we needed salt. We found a Post Office, but they had run out of stamps. We must go to the head Post Office in the town centre. We found the telephone office, but it did not sell phone cards; they were on sale elsewhere, two kilometres distant. We set out, passing gaily clad gypsies, long skirts trailing, selling dried melon seeds, and an old man, proud possessor of a pair of bathroom scales, who would weigh you for a few lei. We discovered the largest supermarket we had yet found in Romania in the basement of a department store. It had a 'down' escalator, but no 'up', the reverse of what one would expect. There were no trolleys, since no Romanian could afford to fill one. We were by now existing very simply; we had run out of butter, salt, mayonnaise, and longlife milk, and had not seen a lettuce or a cucumber since Hungary. Laurel happily bought mayonnaise and butter, but the supermarket was out of salt.

Bill tried unsuccessfully to sleep in the afternoon. He was tense and jumpy all day, so we went out to dinner to the quayside restaurant 'On Plonge'. Constanţa's élite dined here; they possessed cars, leather jackets, and pampered dogs. We enjoyed fried mussels and zander with three sauces: mayonnaise, ketchup, and a runny garlic sauce. It was the best and most expensive meal we had in Romania, and with wine and beer it cost us 31,000 lei, or £9.68.

Bill had to take a sleeping pill that night, even though he was relieved to be safely in port. The wind finally turned to the north-west, but strengthened and produced an uncomfortable scend in the harbour. Fishing boats came in for shelter, and all boats lurched and heaved in their berths as Bill tossed in his. The rain was heavy, accompanied by wild thunderstorms all night.

The weather became worse, and Bill came down with Ceauçescu's revenge, which made him even more irritable. The swell entering the harbour made every rope creak and grumble as *Hosanna* would not keep still. There was no question of moving on. Laurel climbed the cliff and hit a treasure trove: a plastic sachet of salt in a kiosk that otherwise sold beet and cabbages. She found a barber and, using the *Guid de Conversaţie* (Cut me my hair very short from the front and longer from behind), had her hair cut by a lady who, despite an impressive array of modern basins, taps, spray heads and running hot and cold, indicated with calm resignation that nothing worked, and washed Laurel's hair in a bucket of soapy water. The cut which followed was far from the worst she had had, and several minutes were occupied in a relaxing friction massage, right down to the shoulder blades. And all for about £2.50.

After another night of rolling and creaking, we rose to find that one of the cats had brought a present of a dead rat, minus a chewed hind leg. Rattus rattus; the worst kind, the plague carriers. We hoped the cat had killed it and not found a corpse. Dead rats on board are feared by sailors, with good cause; the Black Sea was ever a reservoir of the Black Plague. We shook flea-powder liberally about, including over ourselves and the cats, to their disgust.

Both Bill and the weather improved as the day went on. We realised with a shock that our visas would expire tomorrow, and the paper-work involved in renewing them was unthinkable. We informed Authority of our decision to leave at 1320, documentation took until 1600, when we sailed with a forecast of calm weather, rolling a bit, with the wind a northerly force 3.

We were able to use our sails, but not very effectively. Bill had decided against calling at a Bulgarian port. *Sea Lion* had reported that the officials were objectionable and obstructive, arresting people for minor or imaginary infringements, the fines for which were pocketed without receipt, and again demanding a visa at $66 per person at every port. A Bulgarian we had met confirmed this: he said that control of the port of Varna was in the hands of some of the worst remnants of the old Communist administration. They could well lose their jobs before long, he said, and were making themselves a fortune while they could. Corruption in England is tiddly-winks by comparison.

The moon was big and bright, and nightwatches were under a skyful of stars. The day that followed was lit by the sun sparkling on a sea of dolphins. Greens say the Black Sea is polluted and dead, but dolphins were living there.

Under a full moon on the second night we arrived off the mouth of the Bosphorus. Bill wanted to pass through in daylight, and a small anchorage at Eski Fanalaki, a couple of miles to the east of the entrance, was recommended by the Admiralty Pilot. Unfortunately it was blocked by a mass of unlit tunny drift nets, close to the surface. These nets, guarded by small boats who appeared and disappeared on the radar and waved warning lamps when we got too close, were quite invisible (so the tunny could not see them, the Turks said, logically), and we found it impossible to penetrate them. So instead of anchoring for a rest we headed offshore and steamed slowly in a series of broad circles off the shipping route, until dawn.

We have on board an old Admiralty Pilot of the Black Sea, often better for the yachtsman than the modern versions. One swaps the up-to-date information for that intended for low-powered steamships or sailing vessels.

We quote from the Black Sea Pilot, 11th edition: '... the absence of well-defined landmarks makes it difficult to distinguish the northern entrance to the strait, and owing to mirage, Rumeli lighthouse is difficult to identify at a distance.' It goes on: 'In thick and foggy weather... a vessel should endeavour to ascertain her position by sounding. Depths of 50 to 55 fathoms, mud and shell, would be an indication of her being off the coast eastward of the entrance; she should then stand cautiously southward, and if the depths shoal rapidly to 45 fathoms with the same bottom, she may steer westward until sand and shells are obtained, when she would be in the fairway to the entrance.

'If, on the other hand, mud alone is found at 50 to 55 fathoms, the vessel will be off the coast westward, and might stand south-eastward till the depths shoal to about 45 fathoms, mud and shell; the vessel will then have passed just eastward of the entrance and can proceed as directed above. If a depth of 37 to 40 fathoms, sand and shell, be first obtained, a course may at once be steered southward for the strait.'

This, to Bill, is pure and useful poetry. He ranks it with anything written and published by the literati, both for content and for succinct yet precise prose. He reads such works to himself over and over again, and often to other people. He observed the soundings on the depth-meter, but we no longer have means of arming our lead with tallow to find out the nature of the bottom. We have radar and GPS instead, which makes it easier, but dull.

A strawpink moon was setting as the sun rose into a band of mist at 0640 on Saturday 9 September, climbing out of the calm and oily sea. Bill checked the compass by comparing its bearing on rising with the one he worked out from the Amplitude tables in *Inman*'s. He likes to check it every day, and especially before tricky passages. Laurel altered course for Rumeli lighthouse, following behind a tug and tow so that we did not impede them with our slow progress. On Rumeli Point the buildings were clustered on the black rocks round the white lighthouse tower, flanked by two slender minarets. The entrance was busy with shipping, much of it Russian and Ukrainian. We were off Rumeli castle at 0840, and shortly afterwards were stopped by the Turkish health authorities in their launch. No, we had no problems with dead rats on board, we answered with literal truthfulness, cursing the cats. Nobody had any infectious diseases. Or, *affedersiniz*, (excuse me) diarrhoea? Nor that either. The officials were very solemn. They needed our ultimate destination. We gave them Limnos in Greece. We received a certificate of health and went on southward.

Since we had acquired our sailing instructions a new system of traffic control had been introduced into the Bosphorus. All vessels must now carry VHF radio, and their passages are controlled like that of aircraft in airlanes. One reports as one reaches certain points, is given instructions, and is handed over to the next controller further down. The language used is English, except for Turkish local shipping. The Turkish controllers understood, and were understood by, officers in ships of all the nations that streamed through these busy straits (demonstrating the value of our tongue as a tool of communication) but they found our own native English difficult to understand if we used words and phrases other than the standard ones that they had learnt. There is need of an agreed basic English vocabulary and syntax for international communication; paradoxically, we English will have to learn how to speak our own language! We have too many words for the same thing.

Through the misty early morning we went down the Straits, though in the bustling traffic Bill had little time to enjoy their beauty, and had to get help from Laurel to identify landmarks as we swept southward with a favourable current. The waterside residences were picturesque and well kept, and there was a refreshing absence of ruin and rubbish and decrepitude. Fine old wooden houses with elegant balconies line the European side of the strait, which is narrower than the Danube. It was thrilling to travel between Asia and Europe, almost able to touch both continents. We had visited Istanbul before, but this was the first time we had come by sea, and as we passed the Golden Horn and Galata bridge, the view of Istanbul seen from the water was magnificent, breathtaking: probably the biggest and most beautiful city we had seen in five months travelling.

The cry of a muezzin reached us across the water, echoed after a moment by nearer and further chants, an interweaving of praise and exhortation. We recognised Topkapı on its clifftop, the Blue Mosque on the hill and Santa Sofia behind it, and then we were crossing the big ship anchorage to the marina at Ataköy, arriving at 1030.

It would be an expensive night, at $64, but worth it. We taxied into town to complete the formalities. They took just as long as the Romanian ones, but the atmosphere was different. There were smiles and jokes, no guns in evidence, chairs to sit on, and if the delay was long we were brought glasses of tea or coffee.

Port office; sign transit log and stamp. Health office; fill in form and stamp. Harbour-master; certificate of Registration, one stamp. Police; transit log, one stamp. Customs; transit log, one stamp. It was the visas that caused the most delay. It was Saturday and the frontier police had run out of visas, which were sticky-backed like postage stamps.

While we sat and drank our tea an agent in tight jeans minced in from a Cruise liner, with a plastic bag advertising 'Black Velvet Lingerie'. We surmised that the lingerie was for himself, since he could not keep his eyes away from his image in a wall mirror, continuously primping and rearranging his lustrous locks. The bag contained a huge pile of American passports to be processed. The tourists are excused all this waiting about, they were off sightseeing, while the agent did the work. They'll never know what they missed, apart from the glass of tea. One of the police greeted the agent with great affection, long kisses on both cheeks and much holding of hands. The agent was a linguist, and was asked to explain something to an untidy and bewildered Ukrainian lorry driver. The agent used many words in different languages, most of which we understood (Basic Interlingua?). He cannot come into Istanbul, he must *vai via*, (Go away, Italian), back to Odessa. His visa is *in ordnung* (in order, German), but the police are not happy. 'Am I a Bandit?' asks the poor Ukrainian. The police look the other way. Whatever his crime, he is not being thrown into gaol. That would surprise the Americans, who judge the Turks by *Midnight Express*.

The visas arrived, and we were free to go, all stamped with a smile and *in ordnung*, and knowing that we could call where we liked in Turkey with no further paperwork until we checked out for Greece. The feelgood factor was high. As Laurel said, 'In Romania they kissed my hand, but never offered me a chair.'

On the way back we stored up at a supermarket, which had a European's idea of 'everything' (except pork). We got milk, lamb, stuffed mussels, iceberg lettuce, leeks and cucumber and purslane, all wonderfully fresh and tempting things that we had not had for months.

We ended our 'day out' at a restaurant, fearing to fall asleep, but pigging out on fried aubergines and grilled lamb *beyti*, lots of green salad and a bottle of wine.

We anchored for four days' rest in Çam Limani in the Princes Islands. Summer had returned. We were the only boat in the bay as we barbecued the goodies we had bought in Ataköy's supermarket. Then we got away from the traffic separation scheme to sail the southern shore of the Sea of Marmara to Erdek.

Here the harbour was crowded, and we stopped, thinking that we might have to look elsewhere, when men came running and waving cheerfully. They moved a large trawler and beckoned us into its place. We had not found such a welcome since Herr Rammelmeyr's at Saal. And Oh! the good restaurants after the sullen mediocrity of Eastern Europe. Waiters that swept the crumbs up between courses, who knew how to serve wine, and gave us food cooked to perfection at such a modest price.

We moved on to the more primitive village ports: to Kalabiga which lives on sardines, and the export of pottery clay, liberally spread over the quay, which we did not notice until it rained and we returned on board with our shoes like gigantic suet puddings. The cats were hilariously disconcerted when the same thing happened to their paws. No soigné restaurant here; we happily ate köftes and burghul with tomato salad like everyone else. But the taste of those tomatoes!

After a reunion with *Rainbow*, who had found Turkey as good as we had promised, we cleared out at Çanakkale. To the Customs downstairs, then upstairs, then the Frontier Police the other side of town, the Customs upstairs, then down, then to the Harbour-master half a mile away, back to the Customs downstairs, up and then down again, and finally to the Harbour-master again. Bill had to do this; the stairs and the distance were too much for Laurel, but she could pull much more physical weight now standing her watch at sea, so we were even.

We anchored that night under the conspicuous memorials to the 500,000 who lost their lives in the Dardanelles campaign. It is a sober anchorage; the sun was sinking, blood red, as we recalled the many fields of slaughter that our five month journey had led us through. Their images crowded into our minds. Counting only those from the 19th century, we saw again the shell-pocked fields of the Somme, splashed with blood and poppies.

We saw the steep hills and dense misty forests of the Ardennes, home of mythical horsemen and legendary knights, a terrain thought by the French to be too difficult for Runstetdt's Army to penetrate, and the heartbreaking and contemptuous speed with which the Germans crashed through it, annihilating the French Cavalry and adding more ghostly horsemen to the sum of souls.

We saw the land round Verdun, where bloody stalemate piled half a million skullbones in the Ossuary, and pierced the bosom of the land with half a million crosses.

Our image of the most recent of wars in Serbia and Croatia was the most harrowing and the most vivid, because we had come so close. We thought of Vukovar, destroyed in so recent a November, and the row of broken cranes standing by the River Danube.

The anchorage at Gallipoli was unbearably full of ghosts.

We left at first light, running with all sail set for the 70 miles to Limnos, and, shaking off the grim dreams of the night before, began to think of the lighter side of the journey, the quirks, the oddities, even, God help us, the fun of it.

The fact that we had not found a single postcard in Romania.

That in the land of Caviar, we had regrettably failed to eat any.

That the brochures of the Balkans obtained in England had been full of costume and colour and embroidered ribbons, and from Hungary on we had seen none of this hotel-based folklore. We had danced not one dance, nor sung one song, and had met almost nobody but officials. Life on the River, we concluded, was far from folklorique. Our longheld dictum, that you must moor in one place for at least four days before the locals begin to talk to you, had proved as true as ever.

Laurel now knows the word for onions in fourteen different languages, and how to say, in Romanian: 'Give me, please, another morsel, smaller and not so fat.'

Bill's abiding respect for the Captains of the great rivers of Europe has increased beyond his expectations.

One of the most extraordinary and recurring features of this down-river passage, which passed through ten countries, was being told in each country that the next and further would be full of idiots, rogues, thieves, rapists, *tricheurs*; all these awaited us after the next frontier, no matter which it was. Few of these warnings stood the test of experience. One of the ship's cats was raped in France, and the same cat was almost kidnapped in Turnu Severin. We were robbed in the B & Q car park in England before we left. We have described the mischief suffered in well-regulated Schweinfurt. The only pirates we met were Budapest taxi drivers. In Eastern Europe our trial, if anything, was by State Bureaucracy, and the grim feeling of total incomprehension and mistrust of our way of life. Owning your own boat, and cruising in it, is deeply suspect.

The Greeks, however, have always understood boat ownership, especially in the islands where everyone has a little boat the way landsmen have bicycles. In the last 25 years they have profited by their understanding, and made it easier for yachts to enjoy their waters.

Formalities are different in Greece. Hellas was playing France at soccer. 'Avrio! Come back tomorrow,' said the Harbour-master. Greece won 3-0. Next morning our transit log was issued in minutes as the staff re-lived the match. '*Hosanna*. You were here before, two years is it?' said the Harbour-master. 'Yes,' we said. 'We took Hosanna back to England through the French Canals*, then we came down the Danube, and here we are again.'

Full circle.

* *Watersteps Round Europe*, published by Adlard Coles Nautical in the UK and Sheridan House in the USA.

APPENDIX 1

Plan of Hosanna

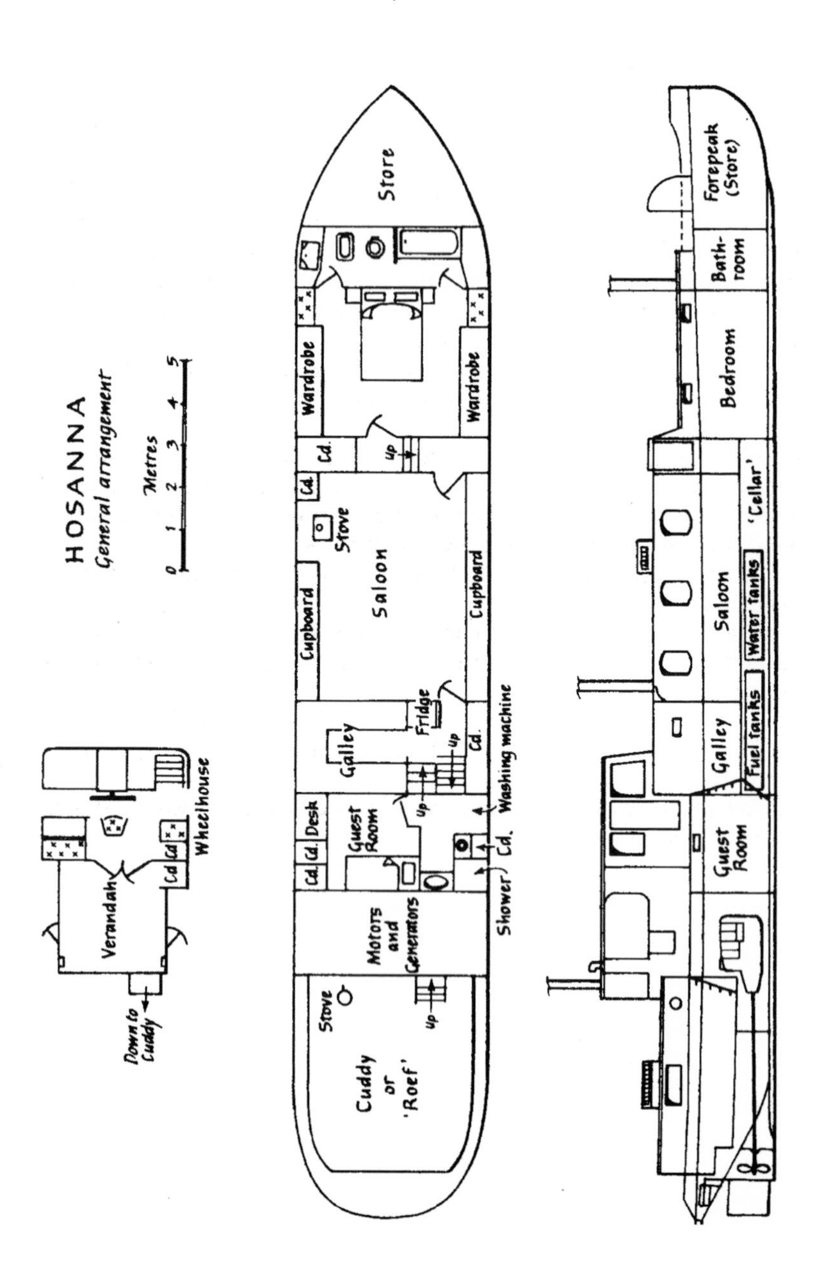

APPENDIX 2

Advice for those contemplating a voyage down River Danube

• The voyage from Mainz to Sulina takes a minimum of 3 months of very hard travel. Allow much more if you wish to pause en route. Wintering on River Danube is not advised. Much of it freezes in winter, and the floods can be devastating. In our view, the last possible wintering place is Rammelmeyr's at Saal, preferably out of the water.
• The Danube floods almost every spring. There is a drought almost every summer. Thus too much water in the Upper Danube, too little in the Lower. It is as well to have more than two persons aboard to avoid fatigue. Have binoculars with sunfilters.
• There is much large débris in the river. Boats with underhanging screws are not advisable, but twin screws are. Take spare screws if they are not in cages.
• Take emergency provisions as for a long sea voyage; you may not need them, but they will vary your diet. You'll need to bake bread.
• Have tankage for a minimum of 1800 kilometres (1000 nm) fuel as diesel stations are rare. Have 4 weeks fresh water.
• Travel health insurance with a fly-you-home medical clause is desirable.
• A return voyage upstream is slow and expensive, owing to the current. Most boats need a tow. A private enterprise deal with a tug-master is possible.
• Good guides are available for the German canals and rivers, and the Danube as far as Mohács, but there is nothing reliable thereafter. (1996).
• We pay our respects to those who preceded us, and wish good luck to those who follow.

Index of Places